Economic Policy Making in China (1949–2016)

This book explores the key ideas and the key people who were responsible for the development of China's economy from 1949 through 2016. It discusses how economic policy evolved, how economic policy was formulated and how the role of economists in decision making evolved. It considers the interplay between ideological and practical questions, provides biographical details of key economists and includes a clear annotated chronology of events. The book is especially valuable because the author, as a senior World Bank official, was a close observer of the situation and, to some extent, a key participant.

Pieter Bottelier is a Visiting Scholar at Johns Hopkins University School of Advanced International Studies in Washington, D.C. He became fascinated by China's economic reforms and development when he served as Chief of the World Bank's resident mission in China in the 1990s.

Routledge Contemporary China Series

China's Soviet Dream
Propaganda, Culture, and Popular Imagination
Yan Li

Deng Xiaoping and China's Foreign Policy
Ronald C. Keith

Corporate Social Responsibility Reporting in China
Evolution, Drivers and Prospects
Jieqi Guan and Carlos Noronha

China's Generation Gap
Jiaming Sun and Dongmei Cheng

China Reclaims World Power Status
Putting an End to the World America Made
Paolo Urio

The Economic Roots of the Umbrella Movement in Hong Kong
Globalization and the Rise of China
Louis Augustin-Jean and Anthea H.Y. Cheung

China's Hydro-politics in the Mekong
Conflict and Cooperation in Light of Securitization Theory
Sebastian Biba

The Power of Relationalism in China
Leah Zhu

Economic Policy Making in China (1949–2016)
The Role of Economists
Pieter Bottelier

For our full list of available titles: www.routledge.com/Routledge-Contemporary-China-Series/book-series/SE0768

Economic Policy Making in China (1949–2016)

The Role of Economists

Pieter Bottelier

Routledge
Taylor & Francis Group
LONDON AND NEW YORK

First published 2018
by Routledge
2 Park Square, Milton Park, Abingdon, Oxon OX14 4RN

and by Routledge
605 Third Avenue, New York, NY 10017

First issued in paperback 2021

Routledge is an imprint of the Taylor & Francis Group, an informa business

British Library Cataloguing-in-Publication Data
A catalogue record for this book is available from the British Library

Library of Congress Cataloging-in-Publication Data
Names: Bottelier, Pieter, author.
Title: Economic policy making in China (1949–2016) : the role of economists / Pieter Bottelier.
Description: Abingdon, Oxon ; New York, NY : Routledge, 2018. | Series: Routledge contemporary China series ; 187 | Includes bibliographical references and index.
Identifiers: LCCN 2017052063 | ISBN 9781138306318 (hardback) | ISBN 9781315141725 (ebook)
Subjects: LCSH: China—Economic policy—1949– | Economists—China.
Classification: LCC HC427.9 .B63 2018 | DDC 330.951/05—dc23
LC record available at https://lccn.loc.gov/2017052063

Typeset in Times New Roman
by Apex CoVantage, LLC

ISBN 13: 978-1-138-30631-8 (hbk)
ISBN 13: 978-0-367-43849-4 (pbk)

Book DOI: 10.4324/9781315141725

For Grace, whose piano performances and master classes in China in the 1990s contributed to the country's "opening up" and a revival of interest in classical music.

Contents

Preface and acknowledgements

The genesis of this book is my curiosity about the contributions of Chinese economists to economic policy making in China since the beginning of communist rule. China's rather sudden emergence as a global economic power in the last few decades remains a puzzle to most. How could they have achieved so much, following policies that were quite unorthodox and sometimes wrong in Western eyes?

Management of the economy under Mao Zedong was totally subordinate to politics. It was only after Mao's death and the arrest of the "Gang of Four" in 1976 that technocrats gained influence on economic policy making in China. From then on, management of the economy became increasingly driven by non-ideological, pragmatic considerations until, in recent years, under the leadership of Xi Jinping, political considerations began to dominate once again, or so it seems.

The story of China's economic miracle and the names of most top political leaders since 1949, Mao Zedong, Hua Guofeng, Deng Xiaoping, Hu Yaobang, Zhao Ziyang, Jiang Zemin, Hu Jintao and Xi Jinping, are well-known, but who were the economists who contributed, or tried to contribute, to the policy-making process? What and where did those "theoreticians", as they were often called, study? What did their analysis of China's economy tell them and what was their policy advice? Who were their professional peers abroad? How effective were they in their roles as analysts and advisors?

When I started working on this project, I aimed at limiting my efforts to the period since Deng Xiaoping's "opening up and reform" policies of the late 1970s and early 1980s. However, I soon realized that it is hard to understand and explain the direction and content of those policies without reference to economic developments and policy making during the preceding decades under Mao Zedong and his immediate successor, Hua Guofeng. So, I broadened the scope of this study and went all the way back to 1949 when, on 1 October, Mao proclaimed the establishment of the People's Republic of China and pursued policies aimed at creating a socialist economic system, initially on the Soviet model.

I had the opportunity to observe first-hand how economic policy is made in China when I headed the World Bank's office in Beijing in the early and mid-1990s. The political system had then recovered – more or less – from the Tiananmen disaster of 1989, and economic reform efforts were resumed with vigor and a clear sense of purpose. It was in many ways a unique period. I was greatly impressed by the professionalism and dedication of senior officials I interacted with in overseeing the World Bank's huge financial and technical assistance program for China during those years. My Chinese counterparts were keenly interested in learning from international experience and frequently used international development agencies such as the World Bank, as sources of knowledge and advice. There was no arrogance or defensiveness on their part. They weren't afraid of loan conditionality – on the contrary – they welcomed it as an instrument to promote development. Many went abroad for study on foreign scholarships. The World Bank undertook hundreds of studies on various aspects of China's economy – often jointly with Chinese counterparts – to inform and guide the policy-making process. There were numerous conferences and seminars to discuss ideas, learn from international experience and train officials.

This book draws on my work experience in China, on numerous discussions with Chinese officials and academics over many years and on my study of relevant Chinese and other literature (see the bibliography). After I left the World Bank in 1998, I taught courses on China's economy at several American universities and found that teaching is sometimes also the best way to learn. I was at first afraid that my very limited knowledge of the Chinese language would be an absolute obstacle to undertaking this study, but that fear began to recede when I discovered that the available literature in English by or about Chinese economists and economic policy makers, is in fact, enormous. Another concern I had was that Marxism and other socialist theories on which much of China's economic policy making since 1949 relied, had been studied to death and that I wouldn't be able to do more than reinvent the wheel. I discovered, however, that the study of Marx and other socialist thinkers is en vogue again today.

Since the main purpose of this book is to identify and assess the contributions of Chinese economists to the country's economic reform and modernization efforts, the selection of people to be covered by this study became very important. It is obviously impossible to be comprehensive in this regard. Choices had to be made. I consulted many Chinese economists and some government officials I got to know over the years to solicit their opinion as to who the key economists were or had been. In the end, I made a list of 20 "theoreticians" I would focus on in particular, including Gu Zhun, Sun Yefang, Xue Muqiao, Du Runsheng, Yu Guanyuan, Liu Guoguang, Ma Hong, Dong Furen, Gao Shangquan, Wu Jinglian, Li Yining, Zhao Renwei, Wang Mengkui, Lu Mai, Zhou Xiaochuan, Li Jange, Lou Jiwei, Chen Xiwen, Lin Yifu and Guo Shuqing. I decided not to include Chen Yun in this list, not because his contributions to economic policy making weren't important – they were! (during the Mao and the Deng periods) – but because he was, in my view, primarily a politician. Many others who made important contributions are not even mentioned.

Not all of the 20 included in Chapter 3 were professional economists the way we understand that term today. Some, particularly the older ones – the first eight are dead – were what we would call today political scientists or historians with a special interest in economics. Gu Zhun, first on the list above, because he is regarded by many in China as the father of market reforms under Deng Xiaoping, was primarily trained (and professionally active) as an accountant. The last 12 in the list above are all alive today and schooled not only in socialist theories, but also in modern western economics.

All Chinese economists wishing to contribute to the policy making process, whether old or young, have to be politically astute. The One-Party State, even when the political leadership is inclined to take technical analysis and advice seriously, creates an intense political environment from which there is no escape.

Until the mid-1990s, most Chinese professionals in leading government or academic positions were trained abroad, often in the USSR. Since that time, the proportion of Chinese professionals who received all or most of their academic training in China, has sharply increased. Many also received at least some academic training in advanced economies such as the US, Japan, Australia, New Zealand and Western Europe.

I am writing this book in the first person because most assessments and opinions expressed are my own. There is no 100% "objective" or scientific way to assess the contribution of individual economists to policy making or to describe the issues they struggled with. Sometimes those issues and the way they were understood were obscured by ideological preconceptions. No two economists would come to the exact same conclusions as to who were the prime movers driving China's economic policy-making process since the start of market reforms in the late 1970s. Another reason for the personal and selective nature of this study is that, as already mentioned, there were many more economists involved in shaping China's economic reforms than I could cover in this book. Another limitation I encountered is that I did not always understand the theoretical socialist jargon used by older Chinese economists in their books and articles. As I try to explain in the first chapter, in the process of researching this book, I was often surprised and/or puzzled by unexpected turns of events and decisions (or non-decisions) in the evolution of China's economic policy making. I found that there are quite a few common misunderstandings in the West about what happened (or did not happen) in China's reform process and why.

It is impossible to properly acknowledge and thank all those who helped me in writing this book. I want to mention a few though. Lu Mai of the State Council's DRC (Development Research Centre) Foundation in Beijing was the main force behind a project to translate into English numerous articles by Chinese economists and publish them in a series of ten books called "Chinese Economists on Economic Reform". I benefitted greatly from Lu Mai's work. Foreign Languages Press in Beijing, a government-owned printer, which translated and published many books by Chinese economists who are virtually unknown in the West. I also want to thank Professors Anthony Saich and David Lampton, who offered me an opportunity to teach graduate courses on China's economy at Harvard and at Johns Hopkins University after I left the World Bank and inspired me with their great knowledge of China. Nancy Hearst, chief librarian of the Fairbank Center in Cambridge, helped me find many publications in English by Chinese economists. Ms. Li Li of the World Bank's office in Beijing put me in touch with Chinese economists (or relatives in case they were deceased) for interviews and found many publications in English in China for my project. Others whose knowledge of or experience in China inspired me greatly, or supported my project in other ways include Ezra Vogel of Harvard University, Fan Shitao of Beijing Normal University, Zhang Xiaotong of Wuhan University, Bert Hofman, current head of the World Bank's office in Beijing, Anna Yan, my RA at Johns Hopkins University's School of Advanced International Studies (2015/16), Natalie Lichtenstein, Ed Lim and Carol Hamrin. I am also grateful to many former students in the U.S. who kept me on my toes with incisive questions and colleagues at Johns Hopkins SAIS and the Kennedy School at Harvard, including especially David Lampton, Tony Saich, Ezra Vogel, Carla Freeman, David Brown, Anne Thurston, Zhaojin Ji and Zhou Dunren, retired professor (of Fudan University in Shanghai) and a personal friend for many years.

Acronyms and abbreviations

ABC	Agricultural Bank of China
AFC	Asian financial crisis
AMC	Asset management company
BN (or bn)	billion
BOC	Bank of China
BOCOM	Bank of Communications
CC	Central Committee (of the CPC)
CCTV	China Central Television
CEFC	Central Economic and Finance Commission
CIBM	China interbank bond market
CIRC	China Insurance Regulatory Commission
CITIC	China International Trade and Investment Company
CMC	Central Military Commission
COE	Collectively owned enterprise
CPC	Communist Party of China
CPPCC	Chinese People's Political Consultative Conference
CPSU	Communist Party of the Soviet Union
CR	Cultural Revolution
CSRC	China Securities Regulatory Commission
DRC	Development Research Centre (of the State Council)
EDI	Economic Development Institute (of the World Bank)
EE	Eastern Europe
EM	Emerging market
FDI	Foreign direct investment
FEC (1)	Foreign exchange certificate
FEC (2)	Finance and Economy Commission
FIE	Foreign-invested enterprise
FYP	Five-Year Plan
GATT	General Agreement on Tariffs and Trade
GDP	Gross Domestic Product
GFC	Global financial crisis (of 2008/9)
GITIC	Guangdong International Trade and Investment Company
GLF	Great Leap Forward

HK	Hong Kong
HRS	Household responsibility system
IAP	Interim adjustment plan
ICBC	Industrial and Commercial Bank of China
IDA	International Development Association (of the WB group)
IMF	International Monetary Fund
IMS	International monetary system
IRS	Internal Revenue Service
JV	Joint venture
KMT	Kuomintang (Chinese Nationalist party)
MLP	Medium – long-term plan
MN	(or mn) million
MOF	Ministry of Finance
NDRC	National Development and Reform Commission
NEP	New Economic Policy (Lenin's)
NPC	National People's Congress
OECF	Overseas Economic Cooperation Fund (Japan)
OTC	over the counter (trade)
PAYG	pay as you go
PBoC	People's Bank of China
PICC	People's Insurance Company of China
PLA	People's Liberation Army
Plenum	plenary Session (of the CPC's Central Committee)
PM	Prime Minister
PRC	People's Republic of China
RMB	renminbi (name of China's currency)
ROC	Republic of China (Taiwan)
SC	Standing Committee
SDR	Special Drawing Right
SEI	strategic economic industries
SEZ	special economic zone
SME	small and medium-sized enterprise
SOE	state-owned enterprise
SPC/SDPC	State Planning Commission (renamed State Development Planning Commission in '98)
SR	senior
STA	State Tax Administration
SWF	Sovereign Wealth Fund
TA	technical assistance
UN	United Nations
UNDP	United Nations Development Programme
US	United States
USSR	Soviet Union
VAT	value-added tax
VP	Vice President

WB	World Bank
WE	Western Europe
WFOE (or WOFE)	wholly foreign-owned enterprise
WTO	World Trade Organization
XR	exchange rate

Annotated chronology of economic policy making in China, pre-1949–2016[1]

Date(s) or period	*Explanation*
Late '31 First CPC central bank (in Jiangxi Soviet)	Establishment of the CPC's first commercial and central bank in the Jiangxi Soviet; it was headed by Mao's younger brother Mao Zemin. The bank had a silver mint and issued paper money in CPC/PLA-controlled areas. (The bank's financial reserves and equipment were taken along on the "Long March" in '34 but abandoned after the Zunyi meeting in early '35). The CPC established other central banks and currency systems in other CPC/PLA controlled areas before '49.
15 Jan. '35 Mao becomes chairman of the Politburo	During the "Long March" (Oct. '34–Oct. '35), at a meeting in Zunyi (Guizhou), Mao Zedong was elected chairman of the Politburo and thus became the CPC's top political leader and economic strategist. He became chairman of the Central Military Commission (CMC) Nov. '35 in Ya'nan, after the Long March.
Jan. '40 Mao's essay "On New Democracy" published	According to this important essay, the economic basis of the "New Democratic Society" – a political-economy system that would be installed when the then still existing anti-Japanese "United Front" (of Mao Zedong's CPC and Chiang Kaishek's KMT had succeeded in driving out the Japanese and the CPC had succeeded in leading China's socialist revolution – would be a mixed economy, including private enterprises and SOEs (banks, natural monopolies and very large enterprises). The mixed economy would last a "long time" (then understood to mean decades) before the transition to socialism could start. However, the New Democratic Society would make sure that capitalism would never again be able to dominate the livelihood of the people. In Mao's thinking at the time, China's socialist revolution would be primarily for the benefit of small and landless peasants, who would receive agricultural land confiscated by the state from "landlords". His ideas about the future organization of China's economy were like Lenin's, as expressed in the latter's "New Economic Policy" (NEP), introduced in '21 towards the end of the Russian Civil War, following the Bolshevik Revolution of October '17.

(*Continued*)

(Continued)

Date(s) or period	*Explanation*
'41 Hu Qiaomu becomes Mao's personal secretary	Hu served in that capacity for over 20 years and became a very influential Party theoretician and senior official in several key functions. He played a major role in designing economic and other policies during the Mao era and beyond – usually "behind the scenes". After Mao's death, Hu became a supporter of market-oriented economic reforms. He was appointed as the CASS's first president when it was established in May '77. His report to the State Council of July '78 helped set the stage for the critical 3rd Plenum of the 11th CC of the CPC in Dec. of that year. Later, Hu's conservative instincts seem to have returned. He co-led the Party's anti- "spiritual pollution" campaign in '83/'84 and fought for conservative causes until his death in '92.
1 Sept. '42 CC meeting	The meeting adopted the "Decision on Centralized Leadership and Adjustment of Relations Among the Party Organs in the anti-Japanese Areas". This was effectively a decision to follow the Soviet model of Party control over the state, (including the military) once the CPC had prevailed over Chiang Kaishek's KMT and had become China's leading political party, as anticipated by the CPC. Party control did indeed become the model for China's system of government after establishment of the PRC in '49.
11–19 June '45 7th Party Congress (in Ya'nan) ('45–'56)	Mao's political report "On Coalition Government" confirmed that in the anticipated "New-Democratic Society" under CPC rule, there should be adequate room for capitalism to co-exist with socialism. Unlike foreign imperialism and domestic feudalism, which had to be resisted, "the development of domestic capitalism under the New Democratic Society has no harm, but only benefit", according to Mao's report. But, on the future of agriculture a major split in the Party soon emerged. One group (supported by Liu Shaoqi, #2 in the Party and Deng Zihui, Chief of the Party's Rural Work Department) argued that farmers should have the right to buy, sell and lease land, hire labor and borrow money, while another group (supported by Mao) thought that farmers should be organized in cooperatives so as to achieve the "socialist transformation of agriculture" more quickly. Disagreements within the CPC over the organization of farming and the allocation of agricultural land characterized domestic political conflict during the entire Mao period. (Similar disagreements had arisen in the USSR after Lenin's death in '24; Lenin's successor Stalin abolished the former's NEP and introduced compulsory collective farming in '28).
10 Oct. '47 Mao declaration	Mao stated that Chiang Kaishek's "dictatorship" would be replaced by a "People's Democracy" (also called "New Democracy"), which would safeguard freedom of speech, press and association. He envisaged that China would gradually (over a "fairly long" transition period) develop light and heavy industries while transitioning from an agricultural to an industrial economy.

Date(s) or period	*Explanation*
Aug. '48 Introduction of "Gold Yuan" by the Nationalist Government	To fight inflation, the Nationalist Government in Chongqing introduced the Gold Yuan (replacing the earlier paper yuan at the rate of 1 for 3 mn). However, continued fiscal profligacy and money printing by the Government in Chongqing, soon undermined the value of the Gold Yuan, triggering hyperinflation.
Sept. '48 Statement by Liu Shaoqi at Politburo meeting	With Mao's support, Liu Shaoqi stated that during the "New Democracy" period – following the anticipated overthrow of Chiang Kaishek's Government- the CPC would "partner with the bourgeoisie" for 10–15 years before the transition to socialism would start. (The main reason for this relaxed timetable was concern that the CPC would be too weak and the country too poor to realize socialism more quickly. After *starting* the transition, *achieving* socialism was thought to require another 10–15 years).
Dec. '48 Establishment (in Shijiazhuan, Hebei) of the People's Bank of China (PBoC) and first issue of the renminbi (RMB)	To fight hyperinflation and control the money supply in areas already liberated by the PLA in northeastern China, the CPC established its own commercial/central bank in Shijiazhuan, Hebei (by merging three regional commercial banks), which introduced a new currency, the renminbi, to substitute for the Nationalist Government's yuan (and other currencies that were then circulating in the northeast.) To further promote financial stability, the newly created People's Bank of China (PBoC) also started a system of deposit accounts indexed to fixed quantities of basic consumer goods (rice, cotton cloth, cooking oil and coal). The economist Xue Muqiao is believed to have provided the theoretical foundation for these anti-inflation policies. After 1 Oct. '49 PBoC was moved to Beijing and later became China's central bank. It absorbed remaining Nationalist banks in '51 and served as China's only financial institution ("mono-bank" system) until '79 (the year after the 3rd Plenum of Dec. '78). The CPC's pre- and post-'49 anti-inflation measures were generally quite successful; currency substitution (RMB for yuan) was repeated at the national level after the PRC had been established and reinforced by other measures aimed at financial stabilization, such as, e.g., indexed deposit accounts.
March '49 2nd Plenum of the 7th CC	This Plenum confirmed the CPC's commitment to constructing a "New Democratic Society" and an economic system in which capitalism and socialism would co-exist for an extended period. However, the "transition to socialism" would not start immediately upon the establishment of "New Democracy" and might take decades. Economically, the PRC would be mainly oriented on the USSR, but Mao also indicated that he was interested in developing economic relations with Western capitalist countries. (Mao's earlier interest in having good relations with the US and in receiving US arms for the PLA is documented in Joiner (2009) and in Tuchman (1972).)

(*Continued*)

(Continued)

Date(s) or period	*Explanation*
June–Sept '49 Creation of the CPPCC and adoption of a provisional Constitution of the PRC	When it was clear that the communists would prevail in China's domestic civil war, the CPC organized the "Chinese People's Political Consultative Conference" to prepare for the establishment of a new regime to replace the KMT-dominated Nationalist Government of the Republic of China (ROC). The first CPPCC (Sept. '49), attended by the CPC and eight (aligned) political parties, approved a "Common Program", which served as a provisional Constitution of the PRC (until the first formal Constitution was enacted in '54). The "Common Program" protected private property and private enterprise.
1 Oct. '49 (1) Establishment of the PRC with a "tilt toward the Soviet Union" (2) China's membership in multilateral organizations stays with the ROC (Taiwan)	(1) Establishment of the PRC marked the start of Mao's "New Democratic Society", including a "tilt" toward the USSR. The "tilt" had political and economic dimensions. Mao and his fellow leaders were impressed by the USSR's economic achievements under Stalin and convinced of the innate superiority of socialism over capitalism. They wished to emulate the Soviet economic system, which was the only socialist model available then, but, as previously agreed, China's transition to socialism would not start immediately. The PRC's first Government included representatives of the CPC and aligned political parties in the CPPCC. A popular slogan of the CPC was "the USSR today is our tomorrow". However, Mao's admiration for the Soviet economic model later turned into doubts and reservations. His book "Critique of Soviet Economics", written during and after the Great Leap Forward (but not published until '67) took issue with key aspects of Stalin's economic policies. This explains part of the background to the emerging Sino-Soviet split that broke into the open in '60. However, in '49, the USSR was the first country to recognize the PRC and establish full diplomatic relations with it. Only a few (small) Western countries (Switzerland, Sweden, Denmark, Finland and Liechtenstein) recognized the PRC relatively quickly (in '50). The UK also recognized the PRC Government as the Government of China, but, partly because of disagreements over the ownership of military assets in Hong Kong, posted a low-level Chargé d'Affaires ad-interim in Beijing. France was the first major Western country to fully recognize the PRC and exchange ambassadors (Jan. '64), and French President Pompidou was the first leader of a major Western country to visit the PRC (Sept. '73). Initial PRC *economic* policies included: (a) ending "feudalism" in agriculture by extending land reforms to all of China (except Tibet); (b) substituting the renminbi for the yuan; (c) closing the Shanghai stock exchange; (d) nationalizing remaining private financial institutions (in '51); (e) nationalizing "comprador-capitalist" enterprises (companies owned by foreigners and members of the expelled KMT); (f) allowing companies owned by local Chinese who were sympathetic to the CPC (referred to as "national capitalist" enterprises) to continue as such – until they were required to form JVs with SOEs a few years later. (Mao initially encouraged private investment in "national capitalist" enterprises);

Date(s) or period	*Explanation*
	(g) unifying management of the national economy under the Central Economic and Finance Commission (CEFC) headed by Chen Yun, and (h) introducing a balanced Central Government budget (until the reforms of '84, the state budget made no distinction between government administration and SOE management.) Pre-existing *political* parties had already been combined in the CPPCC under the leadership of the CPC a few months earlier. The CPC and the CPPCC initially shared power under a "Common Program", which served as the PRC's de-facto Constitution until a formal national Constitution was adopted in '54. China's current Constitution, reflecting decisions of the 3rd Plenum of the 11th CC of the CPC in Dec. '78, was adopted in '82 (and amended in '88, '93, '99 and '04). Non-CPC members initially held about half of all top government positions in the PRC. (2) Since no major Western countries recognized the PRC until much later, Chiang Kaishek's Government of the ROC (which had fled to Taiwan) continued to represent China in multilateral organizations, such as the UN (until '71) and the Bretton Woods institutions (until '80).
Dec. '49–March '50 Mao's first visit to Moscow resulting in a Sino-Soviet aid agreement	Mao spent 2.5 months in the USSR. Stalin had long been more supportive of the KMT than the CPC and initially did not endorse the communist revolution in China. Nonetheless, during Mao's first visit to Moscow, he and Stalin signed a "Treaty of Friendship, Alliance and Mutual Assistance" under which the USSR would provide development assistance (loans and TA) to China. However, serious political tensions developed between the two nations in the second half of the '50s, and the Treaty was terminated by Stalin's successor Khrushchev in '60.
'49–'52 (1) Land reform (2) Creation of new economic institutions	(1) While ownership of all land was vested in the state, the right to use agricultural land (as well as farming equipment and farm animals) was allocated to individual peasants working the land. The Agrarian Land Reform Law was passed in '50. Previous landowners were not compensated for the loss of their property. Many of them were executed or sent to rural camps for "re-education". The redistribution of agricultural land (to poor peasants) started before the PRC's establishment in '49 in areas that had been liberated by the PLA. Agricultural productivity fell in response to these initial land reforms, which led to further reforms in the following years. (2) After the PRC had been established (1 Oct. '49), a new institution was created to manage the economy and plan for the future: Central Economic and Finance Commission (CEFC), headed by Chen Yun. A few years later (in '52) additional economic institutions were created: the State Economic Commission, the State Planning Commission, the State Statistical Bureau and the National Price Commission. The economist Xue Muqiao had leading roles in all of these, at different times. A ministerial State Council or Cabinet, was created in late '53.

(*Continued*)

(Continued)

Date(s) or period	*Explanation*
6–9 June '50 3rd Plenum of the 7th CC	At this Plenum of the CC, the first after the PRC's establishment, Mao warns against moving to socialism too quickly. (Rural land reforms were ongoing and popular support for the CPC was still patchy in some areas).
'50–'53 Korean War	The war required a reallocation of scarce resources for military purposes and delayed China's economic development. It also led to a break in relations with the West and an extension of the Cold War to China.
Dec. '50 US imposes comprehensive trade embargo on China, isolating the country both economically and politically from the West	After PLA "volunteers" entered the Korean War on North Korea's side (Oct. '50), the US imposed comprehensive unilateral trade sanctions on China, which, six months later, following a UN resolution, became multilateral. (The US trade embargo on China wasn't lifted until '71 in connection with preparations for President Nixon's visit to China in early '72.) The US Navy positioned its Seventh Fleet between mainland China and Taiwan, making it effectively impossible for Mao to complete the civil war by invading Taiwan.
'51 Consolidation of the banking system	During the year, PBoC Governor Nan Hancheng oversaw a financial assessment of all remaining Nationalist banks in China. The ones with negative net worth were closed, and the ones with positive net worth were absorbed by the PBoC, which then served as the country's only financial institution (in a "mono-bank" system) until '79.
Feb. '51 Ordinance on Labor Insurance – launch of a (Soviet-style) social security system	State- and SOE workers (and their families) in urban areas became eligible for a basic ("defined benefit") pension-, health- and occupational injury benefits – financed on a PAYG basis, as in the USSR. This system, which did *not* cover non-state and rural workers, remained in place until the mid-'80s when the "pooling" of social security obligations among SOEs in the same jurisdiction, became common. From the mid-'90s, the social security system was gradually reformed to include non-state workers and to extend coverage to unemployment, disability and maternity leave. (Part of the state-mandated pension system was turned into a *funded, individual-account* ("defined contribution") system in '96. Health insurance for urban residents – other than state- and SOE workers – was then privatized. A National Social Security Fund was established in '00. From the early 2000s, various schemes to provide modest social security benefits to rural residents, were introduced.)
18 May '51 UN General Assembly Resolution	A US-sponsored UN resolution imposed a comprehensive trade embargo on China, further isolating the country from the West and increasing its economic dependence on the USSR.
Late '51–'52 (1) Mao launched the Three-Antis campaign followed by the Five-Antis campaign to purify the Party and target capitalist sympathizers (2) Dismissal of Gu Zhun	(1) Mao's first political "campaign" after establishing the PRC in '49 was aimed at getting rid of *corruption, waste and bureaucracy* within the Party. This "Three-Antis" campaign (also called "Struggle Against Three Evils"), which was supported by Chen Yun (head of the CEFC), was soon followed by the "Five-Antis" campaign (against *bribery, tax evasion, stealing state assets, underpaying labor or under-providing raw materials in manufacturing and stealing state economic intelligence*), which targeted China's then still important *capitalist class* running traditional capitalist industrial and commercial units. Chen Yun did not support this follow-up campaign but made no effort to stop it. (A 3rd campaign, sometimes referred to as the

Date(s) or period	*Explanation*
	"thought-reform campaign", aimed at shifting influence on university curriculums from the West to the USSR.) (2) It is not clear what the connection (if any) was between the "Three-" and "Five-Antis" campaigns and the dismissal in '52 of Gu Zhun, director of Shanghai's Financial- and Taxation Bureaus. Since Shanghai was the Central Government's most important source of fiscal revenues, this was an important development. Gu Zhun later became one of Mao's most outspoken critics and an advocate of market (and political) reforms.
'52 Publication in Chinese of Stalin's book *Economic Problems of Socialism in the USSR*	The publication in Chinese (by the People's Publishing House) of this book by Stalin, General Secretary of the CPSU since '22, had significant influence on Mao (who then still looked at Stalin as a role model) and his associates. The book (which had been published in Russian in '51) may have contributed to Mao's decision to "propose" (on 24 Sept. '52) starting China's transition to socialism immediately and accelerate the pace of transition. It also helped shape priorities for China's 1st FYP, '53–'57. (Stalin's book, published in English in New York (also in '52), contains his comments on a draft textbook, *Marxist Political Economy*, which was discussed at a conference in Moscow in Nov. '51, and his responses to speakers at that conference.)
24 Sept. '52 Meeting of the CC Secretariat to discuss priorities for the 1st Five-Year Plan and China's transition to socialism (Source: Wu Jinglian & Ma Guochuan 2016, p. 34)	At this meeting, Mao confirmed, as had already been decided at the 2nd Plenum of the 7th CC of March '49, that China's transition to socialism would take a long time, but unexpectedly "proposed" that the transition should start immediately, rather than after a long waiting period, as originally intended. This "proposal" later became known as Mao's "General line for the Transition Period and the Acceleration of the Chinese Socialist Transformation". It is not entirely clear what prompted Mao's "proposal". It is possible that his reading of Stalin's book *Economic Problems of Socialism in the USSR* and the extension to China of the Cold War (as a result of the Korean War) played a role in the evolution of his thinking. It is also possible that Mao wanted to impress Stalin, who had expressed concern that the new communist Government in Beijing might slide off toward "Yugoslav-type socialism" by placing too much emphasis on democracy and nationalism. Yet another possible reason for Mao's unexpected "proposal" is that he had concluded that the only way to raise the additional financial resources needed to finance the 1st FYP's industrialization projects was to collectivize agriculture. The fact that around that same time, the Government "unified" its system for procuring and selling grain, lends weight to the suggestion that Mao's "proposal" was motivated by financial/fiscal considerations.
1952–'53 Creation of SPC, State Council and phasing out of CEFC	When the PRC was created, all national economic and financial matters were the responsibility of the CEFC, headed by Chen Yun. The State Planning Commission (SPC) was created in '52 to take over certain CEFC functions. After a formal ministerial State Council (Cabinet) was created in late '53, the CEFC was phased out, but Chen Yun remained a central figure in national economic management.

(*Continued*)

(Continued)

Date(s) or period	*Explanation*
'53–'57 1st Five-Year Plan (FYP)	The two main objectives of China's 1st FYP, prepared with TA from the USSR, were: (1) Rapid industrialization through investment in heavy (incl. military) industries, following the USSR's model. (To achieve this objective, the plan included 156 major industrial projects that would be (and were) implemented with USSR financial support and TA; and (2) To increase agricultural production through collectivization (also following Stalin's Soviet model). Although most industrial targets were achieved, agriculture slowed and grain rationing was introduced in urban areas in '53 (which wasn't discontinued until 40 years later). Rationing was later extended to many other consumer goods. The 1st FYP marked the beginning of central planning and comprehensive price controls for key commodities and services. The nationalization of remaining private enterprises was accelerated.
15 June '53 Politburo meeting to consider Mao's "proposal" to start China's transition to socialism immediately and to accelerate the pace of transition	On 24 Sept. '52, Mao had "proposed" to start China's transition to socialism immediately (as part of the 1st FYP). During the June '53 meeting, opposition to this idea was expressed by Liu Shaoqi (#2 in the Party), to which Mao responded by accusing Liu of "rightist opportunism". This appears to have been the beginning of a serious political split between the Party's two top officers. The split, which both leaders initially made efforts to hide, intensified over time, involved other leaders and ultimately led to Liu's tragic death during the Cultural Revolution in '68. The 15 June '53 meeting was also important because it considered a report by Politburo member Li Weihan suggesting that the best way to transition to socialism quickly was through a system he called "state capitalism". The Politburo accepted Mao's "proposal" to start the transition to socialism immediately (as part of the 1st FYP) and the idea that completion of the transition would take a "long time". Mao's "proposal" was later submitted to the Party as a whole in the form of a report by the Propaganda Department dated 28 Dec. '53, entitled "Struggle to Mobilize All Strength to Build Our Country into a Great Socialist One, an Outline for Study and Propaganda of the Party's General Line for the Transition Period".
15 Oct. '53 Mao meets with CPC theorists	Mao explained that his ideas for socialist transformation (which in mid-'55 became known as the "General Line for the Transition Period and the Acceleration of the Chinese Socialist Transformation") were aimed at "solving the problem" of private ownership and at eliminating the bourgeoisie.
Fall '53 Creation of State Council (Cabinet)	Together with the creation of SPC in the Fall of '52, the creation of a ministerial State Council (Cabinet) a year later was the most important national institutional economic development of the early '50s. Next to the Party's CC and Politburo, the State Council began to function as China's main center for economic policy making. Chen Yun's CEFC, which had been responsible for national economic and financial matters since '49, then became redundant and was gradually phased out.

Date(s) or period	*Explanation*
Feb. '54 4th Plenum of the 7th CC formally adopts Mao's "General Line" for socialist transformation	At this Plenum, Mao's "proposal" of 24 Feb. '52 to start the transition to socialism immediately and accelerate its pace was formally approved by the CC. This decision was reflected in the PRC's 1st national Constitution, which was adopted by the 1st National People's Congress (NPC) in September of that year.
20 Sept. '54 1st Session of the 1st NPC adopted the 1st National Constitution (which was effectively suspended less than a year later)	The PRC's 1st Constitution, endorsed by the CPPCC at earlier meetings, was formally approved by the NPC at its 1st official meeting. It reflected Mao's "General Line" and all major institutional developments since '49; it transformed China into a Soviet-style One-Party State (as had been recommended by Stalin): from then on, all senior government positions were held by CPC members (or CPC-approved individuals), essentially merging Party and state. Regarding agriculture, the '54 Constitution said, "*. . . the state protects, according to the law, the right of peasants to own land and other means of production*". Less than a year later, this clause was ignored when, over the objection of Deng Zihui (head of the Party's Central Rural Work Department and vice PM) and his deputy, Du Runsheng, Mao started a process of agricultural collectivization as part of a "socialist upsurge". (For all *practical* purposes, the '54 Constitution was then suspended. It wasn't until '75, during the Cultural Revolution (before Mao's death). that a new Constitution, reflecting (severely restricted) human rights and focusing mainly on security issues, was approved. The '75 Constitution was superseded by yet another Constitution in March '78 (after Mao's death and the arrest of the "Gang of Four"). China's current Constitution was enacted in '82 and amended in '88, '93, '99 and '04.
July '55 Mao presents his report on the need for collectivization in agriculture and orchestrates a "socialist upsurge" in rural China	Mao's report "On the Co-operative Transformation of Agriculture" explained why collectivization was necessary to increase agricultural productivity (through mechanization and other means). The report, which ignored the '54 Constitution on peasant rights, may have been inspired by Stalin's example in agriculture. It marked the start of a year-long campaign against rightist "deviationism" by "errand" comrades such as Deng Zihui (head of the Party's Central Rural Work Department and vice PM), who had objected to Mao's collectivization plans for agriculture. Farmers (except in Tibet) were urged to join voluntary producer cooperatives, which, about a year later, were converted into state-led "higher co-ops" (essentially collective farms). The collectivization process, which was completed in '56, gradually ended private farming while intensifying divisions within the Party on the future organization of agriculture. (The collectivization of agriculture was mirrored in the collectivization of small-scale handicraft industries.) A decline in grain output, due to farmer resistance to collectivization, led to a temporary reversal of the collectivization policy in some areas in '56 and '57. In '58, collective farms were absorbed in even larger "People's Communes", as part of the disastrous Great Leap Forward (GLF).

(*Continued*)

(Continued)

Date(s) or period	*Explanation*
Oct. '55 Meeting of the All-China Federation of Industry and Commerce	Mao calls on owners of private industry and commerce to "be ready for communism". Except for a small amount of wholesale and retail trading, all remaining private enterprises had been nationalized by the middle of '56, the year that, according to the opening session of the 8th Party Congress in Sept., marked the completion of China's transition to socialism. (By then, the Chinese economy had effectively become a Soviet-style centrally planned, command economy.)
25 Feb. '56 Khrushchev's "secret" speech denouncing Stalin	During the 20th Congress of the CPSU in Moscow, Khrushchev severely criticized his predecessor Stalin (who had died in '53) for alleged policy failures and for encouraging the adulation of his person (personality cult). The speech, marking the start of "de-Stalinization" in the USSR, had a strongly negative effect on Sino-Soviet relations; Mao still admired Stalin who was his role model in the early '50s. (Despite his objections to Khrushchev's speech, probably inspired by the USSR's Sputnik success the following year, Mao visited Moscow again in Nov. '57 to strengthen bilateral relations and to seek additional assistance).
25 April '56 Mao's speech on the "Ten Major Relationships"	Presenting the conclusions of a comprehensive review by PM Zhou Enlai of Soviet political and economic experience, in preparation for the 8th Party Congress in Sept., Mao identified 10 major relationships that should be taken into account in constructing socialism in China: (1) heavy and light industry, (2) coastal and interior industry, (3) economic development and defense, (4) the state and its enterprises, (5) central and local Government, (6) Han Chinese and ethnic minorities, (7) Party- and non-Party members, (8) revolution and counter-revolution, (9) right and wrong and (10) China and other countries. Mao concluded that a major defect of China's economic system was an over-concentration of power in the Central Government. His speech became a guide for design and implementation of administrative de-centralization in '58 as part of the GLF. The speech challenged key aspects of the Soviet economic model, which, in Mao's opinion, was overly centralized, depended too much on extracting financial resources from peasants (called "primitive accumulation") and relied too much on heavy industrialization. (Probably influenced by Khrushchev's speech of 25 Feb. (criticizing Stalin), this was the first time since 1 Oct. '49 that Mao publicly distanced himself from the Soviet economic model.)
15–27 Sept. '56 1st Session of the 8th Party Congress (56–69); confirmation that socialism had been achieved	The 8th was the first Party Congress since the PRC was established in '49. It determined that China's transition to socialism had been completed and approved the 2nd FYP ('58–'62) which, like the 1st FYP ('53–'57) was based on the Soviet economic model. (In '58, the 2nd FYP was essentially replaced by the GLF.) The Congress also adopted the Constitution of the CPC (which in its preamble said: the "aim of the Party is the achievement of socialism and communism in China") and approved Mao's proposals for the new "Economic Management System" reform that were based on his "Ten Major Relationships" speech of 25 April. The new "Economic Management System" reform was aimed at pumping new life into the lagging Chinese economy and at differentiating China's path to socialism and communism from the USSR's. The essence of Mao's new "Economic Management

Date(s) or period	*Explanation*
	System" was decentralization (i.e. delegating economic decision-making power and control over SOEs to local Governments), combined with central planning. (By the Fall of '56, China's economy was totally state-owned and/or state-controlled: all non-state enterprises that had survived earlier nationalization drives, except collectives and some state-private JVs that had been formed in the '50s, had been nationalized. Agriculture and handicraft industries had been collectivized. Private financial institutions had been merged into PBoC already in '51. Private traders and shop keepers had become "distributors" for state trading companies or members of cooperative stores. All foreign trade was conducted by a dozen state-owned import-export corporations.) Despite Mao's original intention (as expressed in his publication "On New Democracy" of '40) to delay the start of China's transition to socialism and to implement the transition over "quite a long time", the 8th Congress determined that the transition had been completed already in '56. During the "Let a Hundred Flowers Bloom and a Hundred Schools of Thought Contend" campaign that followed the opening Session of the 8th Party Congress, several leading economists, incl. Sun Yefang and Gu Zhun (obliquely) protested Mao's approach to improving living standards in China, because, in their opinion, it could not work in practice. They, like Deng Zihui before them, were accused of "revisionism", for which they were made to suffer later, especially during the Cultural Revolution (CR).
'56–'78 Period of Soviet-style centrally planned, command economy.	During this 22-yr period, which included the GLF ('58–'60) and the CR ('66–'76), free markets (and private ownership of means of production) were officially not permitted. In line with shifting ideas on national economic management, there were several cycles of administrative *de-* and *re*-centralization. Until they were withdrawn from China in '60, Soviet experts served as political, technical and economic advisors; they also transformed economics education in China by convincing the CPC that Stalin's economic system should be the only acceptable basis for economic theory. In the absence of capital markets, the financing of SOE investments and maintenance expenditures, required fiscal appropriations by the parent ministry in Beijing. Because of farmer resistance to collectivization, there was a partial and temporary return to private farming (under the "household responsibility system" (HRS) in some rural areas in '56 and '57.
Late '56–Fall '57 "Let a hundred flowers bloom and a hundred schools of thought contend" movement followed by an Anti-Rightists campaign and a parallel "Rectification" campaign	After initially inviting criticism of his new "Economic Management System Reform" (through the "Let a Hundred Flowers Bloom and a Hundred Schools of Thought Contend" campaign), Mao clamped down on opponents in a vicious "anti-rightist" campaign, managed by Deng Xiaoping, then the CPC's "Secretary General" and director of the Party's "Office of the Anti-Rightist Movement". In parallel, from May '57, the Party conducted a "Rectification campaign" (as it had done in Ya'nan in the early '40s) to stamp out "erroneous" lines of thinking and behavior in the Party. The Anti-Rightists campaign slackened in '58 but was resumed with vigor after the Lushan meeting of July/Aug. '59.

(*Continued*)

(Continued)

Date(s) or period	*Explanation*
20 Sept.–9 Oct. '57 3rd Plenum of the 8th CC; approval of the Great Leap Forward, essentially replacing the 2nd FYP	After the formal approval of Mao's "proposal" for a "Great Leap Forward" (the term was coined by the *People's Daily* in an editorial dated 13 Nov. '57) and its launch in May '58, the GLF was effectively discontinued in late '60, when Mao finally recognized its catastrophic economic and social effects. The GLF essentially replaced the 2nd FYP ('58–'62), which had been prepared under the leadership of Chen Yun, then Vice Chairman of the Party, and PM Zhou Enlai. The ignominious fate of the 2nd FYP was one of the factors that contributed to growing "distance" between Mao and other senior Party leaders, such as Liu Shaoqi, Chen Yun, Zhou Enlai and Deng Xiaoping. Disagreement with Mao over economic policy was one of the factors that led to Liu Shaoqi's tragic death during the CR (in '68) and to Zhou's speech on "Four Modernizations" in Jan. '75. The GLF also reflected Mao's wish to differentiate China's transition to socialism and communism from the USSR's and to show that China could do it better and more quickly (e.g., through the introduction of large-scale "People's Communes" in agriculture.) Since the 1st Session of the 8th Party Congress of Sept. '56 had determined that China's transition to socialism had been completed, logically, the next step was transition from socialism to communism. According to Marxist theory, communism required ownership of all means of production by "the whole people" (i.e. the state on behalf of all people). Collective ownership of farms was at odds with this requirement. Although the large "People's Communes" did not represent "ownership by the whole people", they were closer to that ideal than the smaller collective farms. (The record is not clear on whether Mao intended to use the GLF to transition from socialism to communism as defined by Marx. What is clear, however, is that he wanted to *catch up* with steel output and other major industrial production in Great Britain *in 15 years* and to *surpass* the US. Whatever Mao's reasons for launching the GLF, it was based on unrealistic output targets and caused very serious social and economic problems (including widespread famine due to a sharp drop in grain output and disease). Local Governments routinely falsified economic reports to disguise the reality of falling grain output. During and after the GLF Mao wrote *A Critique of Soviet Economics*, a book (not published until '67) that explains his objective to quickly transform China from a poor agrarian economy into a modern industrial society to thus avoid the kind of economic problems he saw developing in the USSR. The GLF also involved the forced mobilization of labor for public works (such as dams and irrigation projects) and the application of new agricultural techniques (deep plowing and close-planting, as recommended by Soviet "experts") as well as the construction of numerous "backyard furnaces" for making pig iron.

Date(s) or period	*Explanation*
30 March '58 Special meeting of the CC	To promote agricultural productivity in line with GLF objectives (and presumably also to facilitate the extraction of financial resources from agriculture to finance industrialization), it was decided to consolidate the then existing 740,000 "higher coops" (collective farms) into 26,000 huge "People's Communes" (with communal kitchens and canteens). Communes were also responsible for the processing of harvested crops, some other light industrial activities, military training and social services. Peasants in Communes were organized in "Production Brigades", which were sub-divided into "Production Teams". However, the Commune as a whole was initially the basic accounting- and production unit. (Later, the "Production Brigade" would become the basic unit of account, and during the CR, it was the "Production Team".)
3 May '58 4th Plenum of the 8th CC	In accordance with the decentralization objectives of Mao's new "Economic Management System", the meeting decided to transfer day-to-day control over 88% of all SOEs to local Governments. However, the incentive framework for SOEs remained otherwise unchanged, which meant that SOE efficiency problems were not addressed in a meaningful way.
5–23 May '58 Second Session of the 8th Party Congress	At this Session, Mao's ideas on "The Ten Major Relationships" as expressed in his speech of 25 April '56 became official Party policy and the GLF, which had already been approved by the CC at its 3rd Plenum of Sept./Oct. '57, was launched. In a major speech, Liu Shaoqi referred to the Party's plan for the GLF as the "General Line for Socialist Transformation". Since the 1st Session of the 8th Party Congress in Sept. '56 had concluded that China had already completed its transition to socialism, it is not entirely clear what Liu Shaoqi meant by the phrase "General Line for Socialist Transformation". Because he didn't explicitly say that China would transition from socialism to communism, it is possible that the word "transition" in his speech referred to a further deepening of socialism. Whether Liu and Mao had different objectives for the GLF (communism *or deeper socialism*) is unclear.
July '58 State Council meeting	Again, in accordance with Mao's new "Economic Management System" (which had been approved at the 1st Session of the 8th Party Congress in Sept. '56) and his decentralization objectives, the State Council decided to give Local Governments authority to approve and fund most local construction projects. Local Government revenues were strengthened for that purpose.
2–10 Nov. '58 First Zhengzhou conference to review the GLF	Concerned about negative reports about the GLF, Mao called on the Politburo and other officials to review the situation and to discuss "theoretical issues related to the building of socialism". (Most economic problems were then thought to be the result of isolated cases of hunger and disease.) With the concurrence of Chen Yun, Mao expressed concern that some GLF production targets (e.g., for steel) were not realistic and proposed "cooling down" the GLF by giving peasants more time to rest. However, other, more dogmatic, Party leaders, insisted on pursuing original GLF targets and prevailed at this meeting.

(*Continued*)

(Continued)

Date(s) or period	*Explanation*
Dec. '58 6th Plenum of the 8th CC	This Plenum adopted the "Resolution on Some Questions Concerning the People's Communes", which recognized the unwieldy size of Communes as a problem. A decision in principle was made to reduce their size. But there was no proposal then to discontinue forced collectivization (or to permit grain imports). On the contrary, the Plenum confirmed that collective farming was necessary for the "transition to socialism". There was much discussion on theoretical issues, such as the difference(s) between socialism and communism and between collective ownership and "ownership by the whole people" (as required in mature Marxian communism). Mao instructed all cadres to read Stalin's *Economic Problems of Socialism in the USSR*.
Late Feb.-early March '59 Second Zhengzhou conference to review the GLF and to discuss theoretical issues related to socialist transformation	This follow-up conference of Mao, the Politburo and other officials (to discuss the GLF and theoretical issues concerning socialist transformation) confirmed the decision "in principle" of the 6th Plenum of Dec. '58 to reduce the size of People's Communes. It was decided then to make the smaller "Production Brigade" the basic accounting unit instead of the larger Commune. However, these new arrangements were not immediately implemented. They were confirmed, yet again, at a Politburo meeting in the Fall of '60 and at the 9th Plenum of the 8th CC in Jan. '61. It was also decided at the second Zhengzhou conference to permit "sideline" production of certain crops on small individual plots. Partly because of false reporting by local Governments, Mao and other top leaders still did not have a complete picture of the economic and social disaster that was unfolding as a result of the GLF.)
April '59 Shanghai conference of economists to discuss GLF failures	To discuss theoretical issues related to socialist transformation and problems generated by the GLF, a group of prominent Chinese economists, including Sun Yefang and Xue Muqiao, met in Shanghai. With regard to GLF-related problems, the conference concluded that the problems were due to *tensions in the relationship between plan and market in a socialist economy*. Further public discussion of this sensitive topic was quashed by Mao at the Lushan meeting a few months later.
2 July – 16 Aug. '59 Politburo meeting followed by the 8th Plenum of the 8th CC in Lushan, Jiangxi	After again reviewing disturbing information on the results of the GLF, Mao expressed concern about "some imbalances" that had developed in the national economy. But there was still no complete knowledge of the very serious, nationwide economic and social problems, including famine, that were developing. A climate of fear and delusion pervaded the Lushan meeting, which led to the historic repudiation by Mao of the famous Marshall Peng Dehuai (based on his letter to Mao of 14 July '59 expressing concern about the social and economic effects of the GLF). Peng, accused by Mao of "anti-party right-wing opportunism", was then the only senior Party leader who openly dared to tell Mao the truth about declining grain production and famine. He was purged at the 8th Plenum of the 8th CC, while Mao intensified the Party's earlier anti-rightist campaign.

Date(s) or period	*Explanation*
Sept. '59 Discovery of major oil reserves in China	The discovery of rich oil and gas reserves in southern Heilongjiang (at a place that was then named Daqing = big celebration) temporarily distracted from GLF problems. Economic policy makers then thought that China would have ample energy and financial resources to underpin the aggressive industrialization strategy that was part of the GLF.
Oct. '59 Publication (on the 10th anniversary of the PRC) of *The Socialist Transformation of the National Economy in China* by Xue Muqiao (and two co-authors)	This was the first comprehensive overview of the Chinese economy, as it had evolved since the establishment of the PRC in '49. It was written by the already famous economist Xue Muqiao and two co-authors. The book was widely read in China and published in English, Japanese, French, Spanish and German by Foreign Languages Press, a government publisher in Beijing. The book (287 pages in the English edition) is essentially an explanation of and apology for China's forced transition to socialism. The book suggests that Xue then still believed in Marxist-Leninist revolutionary theories. (Unlike his professional peers Sun Yefang and Gu Zhun, Xue had not publicly expressed reservations about Mao's economic policies during the "Let a Hundred Flowers Bloom and a Hundred Schools of Thought Contend" campaign of '56/'57.) Xue's book was entirely supportive of the nationalization of remaining private enterprises in the early and mid-'50s, the collectivization of agriculture and handicrafts, and central economic planning. The book did not examine the grave problems caused by the GLF. (Xue Muqiao remained a Marxist throughout his professional career, but after the 3rd Plenum of Dec. '78 played a key role (as an economist and official in several important government positions) in the design and implementation of market-oriented reforms under Deng Xiaoping. His thinking about the importance of free markets and the role of the state in a socialist economy apparently changed fundamentally sometime after the publication of *The Socialist Transformation of the National Economy in China*).
'60–'89 Duration of "Sino-Soviet split"	The deterioration in relations between Mao and Khrushchev following the latter's speech denouncing Stalin (Feb. '56) was compounded by Sino-Soviet disagreements over the future of global communism and relations with the West. (Mao's reasons for differentiating China's path to socialism/communism from the USSR's economic model are explained in his *A Critique of Soviet Economics*, a book comprising essays written during and after the GLF, published in '67.) Another factor in the deterioration of bilateral relations was the USSR's criticism of China's GLF in '59. In '60, Khrushchev suddenly withdrew all Soviet experts from China (almost 10,000 technical and 1,500 political and economic advisors), effectively bringing many construction- and research projects in China to a halt. He also withdrew a Soviet offer to help China build an atomic bomb. One of the consequences of this rupture in bilateral relations was a reorientation of China's economic plans on light industry and agriculture. This contributed to a relaxation of restrictions

(*Continued*)

(Continued)

Date(s) or period	*Explanation*
	on private farming in parts of rural China in the early '60s and subsequent improvements in agricultural productivity. The deterioration in Sino-Soviet relations led to a complete break in diplomatic relations in '62 and to military skirmishes in some border areas in the late '60s. (To the withdrawal by Khrushchev of an earlier Soviet offer to help China develop nuclear technology, Mao responded by mobilizing Chinese physicists for a secret nuclear program. This led to a test detonation of China's own atomic bomb in '64 and a hydrogen bomb only 3 years later.) Sino-Soviet economic relations came to a virtual standstill, and diplomatic relations remained tense until Mikhail Gorbachev's visit to Beijing in '89. Fear of an attack on China by the USSR led Mao to relocate critical industries to central China in '70 and to seek relations with the US. This contributed to Henry Kissinger's secret visit in '71 and President Nixon's visit in early '72.
Oct. '60 GLF disaster finally acknowledged by Mao at a Politburo meeting; Chen Yun and Zhou Enlai then put in charge of an "Adjustment Plan" to rehabilitate the economy	When the full magnitude of the national catastrophe brought about by the GLF was finally apparent to Mao, he offered some mild self-criticism about his role in launching the GLF and left Beijing for several months. When the GLF was discontinued, political and economic confusion ensued. Chen Yun was then asked to head a Central Finance and Economy Small Group to guide national economic rehabilitation, reporting to PM Zhou Enlai. Chen declined to head the Group, but became its most important member, while Li Fuchun became its official Chairman. An interim "Adjustment Plan" ('60–'63) was drawn up with the help of Xue Muqiao. It included, inter alia: (1) administrative re-centralization, (2) a commitment to improve the quality of central planning and (3) approval of grain imports to supplement inadequate domestic supplies. "backyard furnaces" for making pig iron were dismantled, and millions of workers, hired by the government in '58 and '59 to build irrigation schemes, dams and other public works, were sent home. Earlier Politburo decisions (at the 2nd Zhengzhou conference of late Feb./early March '59) to reduce the size of "People's Communes", to make Production Brigades basic units of account and to permit "sideline" production on small individual plots, were confirmed. By reducing the size of Communes, their number increased, from about 26,000 in '59 to 74,000 in '63. In some areas, with the (tacit or open) permission of local politicians, there was a return to private farming under the HRS, which quickly contributed to improved productivity. (After falling by almost 30% between '58 and '60, total grain production began to rise again. In '62 it was almost back to the level it had been in '52, but in the meantime, China's population had grown significantly so that the per capita availability of grain remained insufficient.) Since China had exported grain during most of the '50s (in spite of domestic rationing since '53), the need for imports was a blow to Mao's prestige and the clearest indication that the GLF had failed.

Date(s) or period	*Explanation*
Jan. '61 9th Plenum of the 8th CC – adoption of the Eight-Character Principle	This Plenum officially approved the downsizing of People's Communes and making Production Brigades the basic accounting unit within the (smaller) Communes. This was part of the so-called "Eight-Character Principle", a set of economic policy adjustments following the GLF, put together under the leadership of Chen Yun.
'61–'62 Ad hoc meetings of the Politburo	Ideological disagreements among Party leaders on the role of private farming in a socialist economy persisted. A return to private farming was officially resisted, but nonetheless tolerated in many areas. Officially, the Politburo directed local Governments to restore collective farming, but this directive wasn't always carried out, because Deng Xiaoping, then a member of the Politburo and director of the Party's Organization Department, disagreed with it; he favored private (family) farming under the HRS, which was actually happening in many parts of rural China anyway. The partial return to private farming in the early '60s led to major improvements in agricultural output, rural incomes and the overall economy. To explain his position on this, in a speech on agriculture in '61, Deng quoted an old Anhui saying: "*it doesn't matter whether the cat is black or yellow as long as it catches mice*". (While the economy began to recover (from '62 until the start of the CR in '66), disagreement within the Party on economic policy continued, as is illustrated, e.g., by the fact that the post-GLF administrative *re*-centralization was reversed a few years later. Because the national food supply situation remained precarious in the early '60s (after the GLF had ended), grain exports – mainly loan repayments in-kind to the USSR – were halted, while grain imports (mainly from Australia and Canada) were increased.
11 Jan.–7 Feb. '62 "7,000-Cadres meeting"	At this unusually large work conference of the CC (including thousands of central and local officials) to discuss the economy, Mao blamed himself for some of the problems that had developed during the GLF and repeated the same mild self-criticism that he had offered in Oct. '60. Several other senior leaders also admitted mistakes. While much of the blame for the GLF disaster was put on the weather – some natural disasters did indeed occur – Mao's main explanation was that the Party's knowledge of and experience with socialist construction was inadequate. Despite these "semi-confessions", there was still no honest accounting of the problems caused by the GLF, and nobody was held accountable. On the contrary, the basic "correctness" of Mao's economic policies was affirmed by most speakers at this meeting.
24–27 Sept. '62 10th Plenum of the 8th CC	Mao urges the Party to return to "class struggle", while denouncing private farming and markets as "capitalist".
May '63 Ad hoc meeting of the CC	This meeting launched the Party's "Socialist Education Movement" in rural China to promote *socialist thinking and terminate private farming* (which had spontaneously returned in some areas with the consent of local political leaders).

(*Continued*)

(Continued)

Date(s) or period	*Explanation*
16 May '66 Mao launches the "Great Proletarian Revolution" with his "May 16 Circular"	Having concluded that the Party was backsliding toward capitalism, Mao wanted to rid it of "revisionist elements", (incl. Liu Shaoqi and Deng Xiaoping). He urged "Red Guards" to "smash the Party's HQ", unleashing a period of great social/political turmoil and economic disruption, which lasted until the arrest of the "Gang of Four", a few weeks after his death on 9 Sept. '76). Grain imports were discontinued at the start of the CR.
'66–'76 Great Proletarian Cultural Revolution (CR) period	This was a chaotic era, during which many local Governments ceased to function and were replaced by "Revolutionary Committees". Many cultural monuments were destroyed by "Red Guards" (who tried to eliminate the so called "four olds" – old thinking, old culture, old customs and old habits), while most higher education and scientific research was suspended (until the early '70s or, in some cases, until after the CR). Millions of people were sent to the countryside for "re-education" through living and working with local farmers. (The officially approved 3rd and 4th FYPs ('66–'70 and '71–'75) were essentially ignored, like the 2nd FYP, '58–'62, which had been superseded by the GLF.) In '69 PBoC was discontinued as a separate institution and turned into a department of MOF. During the CR, Chinese people interacting with foreigners were often suspected of espionage. Private farming, which had returned in several areas, was rolled back as agriculture was re-collectivized (but, sensibly, in yet smaller Communes with "Production Teams", sub-divisions of "Production Brigades", serving as basic accounting units). The new (smaller) Communes were encouraged to follow the "Dazhai model", a "Group Responsibility System" (modeled after the HRS for individual farmers) based on the "Production Team". Compensation payments to the private partners in former state-private industrial JVs, were discontinued in '67. Existing pension funds were liquidated. Other than the "work point" system in agriculture (work points could be traded for grain) economic incentives were taboo. There was virtually no private enterprise during the CR. Most daily necessities were rationed and the freedom of movement of people was severely restricted. Grain rationing intensified as cereal imports were discontinued. Numerous intellectuals and people in positions of authority were humiliated and persecuted. (E.g., Sun Yefang was imprisoned and deprived of his CPC membership in the first year of the CR – and not rehabilitated until after Mao's death in '76). As a result of China's *self*-imposed seclusion from the rest of the world, foreign trade shrank to a trickle. The national economy suffered badly, especially in the first and last years of the CR. (E.g. China's share in global GDP fell from 4.7% in '55 to 1% in '77.) In '70 there was another major (politically motivated) administrative *de*-centralization, while key industries were relocated to interior provinces, as part of Mao's so-called "Third-Front" strategy (based on his expectation that war with the USSR was imminent). Fear of Moscow's intentions also led to China's opening to the US, starting with Kissinger's secret visit to China in July '71.

Date(s) or period	*Explanation*
July '71 Henry Kissinger, then President Nixon's National Security Advisor, secretly visited China to discuss normalization of bilateral relations	The visit, which had extremely important long-term political and economic consequences for both countries and for the world, was prepared with Pakistan's discreet assistance. (The Kissinger visit was preceded by friendly ping-pong matches between US and Chinese teams in Japan and China – the so-called "Ping-Pong diplomacy" was arranged with the help of the National Committee on US-China Relations.)
25 Oct. '71 The PRC replaces the ROC in the UN	The UN General Assembly voted to admit the PRC and to expel the ROC (Taiwan). This was an important development in the sequence of events that eventually led to the normalization of US-China relations.
21–28 Feb. '72 President Nixon's visit to China	This visit, which had been prepared by Henry Kissinger during his secret visit to China in July '71 started a process of bilateral and international political and economic changes of great importance for both countries and for the world.
29 Sept. '72 Normalization of China-Japan relations	Following the Nixon visit and intensive "people-to-people" diplomacy, Japan and many other countries, incl. the UK (on 13 March '72) and the Fed. Rep. of Germany (on 11 Oct.'72), recognized the PRC Government, one of the few positive developments during the CR.
Feb. '74 "Third World" concept introduced by Mao	In a meeting with Zambia's president Kenneth Kaunda, Mao explained his world vision. The world is divided into three parts, he said: the "first world" of superpowers (US and USSR), the "second world" of developed countries (Europe, Japan, Canada, Australia, New Zealand) and the "third world" of developing countries (in Asia – including China – Africa and Latin America). The term *third world* thus entered the lexicon of international relations and development economics. Mao's conversation with Kaunda seemed to signal that China wished to distance itself from both superpowers at that time.
Jan. '75 PM Zhou Enlai's Four Modernizations	In his report to the 4th NPC, PM Zhou Enlai repeated his calls for the modernization of: (1) agriculture, (2) industry, (3) national defense and (4) science and technology. (It was an attempt by Zhou to distance himself from Mao's ideology-inspired CR and focus on the need for *economic development.*) Zhou's four modernizations were subsequently enshrined in the CPC's national Constitution and regularly cited as critical national development objectives. (In a posting on "Democracy Wall" in Beijing in '78, human rights activist Wei Jinsheng called for a "Fifth Modernization" (i.e. democracy), an act for which he was imprisoned and later exiled).
8 Jan. '76 Zhou Enlai dies	As a result of events following Zhou's death, the "Gang of Four" gained power. They denounced Deng Xiaoping and his mentor Zhou Enlai. The former fled to Guangzhou. Later that year, after his return to Beijing, he was stripped of his Party and government positions by the "Gang of Four", which had effectively taken over Party leadership from Mao, who was very ill. Soon after

(*Continued*)

(Continued)

Date(s) or period	*Explanation*
	Zhou's death, Deng Xiaoping was appointed Acting PM and a few months later, Mao appointed Hua Guofeng as the CPC's "First Vice Chairman" (i.e. his chosen successor.) Meanwhile, the madness of the CR intensified.
20 Jan. '76 Deng tenders his resignation as Vice PM.	This marks the final break between Mao and Deng Xiaoping, who was accused by Mao of "revisionism". Deng's resignation was not immediately accepted, but he was relieved of his official functions and placed under house arrest (by the "Gang of Four") on 7 April, two days after the "Tiananmen Incident" of 5 April '76.
5 April '76 "Tiananmen Incident"	After Zhou Enlai's death, spontaneous demonstrations (on Tiananmen Square in Beijing and in other cities) to honor him were suppressed by the "Gang of Four". This led to more demonstrations (often against the government) and the alleged killing by police of about 60 protesters and the arrest of thousands, on 5 April. Acting PM Deng Xiaoping, a life-long ally of Zhou Enlai, was held responsible for the "incident" and placed under house arrest on 7 April.
7 April '76 (1) Hua Guofeng appointed 1st Vice Chairman of the CPC (2) Deng placed under house arrest	(1) After the death of Lin Biao in '71, Hua Guofeng had already been tentatively designated by Mao as his successor. He was confirmed as Mao's chosen successor and appointed "First Vice Chairman" of the CPC on 7 April '76. (2) That same day, Deng was stripped of all his official Party and government positions and placed under house arrest (but not expelled from the Party).
9 Sept. '76 Mao dies; Hua Guofeng assumes CPC Chairmanship	Hua Guofeng succeeds Mao as Party Chairman after Mao's death on 9 Sept. '76. Four weeks later, the "Gang of Four" was arrested with Hua's blessings. In accordance with Deng's wishes, Hu Yaobang took over from Hua as Party Chairman in June '81 and continued Party leadership as "General Secretary" after the 1st Plenum of the 12th Party Congress in Sept. '82, when the title "Chairman" (of the Party) was abolished.
6 Oct. '76 Arrest of the "Gang of Four"	This historic event (authorized by Hua Guofeng on the recommendation of some Party elders, including the famous Marshal Ye Jianying and Vice PM Li Xiannian) marked the end of the CR. Hua's decision to give priority to economic development (over ideological "class struggle" was quickly followed by various government-led efforts to understand the reasons for China's economic backwardness at that time. Such efforts included numerous studies (by officials and professional technocrats) on the development experience of other countries and the drafting of proposals for alternative development strategies. A major hurdle, however, was Hua Guofeng's doctrine of the "Two Whatevers".

Date(s) or period	*Explanation*
Feb. '77 *People's Daily* editorial "Learning the Documents Well and Grasping the Key Link", promoted Hua Guofeng's doctrine of the "Two Whatevers"	By promoting the idea that Party members should (1) "resolutely support *whatever* Mao had decided and (2) do *whatever* Mao had instructed", an editorial in the *People's Daily* absolved Mao from responsibility for the disastrous CR. The editorial was apparently also intended to block Deng Xiaoping's reentry into Party leadership positions, but several senior Party elders, including Marshal Ye Jianying and CPC Vice Chairman Chen Yun, wanted Deng to be fully rehabilitated, because they saw in him the leader China needed.
18 April '77 Xue Muqiao writes an open letter about the economy to Deng Xiaoping and Li Xiannian	In this influential letter, written to Deng Xiaoping (when he was still under house arrest) and Li Xiannian (then Vice Chairman of the CPC and chief economic advisor to Hua Guofeng) the famous economist Xue Muqiao alerted Party leaders to fundamental economic imbalances that had developed during the GLF and the CR: too much heavy industry, too little light industry and insufficient progress in agriculture. For the first time, Xue Muqiao openly criticized some of Mao's economic policies, urging the Party to *rebalance* the economy as a matter of priority. Xue blamed the problems in agriculture on a lack of farmer "enthusiasm" to increase output under forced collectivization. In this letter, he does not mention the importance of markets and economic incentives, as he would, with growing intensity, after the 3rd Plenum of Dec. '78. Instead, he stressed the need for better planning by the government.
May '77 Establishment of the China Academy of Social Sciences (CASS)	This, together with the arrest of the "Gang of Four" after Mao's death in '76 and the political rehabilitation of Deng Xiaoping in July '77, was the most important contribution by Hua Guofeng to China's subsequent economic reform and development. The CASS, whose first president, Hu Qiaomu, was then known as a "conservative", quickly became a crucially important semi-independent think-tank, supporting Deng Xiaoping's strategy to fundamentally redirect China's economic development efforts. The initial "heart" of the CASS was the Institute of Economics of the CAS, where several of China's most prominent early reformers such as Xue Muqiao, Sun Yefang, Du Runsheng, Liu Guoguang, Dong Furen and the younger Wu Jinglian, had gotten to know each other. (Gu Zhun, who might have become the most important technocratic reformer, if he had lived longer, died in '74).
16–27 July '77 3rd Plenum of the 10th CC – Deng Xiaoping rehabilitated	During this Plenum, Deng Xiaoping was fully rehabilitated (and reinstalled as a member of the Politburo's Standing Committee, Vice Chairman of the CC and CMC, Vice PM and Chief of the PLA's General Staff). Although he initially had some doubts, Deng's rehabilitation was supported by Hua. About a year and half later, at the 3rd Plenum of the 11th CC, Deng became China's de-facto "Paramount" leader thus marginalizing Hua, who was considered an obstacle to real economic reform by Deng.

(*Continued*)

(Continued)

Date(s) or period	*Explanation*
12–18 Aug. '77 11th Party Congress (Aug. '77 – Aug. '82)	Under the leadership of Hua Guofeng, this Congress affirmed (1) Hua's doctrine of the "Two Whatevers" and (2) the Party's determination to continue Mao's "revolution under proletarian dictatorship" (a popular slogan during the CR).
'77–'78 Many professional conferences and political debates on the question whether "distribution according to work", (incl. bonuses and compensation based on piecework) was consistent with socialism	Intense debates on key economic development and ideological issues in '77 and early '78, involving hundreds of officials and technocrats/economists, eventually led to a Deng Xiaoping-sanctioned article in the People's Daily (5 May '78) confirming that the principle of "distribution according to work" was consistent with socialism. When this controversial issue was finally settled, the formulation of alternative economic development strategies based on *incentives and markets* (combined with official tolerance for social inequality), became politically acceptable. The People's Daily article marked a breakthrough in economic policy making.
'77–early '80s (1) Senior politicians, economists and officials visit many foreign countries, especially Eastern Europe (EE) and Western Europe (WE), to study their economic systems, policies and institutions (2) China taps into multilateral institutions for knowledge about the global economy (3) Chinese professional economists become important players in the national debate on development strategy	(1) After the arrest of the "Gang of Four", having discovered how backward China's economy was then, numerous official study trips were undertaken to learn from other countries. E.g., in '77 Party Chairman Hua Guofeng and PM Zhao Ziyang visited Yugoslavia and Romania. In '78 Deng Xiaoping visited eight countries, incl. Japan and Singapore, while Vice PM Gu Mu led a study mission to WE, which led to a State Council decision in July '78 to lift China's self-imposed ban on borrowing from Western countries/agencies. Yu Guangyuan led study missions to Yugoslavia and Romania. In early '79 Deng, shortly after the normalization of bilateral relations, visited the US, and Yu Guangyuan led a mission to Hungary. (The most probable explanation for the apparent absence of study missions to Russia during those years is that many Chinese scholars and politicians were already familiar with that country.) Several EE countries urged the PRC to join the IMF and the World Bank. In '80, Zhu Rongji (then Vice Chairman of the Import-Export Commission) visited Southeast Asia, Ireland and Sri Lanka. Liu Guoguang headed a task force pulling together information on alternative socialist development experiences. Hungary and Czechoslovakia were thought to offer important lessons for China, even though their approach to price reform was seen by the Chinese as flawed. Of all these study missions abroad, the one led by Gu Mu to France, Switzerland, West Germany, Denmark and Belgium (May/June '78) was probably the most influential. It helped Party leaders reach consensus on what later became China's "reform and opening-up" strategy and on the need to permit borrowing capital from Western countries and agencies to promote China's development. The mission was very impressed by WE's economic, social and scientific achievements and questioned the inevitability of extreme social inequality and revolution in capitalist countries as predicted by Marx and Engels. Though China's orientation on Europe in the late '70s was strong, the two most important sources of inspiration and practical examples for Deng, were Japan's "miracle economy" and Lee Kuan Yew's Singapore.

Date(s) or period	*Explanation*
	(2) After initial interest in EE approaches to economic reform had cooled, China began to focus on the broader international economic experience and, when the PRC had replaced the ROC (Taiwan) as China's representative in the Bretton Woods institutions in '80, often used the IMF and the World Bank as sources of information and advice. (3) The most important Chinese economists (many of whom also served in senior government positions) involved in economic study missions and reform debates during this period were Sun Yefang, Xue Muqiao, Liu Guoguang, Liu Suinian, Zhao Renwei, Liao Jili, Ma Hong, Yu Guangyuan, Dong Fureng, An Zhiwen, Gao Shangquan and Wu Jinglian. Some younger Chinese economists (including, e.g., Zhou Xiaochuan, Lou Jiwei, Guo Shuqing, Chen Xiwen and Li Jange) would later join the ranks of leading economist-reformers.
'77–present Disagreements within the Party and among technocrats on economic reform priorities and strategy persist	After Mao's death and the arrest of the "Gang of Four" in '76, disagreements among Party leaders and technocrats on economic reform priorities and strategy burst into the open and continued, in one form or another, at different levels of intensity, until the present. For convenience, analysts usually distinguish between two schools of thought: "reformers" and "conservatives". In reality, there were, and are, many shades of opinion in between. In '86, a new school of thinking about economic development, led by engineers, emerged. They focused in particular on the acquisition of foreign technologies and the promotion of *indigenous innovation*. While conservatives and reformers agreed on the need for major changes in economic institutions and policies, they often disagreed on the *extent* of change that was needed. The terms of debate between them were more or less settled at the time of the 3rd Plenum of the 11th CC of Dec. '78, but disputes on strategy and priorities continued. Conservative leaders initially opposed a return to private faming, while reformers favored quick de-collectivization under the HRS. Deng Xiaoping, China's "paramount" leader from late '78 through the early 1990s, was very much a reformer at heart, but sometimes sided with conservative leaders for political reasons. Deng supported state-sponsored science and technology development. His successor as Party leader, Jiang Zemin was also a reformer, as was his successor Hu Jintao, although the latter (and his PM, Wen Jiabao) had different priorities –they focused more on social issues and "industrial policy" than on perfecting the market economy. Hu Jintao's successor Xi Jinping (CPC General Secretary since the 18th Party Congress in Nov. '12), affirmed his commitment to Deng Xiaoping's "reform and opening up" policies started in the late '70s, but in practice appears to be giving higher priority to political objectives, corruption fighting and "industrial policy", while promoting "national rejuvenation" and the "China Dream". Though basic ideological differences persist (and from time to time dominate internal debates, like after the Tiananmen "incidents" of '76 and '89), as the economy grew and

(*Continued*)

(Continued)

Date(s) or period	*Explanation*
	became more complex, practical governance questions (such as, e.g., how to organize health care and social security, how to promote sound urbanization and increase the share of domestic consumption in GDP; how to manage the exchange rate and international reserves; how to deal with excess manufacturing capacity and overleveraging) began to dominate debates on economic policy making. Reformers tended to minimize the importance of Marxist theory while emphasizing the need for greater economic *efficiency* and *innovation* (to be achieved through greater reliance on incentives and competition.) Conservatives, on the other hand, tended to emphasize the need for state and Party control (to be achieved through public ownership of the means of production, centralized economic planning and state-led "industrial policy").
Jan. '78 PBoC re-established as a separate agency	At Deng's urging, PBoC, which had been part of MOF since '69 (during the CR), was re-established as a separate agency, but the "mono-bank" system continued until '79, when ABC, BOC and CCB were established as separate commercial banks.
Feb. '78 5th NPC approves Hua Guofeng's 10-Year Development Plan	NPC approved Hua Guofeng's Soviet-style 10-yr Development Plan ('76–'85), which favored heavy-industries and capital-intensive projects. The Plan also aimed at reducing China's international economic isolation by importing advanced equipment (although the country's capacity to pay for the imports and absorb the technologies was doubted by many). The Plan was effectively shelved the following year and replaced by a 3-yr Interim Adjustment Plan favored by Chen Yun and Deng Xiaoping.
Early '78 (1) Spontaneous de-collectivization starts in Anhui and Sichuan (2) CITIC established to attract foreign investment	(1) Eighteen farmers of the Production Brigade of Xiaogangcun village (Fengyang county, Anhui) signed a secret "death pact", agreeing to support each other's families in case of punishment for their decision to break up their Commune and return to private farming under the HRS. (Note: some Chinese sources put this event in '76). Although the HRS (as opposed to the "Small-Group Responsibility System" (Dazhai model) was very controversial then, this spontaneous de-collectivization was quietly supported by local cadres and by Anhui provincial Party Secretary Wan Li, who had criticized the officially mandated Dazhai model of collective farming. Wan Li also saw a return to private farming (on collectively owned land) as the best way to deal with the drought in Anhui that year. Some spontaneous de-collectivization also occurred in Sichuan Province, where Zhao Ziyang was then Party Secretary. However, this (unofficial) beginning of China's post-CR agricultural revolution, was not acknowledged (let alone approved) by the CC. (2) Rong Yiren, a prominent business leader with pre-'49 experience, established CITIC to attract private foreign investment capital.

Date(s) or period	*Explanation*
5 May '78 Article in the *People's Daily* settles a controversial ideological question	An important article (allegedly sanctioned by Deng Xiaoping) reconciled the concept of "distribution according to work" with socialism. Resolution of this controversial issue opened the way for critical market-oriented reforms. The issue had dominated debates on economic reform since the arrest of the "Gang of Four" in Oct. '76. The "Gang" had opposed the principle of "distribution according to work" on the ground that it was a capitalistic principle based on material incentives that were believed to be inconsistent with communist principles.
10 May '78 Article in the journal of the Central Party School challenging Hua Guofeng's "Two Whatevers"	The journal (named *Theoretical Trends*) published a landmark article "Practice is the Sole Criterion for Testing Truth". The article aimed at undermining Hua Guofeng's doctrine of the "Two Whatevers" and at supporting Deng Xiaoping's view that the Party's approach to economic development had to change fundamentally. (For years, Deng had argued that the key to modernization lies in science, technology and education, *not* in ideology.) The article was reprinted in many other Party publications. (Hu Yaobang was then VP of the Central Party School.)
2 June '78 Deng Xiaoping defends the article "Practice is the Sole Criterion for Testing Truth"	In a major speech for the PLA, Deng explained that "seeking truth from facts" (a phrase borrowed from Mao) was consistent with Marxism-Leninism. This speech was another nail in the coffin of Hua's doctrine of the "Two Whatevers".
July '78 (1) State Council approved borrowing from "the West" for development (2) Hu Qiaomu's report to the State Council "Act in Accordance with Economic Laws, Step Up the "Four Modernizations"	(1) With the support of Deng Xiaoping, Vice PM Gu Mu proposed and the State Council agreed that the government should be allowed to borrow money from Western countries and Japan to finance development projects in China. (2) Hu Qiaomu, then president of the recently established CASS and a veteran revolutionary whose conservative credentials were not in doubt, submitted an influential report (which Xue Muqiao had helped write) to the State Council criticizing Hua Guofeng's economic policies by challenging (a) his support for the Dazhai model of collective farming, (b) his theory of the "Two Whatevers", (c) his relative neglect of agriculture and (d) his domestic crude oil policies. It was the first official report on economic policy by a senior Party official since the arrest of the "Gang of Four". The report helped Deng prepare for the historic 3rd Plenum of the 11th CC later that year.
Aug. '78 Signing of Sino-Japanese Treaty of Peace and Friendship	In preparation for Deng's visit to Japan in Oct., the two countries signed a bilateral friendship agreement in Aug. The agreement provided a framework for a large flow of financial aid and TA from Japan (mostly through OECF). During the following 25 years, Japan was the largest external source of financial assistance to China, by far.

(*Continued*)

(Continued)

Date(s) or period	*Explanation*
Oct. '78 (1) Deng visits Japan (2) Start of limited SOE reform in Sichuan	(1) Deng was keen to learn from Japan's impressive development after WWII, and to have good bilateral Sino-Japan relations. This was probably the most important of Deng's four trips abroad that year, during which he visited eight countries. He was the first Chinese leader to officially visit Japan since '49. (2) The Sichuan provincial government launched an experimental program aimed at improving performance of provincially owned SOEs. Six enterprises were given greater management autonomy, including partial profit retention. This initiative marked a major change in the approach to SOE reform, which until then had focused on administrative *de-* or *re-*centralization.
10 Nov.–13 Dec. '78 Central Party Work Conference	This was an extremely important, 36-day "work conference" of Party leaders, key officials and economists/technocrats to discuss China's economic situation and priorities for the future. (It was the first major "work conference" of the CC after Mao's death.) Chen Yun was one of the main speakers. He stressed the need for "balanced" growth and noted that progress in agriculture had been inadequate – reminding his colleagues that per capita grain production in '77 was about the same as in '55. Like many other speakers, he criticized Hua Guofeng's 10-year development plan, which had been approved by the NPC in Feb. Deng Xiaoping, who agreed with Chen's arguments, emerged as the Party's top leader at this conference.
13 Dec. '78 Deng Xiaoping's closing speech for the Central Party Work Conference	This seminal speech entitled "Emancipate the Mind, Seek Truth from Facts and Unite as One in Looking to the Future" (allegedly drafted by Deng with the assistance of Hu Yaobang, Hu Qiaomu and Yu Guangyuan), set the agenda for the watershed 3rd Plenum of the 11th CC, which started five days later. The speech implicitly criticized Hua Guofeng's "Two Whatevers" and his economic policies, while proposing a new approach to economic development based on market-oriented reforms and opening the economy to foreign trade and investment.
18–22 Dec. '78 3rd Plenum of the 11th CC	It is hard to overstate the significance of this Plenum. (The stage for it had been set by Deng Xiaoping's closing speech for the Central Party Work Conference five days earlier, an article explaining the need for fundamental reforms in the *Journal of the Central Party School* dated 10 May '78, and Hu Qiaomu's report to the State Council of July '78.) The Plenum forged a political consensus for reforming the economic system by shifting the work focus of the Party to *economic development*, instead of permanent *class struggle*. While the Plenum did *not* reject Mao or "Mao Zedong Thought", it marked the start of a major transition toward greater political and economic openness, pragmatism (as opposed to ideological thinking), collective leadership and institutional development. Mao's "ideological prison" was closed and the "market for ideas" was the first to be liberalized. Although the Plenum made *economic development* the Party's *top priority*, it did *not* mark a return to capitalism or an acceptance of the view that capitalism and socialism would eventually converge. (Deng Xiaoping and

Date(s) or period	*Explanation*
	his fellow reformers never doubted the economic and moral superiority of socialism. Capitalism was nonetheless admired as a *dynamic* system, from which China could learn to build socialism. However, in the minds of Party leaders and leading technocrat/economists, capitalism was associated with bad things such as social inequality, anarchy, criminality, unemployment, spiritual depravity and imperialism; in their thinking, capitalism was doomed to be overtaken by socialism.) One of the first consequences of the Plenum was that the share of military spending in GDP dropped from 15% during the CR to 3% in a few years. The *political* transition resulting from the Plenum involved the gradual introduction of age- and term-limits for Party leaders, legal system- and other institutional development. This Plenum would probably not have been possible without the widely shared disgust of the horrors of the CR. The Plenum confirmed Deng Xiaoping's rise to top national leadership and endorsed his *pragmatic* approach to decision making (captured by the slogans "practice is the sole criterion for testing truth" and "seeking truth from facts"). Importantly, it was *not* the start of Party-sanctioned de-collectivization in agriculture or general economic liberalization as is often, mistakenly, thought. On the contrary, the Plenum confirmed the Party's commitment to collective farming and officially opposed private farming (except for small-scale "sideline" production). While farm output and input prices were raised, the main focus of this Plenum was on "*Socialist Modernization*", to be achieved through: (a) administrative decentralization, (b) modest, experimental SOE reforms, (c) boosting grain production and (d) making allowances for the emergence of non-state enterprises (as would be confirmed in China's national Constitution of '82). The Plenum was more a *prologue* to the "reform and opening-up" policies that followed than a platform for detailed decision making. The Plenum's most important explicit *decisions* were:
	1. To confirm the importance of Zhou Enlai's "Four Modernizations" (industry, agriculture, national defense and science-technology);
	2. To repudiate the CR and emphasize the importance of *emancipating the mind* and *seeking truth from facts* (the slogan "practice is the sole criterion for testing truth" was popularized);
	3. To raise producer prices for food grains by 20% and an additional 50% for output above quota; government procurement prices for many other agricultural products were also increased, while prices of agricultural machinery and key inputs were reduced (by 10–15%);
	4. To permit "sideline" production on small individual plots (on collectively owned farm land) and private sales at market prices of the output from those plots;
	5. To affirm that Mao had been an *excellent Marxist*, while Lin Biao and the "Gang of Four" had caused great harm to the nation and its economy;

(*Continued*)

(Continued)

Date(s) or period	*Explanation*
	6. To establish a Central Commission for Discipline Inspection. (This anti-corruption commission was headed by Chen Yun from Dec. '78–Oct. '87, when he retired from senior Party positions); 7. To gradually extend "direct democracy" (elections by the people, as was already common practice at the village-level.) This 3rd Plenum implicitly rejected the more rigid and dogmatic Soviet approach to socialism under Brezhnev and undermined residual support for Hua Guofeng's 10-year development plan.
1978–'83 Agricultural transformation and rural industrialization	In addition to the CC's later official endorsement of de-collectivization in agriculture and acceptance of the principle that farmers should be allowed to choose their own system of production under the HRS (on collectively owned farm land) – decisions that weren't made official until 27 Sept. '80 – the Party also approved (in Jan. '82) a system of "land-user-rights" for individual farmers under the control of village committees and welcomed the establishment of commercial "Township and Village Enterprises" (TVEs), which often used industrial assets of former Communes. Many TVEs were genuine *collective* enterprises, but some were essentially private companies disguised as collectives for political reasons ("red hat" companies). TVEs accounted for most of China's industrial growth in the '80s. By '88, they employed 100 MN (surplus agricultural) workers, thus preventing early large-scale migration to cities (which would then not have been able to absorb a large inflow of migrants).
Dec. '78–'86 "Crossing the river by feeling the stones"	Economic reforms during the first 6–7 years following the 3rd Plenum of Dec. '78 were *incremental, partial* and often *experimental* in nature. China's initial approach to reform (from central planning to a market economy-type system) is sometimes described as "enlightened pragmatism"; there was no detailed overall reform plan, no timetable and, apart from a general commitment to socialism, no precise definition of an economic model to be pursued. This approach to reform was described by Chen Yun (at the Central Party Work Conference in Dec. '78) as "crossing the river by feeling the stones"; pragmatic "learning-by-doing". Discussions on the need for a *comprehensive* (or *integral*) approach to reform started already in '79 but didn't affect actual decision making until much later. In '86 the Party approved a *comprehensive* "Economic System Reform Implementation Plan" (proposed by PM Zhao Ziyang), but that plan became a victim of subsequent developments (including the political "disturbances" of '89). The 3rd Plenum of the 14th CC (Nov. '93) approved the next long-term, *comprehensive* reform plan, but it wasn't until China joined the WTO in Dec. '01 that greater clarity (or so it seemed at the time) regarding China's target economic model emerged, along with explicit, enforceable reform commitments.

Date(s) or period	*Explanation*
'79–'81 Preparations for 12th Party Congress	While a Politburo meeting on 27 Sept. '80 decided that farmers would be allowed to choose their own system of production (on collectively owned land), internal Party divisions (between reformers and conservatives) on the direction of broader economic reform, continued. Some leaders, including Chen Yun, favored central planning, while others, including Deng Xiaoping, preferred greater reliance on market forces. During preparations for the 12th Party Congress ('81), Xue Muqiao recommended "*serious market-oriented*" reforms. Others worried that this would blur the distinction between socialism and capitalism. An influential conservative Party leader throughout the '80s, Deng Liqun, was often supported by Chen Yun on economic policy issues.
1 Jan. '79 US-China political relations normalized	As ambassadors were exchanged, the US became the last major Western country to recognize the PRC. This was a development of great political and economic importance for both countries and for the world. Deng Xiaoping visited the US the next month. With the lifting of US trade sanctions against China in '71 (in connection with preparations for President Nixon's visit to China in early '72), bilateral trade relations had been "normalized" almost a decade earlier.
March '79 (1) Finance and Economy Commission (FEC) established (headed by Chen Yun) (2) Theory and Methodology Research Group established (3) Joint letter from Chen Yun and Li Xiannian to CC about the need to "rebalance" the economy	(1) Following the 3rd Plenum of Dec. '78, a Finance and Economy Commission (headed by Chen Yun) was established under the State Council to make specific reform proposals. It was the 3rd time since '49 that Chen Yun was asked to lead a national economic policy making. The first time (in '49), the CEFC was effectively responsible for national economic policies and management (pending the creation of SPC in '52 and a ministerial State Council in '53); the second time was in '62, when Chen Yun was asked (but declined) to lead a "Small Group" to lead China's economic rehabilitation efforts after the disastrous GLF. The FEC created in March '79 included high-level political leaders such as Hu Yaobang and Deng Liqun, as well as professional economists and government officials. It formed 3 sub-groups: (1) on economic reform (under by Xue Muqiao), (2) on economic structure (under Ma Hong), and (3) on technological development (under Wang Daohan). Probably the most important output of this FEC was a book by Xue Muqiao, leader of the 1st sub-group: *China's Socialist Economy, a conceptual framework for China's economic reform towards mature socialism*, recommending, inter-alia, administrative *de*-centralization, greater SOE autonomy and the systematic use of *economic incentives*. That book and Sun Yefang's *Some Theoretical Issues in Socialist Economics* (both published in '79), together with the conclusions of the Wuxi Conference of April '79, formed the intellectual groundwork for China's initial economic reform strategy under Deng Xiaoping. The 2nd sub-group (under Ma Hong) formulated a 3-year "Interim

(*Continued*)

(Continued)

Date(s) or period	*Explanation*
	Adjustment Plan" (IAP) giving priority to the development of coastal provinces and to agriculture and light industry. Hua Guofeng's Soviet-style 10-year development plan ('76–'85), approved by the NPC in Feb. '78, and a 15-year plan that was then under preparation by the SPC, were dropped when the IAP was finalized and approved by the CC in Dec. '80. Then, the 6th FYP ('81–'85) replaced the IAP when it was approved by the NPC on 12 Dec. '82. The work of the 3rd sub-group (on technological development) underpinned external opening-up policies, including the establishment of Special Economic Zones, which became a central focus of reforms a year later. Members of Chen Yun's FEC and its three sub-groups published many (often controversial) reports on economic reform strategy, while some provinces (Sichuan, Zhejiang, Guangdong and Anhui) started SOE reforms on their own. (2) At about the same time, the State Council established a "Theory and Methodology Research Group" (headed by Yu Guangyuan, with Dong Fureng serving as deputy), also reporting to Chen Yun. This 4th sub-group focused on (highly controversial) SOE and COE ownership reform issues. (3) Two political heavy weights, Chen Yun and Li Xiannian (then deputy Chairman of the CPC under Hua Guofeng, wrote a joint letter to the CC expressing concern about China's large budget deficits and other economic imbalances, proposing to "balance" the economy as a matter of priority. The letter questioned the wisdom of Hua Guofeng's 10-year development plan and endorsed Ma Hong's 3-year IAP (which at that point had yet to be approved by the CC). The letter was based, in part, on Chen Yun's *Planning and Markets* report of early March '79, which argued that a socialist planned economy needed a free-market component for small private enterprises.
'79 (1) Three specialized state-owned commercial banks established (2) Resumption of commercial insurance business (3) Publication of Sun Yefang's *Some Theoretical Issues in Socialist Economics* and Xue Muqiao's *China's Socialist Economy*	(1) During the year, three specialized commercial banks were established (or, more accurately, *re-established*): the Agricultural Bank of China (ABC) and the Bank of China (BOC) were legally separated from PBoC in Feb. and March, while the People's Construction Bank (later named China Construction Bank (CCB), was separated from MOF in Oct. This ended the mono-bank system that had been in place since '56. (2) In '79, China resumed commercial insurance by reviving PICC, which had been closed for 20 years. (3) The publication (in Chinese) of several influential books by prominent Chinese economists was made possible by Deng's "defogging" of China's intellectual climate. Sun Yefang's book *Some Theoretical Issues in Socialist Economics* (24 essays written between '56–'78) critiqued central planning and socialist economic policies pursued by Mao Zedong and his successor Hua Guofeng. It reinterpreted Marx's "law-of-value" to prove that autonomous market forces could not be ignored in a socialist economy; Sun firmly rejected *dogmatic thinking*. A somewhat similar book by Xue Muqiao, *China's Socialist Economy* (based on a draft textbook on socialist economics he had written during the CR, when it could not be published for political reasons),

Date(s) or period	*Explanation*
	also came out in '79. *China's Socialist Economy* (Xue's magnum opus) had great influence on economic policy making during the '80s. It was required reading for Party cadres – some 10 million copies were printed. (Slightly amended follow-up editions were published in '81, '86 and '87.) Though couched in Marxist-Leninist jargon and starting from the then commonly accepted premise that "socialism is a superior economic system" (because, in Xue's words, "a socialist system can motivate and give full play to people's enthusiasm since people become the masters of their own country"), the book nonetheless argued that autonomous market forces should be recognized and respected by planning authorities in a socialist economy. The book furthermore argued that: (a) agriculture and light industry should be given priority over heavy industry; (b) greater managerial independence should be given to SOEs; (c) local Governments should be given more economic decision-making power; (e) "rigid" central planning is harmful to economic development; (f) capital formation should generally not exceed 25% of GDP. (In later economic work, Xue argued that private foreign investment should be encouraged, along with domestic private sector development.) In *China's Socialist Economy*, Xue blamed China's economic problems of the late '50s on the "rush" to collectivize agriculture and on excessively high rates of capital formation. (He did not blame the *forced nature* of earlier collectivization, nor did he question the Marxist idea that all major means of production should be state-owned and that agriculture should be collective.) In the next few years, *China's Socialist Economy* was published in several other languages by Foreign Languages Press in Beijing, a government-owned publisher modeled after the USSR's Foreign Languages Publishing House. (In '80, Xue Muqiao published yet another book: *Current Economic Problems in China*, a collection of speeches and essays written *after* the 3rd Plenum of Dec. '78. Like Sun Yefang's '79 book, Xue's book of '80 was published in English in the US in '82, based on edited translations by K. K. Fung. In '86, Xue's *Current Economic Problems in China* was also published in Japanese, in Japan.)
30 March '79 Deng Xiaoping's speech on "Four Cardinal Principles"	Deng's "Four Cardinal Principles" (supplementing Zhou Enlai's "Four Modernizations") meant to convey that the socialist path was the *only* way for China and that there would be *no convergence* of capitalism and socialism in China. Deng's four cardinal principles were that China should: 1. Not deviate from the socialist path; 2. Accept the dictatorship of the proletariat; 3. Accept the leadership of the CPC; 4. Be guided by Marxism-Leninism and Mao-Zedong thought. This speech set the parameters for what officials and technocrats/economist could publicly say or propose. Some were surprised by this speech, as it seemed to suggest that Deng was backtracking from his commitment to radical reform.

(*Continued*)

(Continued)

Date(s) or period	*Explanation*
April '79 Wuxi Conference	More than 300 scholars and officials (mainly from SPC, SSB and CASS) attended this (first major, semi-official) economic conference after the 3rd Plenum of Dec. '78 to discuss the practical meaning of Marx's "law-of-value", the role of SOEs in the economy and future relations between plan and market. Xue Muqiao, then head of SPC's Economic Research Office, opened the conference and, together with Chen Yun, played a leading role in it. Liu Guoguang also participated; he focused on the shortcomings of China's planning system as it had developed since the early '50s.
8 July '79 Equity JV Law (start of legislation covering foreign investment in China)	The NPC promulgated the "Sino-Foreign Equity Joint Ventures Law" (EJV Law), a critical part of Deng's opening-up strategy. It was the first major economic law since the 3rd Plenum of Dec. '78. (The law was amended in '90 and '01 – mainly to relax various restrictions on FDI. On 12 April '86, well before China joined the WTO, NPC adopted the "Law on Wholly Foreign-Owned Enterprises" (WFOE Law), which permitted 100% foreign ownership of certain kinds of enterprises. In the early '90s, NPC adopted the "Sino-Foreign Contractual Joint Venture Law" (CJV Law). On 1 Oct. '16, China changed its prior approval system (for foreign investments) into a registration system based on a national "negative list".)
July '79–end '80 Further partial SOE reforms	In July '79, the State Council decided to extend the Sichuan reform experiment (of Oct. '78) nationwide. When it became apparent that this approach led to reduced fiscal revenues, SOE autonomy was throttled back and an "SOE Responsibility System" (modeled after the HRS in agriculture) was introduced instead. The State Council then also introduced "dual-track" pricing for selected industrial SOEs. One of the main problems during this period (a problem that has never been fully resolved) was that SOE managers faced asymmetric incentives; i.e. profits for the firm and losses for the state. Another problem was – and in many cases, still is – the absence of *hard budget constraints* (identified by János Kornai as a *sine qua non* for a socialist economy).
13 Aug. '79 Start of export promotion and reform of external trade policies	The State Council promulgated "Regulations on Issues Concerning Vigorous Development of Foreign Trade and Increase of Foreign Exchange Revenues". These regulations called on all regions and departments to develop products for export and to increase foreign exchange earnings. Later, with this objective in mind, China's XR was also used as a policy tool. During the '80s, the RMB/USD exchange rate was adjusted several times, and a dual exchange rate system was introduced to influence exports and imports in line with plan priorities. (This multiple XR system was terminated on 1 Jan. '94.) Gradually, from the early '80s, both SOEs and non-state enterprises were given licenses to engage in external trade. (By the end of '07, almost 650,000 enterprises were engaged in foreign trade.) From the late '80s, most state trading monopolies were gradually dismantled.

Date(s) or period	*Explanation*
Sept. '79 4th Plenum of the 11th CC	This Plenum confirmed the conclusions of the preceding (3rd) Plenum of Dec. '78, including the prohibition of land distribution for private farming. Small-scale "sideline" production for private consumption and commercial sale was permitted. However, despite the official ban on private farming, many Communes were in fact dismantled (with the tacit or open permission of local politicians), while the land was distributed to individual farmers, who agreed to work under the HRS/contract system.
Late '70s–early '80s (1) Intense debates and disagreements on the direction of economic reform (2) Visits to China and lectures on economic reform by East European economists and by Milton Friedman	(1) Throughout this period, there were major disagreements among economists/technocrats and political leaders over the direction of and the priorities for economic reform. Nobody wanted to go back to capitalism or Mao-style socialism. Everybody was in favor of establishing a "socialist economic system", but there was no agreement on how to define such a system and how much "planning" would be needed. Most agreed that socialism yields better result when combined with certain elements of a capitalist system. The controversy over private farming under the HRS continued through the early '80s. Those who favored market-oriented reforms (e.g., Hu Yaobang, Zhao Ziyang and many of the technocrat/economists, including Xue Muqiao) used the term "commodity economy" to describe their preferred system, rather than "market economy", a more capitalistic-sounding term. However, Chen Yun, Deng Liqun and other conservative Party elders, who favored a centrally planned, state-controlled economy, with limited "regulation by markets", prevailed. There is no indication that Deng Xiaoping personally participated in these internal debates. The situation changed in Nov. '84, at least temporarily, when the 3rd Plenum of the 12th CC endorsed "market-oriented reforms" and expressed reservations about central planning. During this crucial period, political factions began to form. (2) Prominent EE economists who visited China were: Markimovich (Yugoslav), Wlodzimierz Brus, Oskar Lange (Polish), Michael Kalecki (Polish) and Ota Sik (Czech). János Kornai (Hungarian) visited China later and participated in the historic Bashan Lun (boat) conference of Sept. '85. He became an iconic figure in circles of Chinese intellectuals; his 1980 book, *Economics of Shortage*, was translated into Chinese and became a bestseller in China in the '80s. Kornai argued that even in a socialist economic system, SOEs had to be operationally independent and subjected to *hard budget constraints*. (Kornai preferred to privatize SOEs.) In late '79, the famous American economist Milton Friedman was invited to lecture in China on the principles of a market economy. He visited in Sept.–Oct. '80 and met with PM Zhao Ziyang to discuss price liberalization and associated inflation risks. (Friedman met again with (then CPC General Secretary) Zhao in Sept. '88, when Deng Xiaoping's decision of mid-'88 to quickly liberalize most consumer prices had led to high inflation and economic confusion.) Friedman was reportedly frustrated by his inability to convince his Chinese counterparts of the need to rapidly privatize SOEs.

(*Continued*)

(Continued)

Date(s) or period	*Explanation*
'80s and '90s China receives much development assistance (financial and TA) from many sources	Following the 3rd Plenum of Dec. '78, many foreign aid agencies (including multilateral development banks), UNDP and private Foundations (including the Ford Foundation) provided significant financial- and technical assistance to China. In financial terms, Japan was the largest donor *by far*, followed by the World Bank Group (which, through projects and EDI programs, was also the largest source of TA, staff training and policy advice). Because of Congressional restrictions on official aid to China, the US was a relatively small source of aid to China; other bilateral donors, including Canada, Australia, some European countries and (especially) Japan, were more important. The ADB in Manilla became a major source of financial- and technical assistance in the late '90s. However, throughout this period, China's *domestic* savings financed a much larger proportion of total investment, than official foreign aid and private sector FDI combined. The IMF undertook macro-economic analyses and provided policy advice, but China has not used IMF financial facilities, except the withdrawal of $597.7MN from its reserve tranche in '86 to shore up foreign exchange reserves. (Some official aid continued in the 21st century, even *after* China became a donor country. The Ford Foundation provided financial support for professional training and institution building in many areas, including legal system development and international affairs. It also financed many international conferences and seminars, including the historic Dalian Conference of June '93. Almost all important Chinese reform economists benefited, directly or indirectly, from FF financial assistance.
Jan. '80 Publication of "Preliminary Ideas on the Overall Reform of the Economic Management System"	This seminal report by a group of young economists known as the "Four Gentlemen" (Huang Jiangnan, Wang Qishan, Weng Yongxi and Zhu Jiaming), members of the FEC's 2nd sub-group (under Ma Hong), created in March '79, had great influence on the direction and content of economic reforms in the early '80s. Xue Muqiao, head of 1st sub-group (on economic reform), supported the Four Gentlemen's report with his own paper: "Preliminary Opinions on Economic Restructuring" later in '80.
1 April '80 Foreign Exchange Certificate (FEC) created (as part of a FX balancing policy)	To facilitate the management of China's scarce foreign exchange reserves, the State Council created a special currency for foreign residents and visitors, "Foreign Exchange Certificate". (The FEC was abolished on 1 Jan. '94.) During the '80s and early '90s, the government also required that foreign enterprises in China (as a group) earned their own FX to finance their import needs. This so-called FX balancing requirement enabled the government to treat foreign enterprises separately in national development plans.
April–May '80 PRC replaces ROC (Taiwan) as China's representative in (member of) the Bretton Woods institutions	(IMF in April; World Bank in May.) Deng was keenly interested in tapping into WB resources for China's economic development. WB president Robert McNamara discussed China's membership with Deng in Beijing (April '80). Deng told McNamara: "we are very poor; we have lost touch with the world; we need to catch up; we can do it without you, but we can do it better and faster with you". To establish the PRC's eligibility for WB loans and

Date(s) or period	*Explanation*
	IDA credits, a major baseline study of China's economy was undertaken (Fall '80) by some 30 WB staff and consultants, supported by a large team of Chinese counterparts, including Zhu Rongji and Zhao Renwei. While the IMF provided macro-economic analyses and advice, the WB became China's principal multilateral development partner. During the next several decades, the WB supported China's reforms with numerous (often joint) studies and financing for hundreds of projects (for investment, TA and staff training) all over China (except Tibet). (TA and staff training projects were often executed by EDI and co-financed by UNDP.)
May '80 Establishment of the System Reform Office of the State Council – later enlarged to the form the State Commission for Restructuring the Economic System (SCRES)	The "System Reform Office" was the predecessor of SCRES (established in '82) as an in-house State Council think-tank to help guide the economic reform process. SCRES was initially headed by PM Zhao Ziyang and staffed by young Chinese economists, many of whom were later promoted to high government positions (including, e.g., Lou Jiwei and Guo Shuqing). Xue Muqiao was SCRES's first "principle advisor". Another important advisor was Gao Shangquan, who, from '85–'93, served as SCRES's deputy director and contributed to many important reports during that period. SCRES soon became a very important agency in guiding China's reform efforts; it had a major role in preparing the 7th FYP, which went into effect in '85. One of its main themes was the need for a "coordinated", integral approach to reform. (SCRES was merged with SDPC to form NDRC in March '03.)
Aug. '80 (1) Politburo meeting (2) Regulations issued for "Special Economic Zones" to attract inward FDI (for export promotion)	(1) Hua Guofeng was criticized for his leftish views. This was a further step in a Deng-engineered plan to gradually remove Hua from power and to replace him as Party chief by the reformer Hu Yaobang (which took place in June '81). (2) During the same month, NPC issued regulations for SEZs that had been established in Shenzhen, Zhuhai, Shantou and Xiamen, in April '79. Deng attached great importance to SEZs and referred to them as "windows on the world".(Chen Yun did not like SEZs; he referred to them as "capitalist beachheads"). In May '84, 14 other coastal and inland cities were opened to foreign investment (essentially like the four initial SEZs). In May '85, the Yangtze and Pearl River deltas along with two other coastal areas were designated as "Open Economic Regions". Hainan Island became an SEZ (and a separate province) in April '88. (Pudong was designated an SEZ in '92 (following Deng's "Southern Tour" that year.) Several other coastal and inland areas were designated as "Open Zones" later in the '90s). Fiscal and other incentives were used to attract FDI to SEZs and "Open Zones". By attracting FDI on a large scale, China was able to significantly accelerate economic, technological and institutional development. (In the '00s – China started promoting outward FDI.)

(*Continued*)

(Continued)

Date(s) or period	*Explanation*
18 Aug. '80 Deng Xiaoping's "August 18 talk" signaling the importance of political reform	Deng signaled the importance of *political reform* to complement – and facilitate – economic reform. He complained about insufficient democracy within the CPC. Deng repeated calls for *political reform* in the following years. In his view at that time, *political reform* meant separating the Party from Government and government administration from SOE management.
1 Sept. '80 CC approves private farming in principle	The CC approved a document entitled *Issues Concerning Further Strengthening and Perfecting the Agricultural Production System*. Effectively, this meant that the Party finally accepted private farming based on the HRS as an alternative to collective farming. Later that month, the Party formally authorized local Governments to break up agricultural communes and adopt private farming based on HRS contracting, if farmers so wished.
Sept. '80 Formation of the "Rural Development Group"	A group of about 30 young intellectuals led by Chen Yizi, founded the (unofficial) "Rural Development Research Group", a semi-private think-tank which enjoyed Deng Xiaoping's support. It became very influential in the design of rural reform policies. The Group, working for Du Runsheng's Agricultural Development Center, strongly advocated returning to private farming under the HRS as soon as possible. The "Rural Development Research Group" had been preceded by (and in some ways competed with) a team of four economists known as the "Four Gentlemen", who, in Jan. '80, had published a very influential report entitled *Preliminary Ideas on the Overall Reform of the Economic Management System*.
'80s–early '90s Local Governments design their own preferential policies to attract FDI	The Central Government's SEZ policy was followed by similar initiatives at the local level. Often without Central Government authorization, many local Governments offered tax incentives, land and/or infrastructure to attract FDI. As a result of its successful FDI policies, China became the "workshop-of-the-world" in the '90s.
25 Sept. '80 One-child policy becomes official nationwide	After promoting various *voluntary* family planning programs since '49 (including a "two-child policy" since '64), the Party issued a public letter mandating a "one-child policy" nationwide, with certain exceptions. (Given the paucity of reliable demographic information at that time, it is possible that this policy would not have been introduced if policy makers had known that China's fertility rate had already fallen dramatically (from 6 in the early '60s to about 2.5 when market reforms started in the late '70s). The "one-child policy" was replaced by another "two-child policy" at the 3rd Plenum of the 18th CC in Nov. '13.
27 Sept. '80 (1) Politburo meeting (2) Document No. 75	(1) Almost two years after the 3rd Plenum of Dec. '78, the Party decided that farmers would be allowed to choose their own system of production. This marked the official end of Party-mandated collective farming. (2) In "Document No.75" (issued shortly after the Politburo meeting of 27 Sept. '80) the CPC gave explicit permission to Provinces to return to private farming (with contracting under the HRS). However, some senior provincial leaders continued

Date(s) or period	*Explanation*
	to resist the return to private farming on ideological grounds. Nonetheless, by the middle of '82, private farming under the HRS was common everywhere in rural China.
Dec. '80 CC adopts 3-year Interim Adjustment Plan (IAP)	This was the plan that had been prepared at the suggestion of Chen Yun by the FEC's 2nd subgroup (under Ma Hong). After much discussion among Party leaders, the IAP was adopted in Dec. '80, replacing Hua Guofeng's Soviet-style, heavy industry-oriented 10-year development plan, which had been approved by the NPC in Feb. '78).
'81 (1) Ministry of Finance issued Treasury Notes for the first time since the PRC was established; start of capital market development (2) World Bank's first economic report on China (3) Development Research Centre (DRC) established	(1) Recognizing that financing budget deficits from Central Bank overdrafts (as was common practice under Mao), was not consistent with Deng's economic reforms, MOF began to issue Treasury Bonds for that purpose. Initially, these bonds were not tradable; they were force-placed with state banks at government-determined interest rates. (It took well over a decade for a commercial government bond market to develop and much longer for corporate bonds and broader debt markets to develop. China's domestic debt market has since become the world's 2nd largest (and is slowly opening for foreign investors). (2) Publication for unrestricted distribution (in '83, with government permission) of this multi-volume report, *China. Socialist Economic Development*, marked an important step toward greater "openness". The report was translated into Chinese by the government, widely read by the leadership and used for teaching purposes at Chinese universities. (3) Having established a "System Reform Office" in May '80 (which became SCRES in '82), the reform process was so intense in the early '80s and the need for guidance in that process so strongly felt that the State Council founded another, broader-gauged think-tank directly available to it: DRC. While SCRES ceased to exist as a separate agency when it was merged with SDPC (to form NDRC) in '03, the DRC continues to function as the State Council's main in-house think-tank; it focuses on *economic reform* and other issues).
June '81 Special meeting of the CC. Hu Yaobang replaces Hua Guofeng as Party Chairman	This was the ignominious end of Hua as Party Chairman. However, he remained member of the CC until his resignation in '02. The title "Chairman" (of the CPC) was dropped at the 12th Party Congress in Sept. '82, when Hu Yaobang (Hua's successor as Party leader) became the CPC's first "General Secretary".
27 June '81 6th Plenum of the 11th CC. "Resolution on certain questions in the history of our Party".	This Plenum confirmed that: (1) China had entered the "primary stage of the socialist system", (2) socialism is a superior system, (3) only socialism can save China and (4) socialism is a long transitional stage between capitalism and communism. The Plenum also passed an important resolution, stating that, though Mao Zedong had made errors during the CR, his overall performance had been good. (Deng later specified 70% good.) According to this Plenum, Mao's merits were *primary* and his errors *secondary*. The contributions of Hua Guofeng were assessed mostly favorably, but those of the "Gang of Four" entirely unfavorably.

(*Continued*)

(Continued)

Date(s) or period	*Explanation*
Jan. '82 Formal approval by the CC of the HRS with "dual track pricing" and individual land-user rights for farmers	The Politburo had already decided on 27 Sept. '80 that farmers would be allowed to choose their own method of production, but implementation was very uneven. The decision of Jan. '82 was to formally endorse the HRS system with "dual-track" pricing and to legitimize land "user-rights" for individual farmers. However, all agricultural land continued to be owned collectively (by village committees on behalf of the state). Three years later (Jan. '85), the "dual-track" pricing system was extended to most industrial SOEs.
July '82 First Moganshan (Zhejiang) conference	At the request of some prominent Chinese economists, the World Bank organized a conference on the economic reform experience of EE countries. The team of visiting EE economists was led by Wlodzimierz Brus (Polish) and included Julius Struminsky (Polish), Jiri Kosta (Czech) and Peter Kende (Hungarian). The Chinese team was led by Xue Muqiao, Liao Jili and Liu Zhoufu. The EE economists (who had been trained in modern economics at Western universities and were all living outside their original home countries), demonstrated to their Chinese counterparts certain systemic problems associated with central planning. After the conference, Liu Guoguang and his older colleague Sun Yefang published articles criticizing Soviet-style central planning, while advocating greater SOE autonomy in China.
12–13 Sept. '82 (1) 12th Party Congress (Sept. '82–Oct. '87) (2) Endorsement of the 6th FYP ('81–'85) by the CC (3) Hu Yaobang's title changes from Party Chairman to General Secretary	(1) Reflecting ideology-inspired doubts about market reforms in some leading circles, this 1st Party Congress after the historic 3rd Plenum of Dec. '78, defined China's reform objective as "maintaining the *primary* role of the planned economy, while giving play to the *supplementary* role of market forces in economic regulation." At the same time, the CPC's Constitution was amended to reflect that "the focus of the work of the CPC is to lead the people of various nationalities throughout the country in carrying out socialist, modernized economic construction". (2) A major input into the preparation of this FYP was the study by Ma Hong's sub-group of Chen Yun's FEC, *China Toward the Year 2000*. The main quantitative economic target for the year 2000 explored by Ma Hong's team in that study was a quadrupling of GDP by the end of the century, implying 7.2% annual growth. (In '83, Deng Xiaoping asked visiting WB president Tom Clausen to assess the feasibility of this target and to advise how it could be achieved. Deng's question became the focus of the WB's second major economic report on China.) (3) Hu Yaobang, who had replaced Hua Guofeng as Party Chairman in '81, became the Party's "General Secretary". This change in title was made at Hu's request – he was a humble man and much younger than some of the Party elders. However, Deng Xiaoping (who was recognized as the main architect of China's "reform and opening-up" strategy and who had declined an offer to become Party Chairman), remained de-facto "paramount" leader. Deng called again for *political reform* (i.e. strict separation of Government from Party and government administration from SOE management).

Date(s) or period	*Explanation*
Dec. '82 NPC approves 6th FYP and mandates accelerating economic reforms	Following the CC's endorsement in Sept., the 6th FYP (the first such plan after the historic 3rd Plenum of Dec. '78), was formally approved by the NPC. (It followed the 3-year IAP ('79–'82), which had replaced Hua Guofeng's 10-year plan.) At the same time, recognizing the amazing success of economic reforms since the late '70s, the NPC mandated accelerating and broadening economic reforms. This mandate was pursued with vigor by PM Zhao Ziyang. However, China's approach to national economic reform and development plan did not become *comprehensive* in nature until the next (7th) FYP was launched in '86.
'82 (1) New national Constitution (adopted at the 5th meeting of the 5th NPC in Dec.) followed by amendments in '88,'93,'99 and '04 that increasingly recognize the importance of private enterprise (2) The first version of Ma Hong's report *Toward the Year 2000* becomes available (3) China becomes an observer in GATT	(1) The new national Constitution (sometimes referred to as the "Deng Xiaoping Constitution"), while confirming in its Preamble that the main objective is to further the development of a *socialist system* under CPC leadership, reflects the basic reform decisions of the 3rd Plenum of Dec. '78. The present version of the national constitution, in its preamble, states that the basic task of the nation is to concentrate its efforts on "socialist modernization along the road of Chinese-style socialism". The '82 Constitution restored term limits on senior official positions (which had been part of the original '54 Constitution but not of the March '78 Constitution.) The '82 Constitution and its amendments of '88, '93, '99 and '04, reflect, inter alia, the evolving role of private enterprise in China. (On this subject, the original text says: "The state protects the lawful rights and interests of the individual economy. The state guides, helps and supervises the individual economy by exercising administrative control". The '88 amendment says: "The state permits the private sector of the economy to exist and develop within the limits prescribed by the law". The '99 amendment says: "The non-state sector of the economy, comprising self-employed and private businesses within the domain stipulated by law, is an important component of the country's socialist market economy". The '04 amendment says: "The state protects the lawful rights and interests of the non-state sectors of the economy such as the individual and private sectors of the economy. The state encourages, supports and guides the development of the non-state sectors of the economy and, in accordance with law, exercises supervision and control over the non-state sectors of the economy".) (2) This long-term perspective study on the Chinese economy (drafts of which served as inputs into the 6th FYP, '81–'85), was inspired by the *Global 2000 Report to the President* (a long-term perspective study on the US economy commissioned by President Carter in '77. At the request of the Chinese government, the latter study was presented in Beijing (in July '81) by Gerald O. Barney, director of this study. The *Toward the Year 2000* study was undertaken by a group of Chinese economists under the leadership of Ma Hong, with inputs from many government agencies. The WB's 2nd major economic report on China (which, at the personal request of Deng Xiaoping, was focused on assessing the feasibility of quadrupling GDP by the end of the

(*Continued*)

(Continued)

Date(s) or period	*Explanation*
	century, as suggested in Ma Hong's *Toward the Year 2000* study) was prepared in parallel with Ma Hong's follow-up long-term perspective study called *China 2000*, which had been requested by PM Zhao Ziyang. The follow-up Ma Hong report and the World Bank's 2nd economic report on China, were both finalized in '85 and confirmed that GDP could indeed be quadrupled by 2000, subject to certain conditions. (3) In '82, China began to participate (as observer) in the GATT's "Uruguay Round" of negotiations that eventually led to the establishment of the WTO on 1 Jan. '95. However, China was unable to join the WTO as a "founding member", as it had hoped and expected when it applied for GATT membership in '86.
2 Jan. '83 CPC Document #1 on agricultural reforms promulgated	This document, *Some Questions Concerning the Current Rural Economic Policies*, acknowledged that private farming under the HRS had worked well and should be encouraged. The document also called for the strict separation of government administration from Commune management, thus setting the stage for terminating the Commune system in rural China altogether, which wasn't officially done until the 3rd Plenum of the 12th CC in Oct. '84. (In reality, almost all Communes had already been dissolved by the time Document #1 was promulgated.)
8 Feb. '83 Chongqing designated as pilot city for "comprehensive" urban reform	As a result of a State Council decision, Chongqing became the first large city that could begin planning its development under *national* rather than *provincial* guidance. Since economic reforms thus far had primarily focused on *rural* areas, this decision (when Chongqing was still part of Sichuan Province) indicated that the leadership was getting ready to extend the economic reform program to urban China (as was decided at the 3rd Plenum of the 12th CC in Oct. '84). Later in '83, the city of Wuhan in Hubei Province was given the same "independence" as Chongqing. (PM Zhao Ziyang, a former Party Secretary of Sichuan, was keenly interested in promoting urban development and had already initiated a series of studies on urban development issues in '80.)
June '83 Corporate tax contract system for SOEs launched	SOE taxation played a central role in the struggle to preserve the state's solvency, while the economy was reforming. The continuing slide of fiscal revenues from SOEs (because of poorly conceived/inadequate SOE reforms thus far) caused considerable concern in Beijing. In June '83, SOEs were subjected to a system of "contractual" (usually negotiated) corporate tax obligations, called "taxes for profits". (The fiscal system for SOEs was revised (tightened) in '84 and in '86, but it wasn't until '94 that an effective system of corporate taxation, based on standard accounting and auditing rules, was introduced.)
Sept. '83 Central Bank	The State Council officially appointed PBoC to serve as China's central bank, responsible for monetary policy.

Date(s) or period	*Explanation*
'83–early '84 (1) Campaign against "spiritual pollution" (2) Rectification campaign (3) 8,000 cadres meeting	(1) The year-long *anti-spiritual pollution* campaign (led by conservative Party leaders Deng Liqun and Hu Qiaomu) against "abominations" such as lipstick, sunglasses, long hair, pornography and cheek-to-cheek dancing, was a backlash against some of the societal changes that were beginning to take root as a result of Deng's "reform and opening-up" policies. (2) The *anti-spiritual pollution* campaign ran parallel to a political "Rectification" campaign aimed at purifying Party ideology and at fighting corruption. Both campaigns criticized Hu Yaobang, Zhao Ziyang and their economic reform policies. Conflicts within in the Party between reformers and conservatives intensified once again. (3) The "Rectification" campaign led to a large anti-corruption meeting in Jan. '84 chaired by Party General Secretary and reformer Hu Yaobang (known as the "8,000 cadres meeting") to set high ethical standards for Party officials and dissociate economic reforms from their perceived links to rising corruption. Since the meeting was seen as a challenge to the Party's Discipline Inspection Commission (which was still headed by Chen Yun, a conservative Party elder), it contributed to tensions between reform-oriented and conservative factions in the Party.
Early '84 Change in system for SOE financing; ICBC created	When, as part of the evolving reform strategy, responsibility for SOE financing was shifted from the state budget to the banking system, the Industrial and Commercial Bank of China (ICBC) was created to lend to industrial and commercial SOEs and to take deposits. However, specialized commercial banks were then still subject to the government's annual "credit plan" and functioned effectively as *fiscal agents* of the state until much later. They accumulated *non-performing loans* at face value on their balance sheet, without provisioning, while paying income tax on *accrued (but not yet realized)* interest income. (NPLs only began to be accounted for in the late '90s as part of broader bank reforms, following the Asian financial crisis. The annual credit plan was officially abolished in '96, but the government continued to influence credit allocation by state banks in other ways.)
3–10 Sept. '84 2nd Moganshan conference (on economic reform)	(The 1st Moganshan conference, with EE economists, organized by the World Bank, was held in July '82.) The main purpose of the 2nd one was to discuss the pros and cons of two alternative approaches to price reform: (a) quick and comprehensive (based on market forces), and (b) multiple small, government-managed steps (so as not to threaten economic stability). The conference, attended by many SCRES, DRC and CASS economists, was closely monitored by PM Zhao Ziyang, who agreed with its conclusion that the second approach (b), using "dual-track" pricing, was preferable.

(*Continued*)

(Continued)

Date(s) or period	*Explanation*
Oct. '84 3rd Plenum of the 12th CC. Reform objective defined as "Socialist Planned Commodity Economy"	This Plenum, which aimed at ending confusion and conflicts between reformers and conservatives in the Party, marked another breakthrough in the evolution of China's reform strategy. The Plenum's "Decision on Restructuring the Economic System" defined the Party's reform objective as creating a "Socialist Planned Commodity Economy". Although the Plenum stressed the continued importance of public ownership, it endorsed *diverse* forms of enterprise ownership and *diverse* "operational modes" – meaning that both state and non-state enterprises would play a role in economic development. (These changes in thinking on the role of the non-state, including private enterprises, were reflected in the Constitutional Amendment of '88.) The Plenum also emphasized the importance of market-pricing and market-oriented SOE reforms. The Plenum broke with the traditional view that a planned economy and a market economy were mutually exclusive, but its "Decision" was otherwise ambiguous about the role of "planning". (The term "commodity economy", used in the USSR in lieu of "market economy", was also used in China at that time. By adding the words "socialist" and "planning" to "commodity economy" the Party indicated that it was *not* tolerating capitalism.) Two other important results of this Plenum were: (1) confirmation of the evolving shift in reform priorities from *rural* to *urban* China (which essentially meant promoting organized urbanization and intensified SOE reform) and (2) agreement on the need to use a *comprehensive* approach to the design and implementation of economic reforms; the earlier "learning-by doing" approach ("crossing the river by feeling the stones") was no longer considered appropriate. (The shift to urban reform was a recognition of the fact that industrial progress had lagged agriculture.) For a while it seemed that the conservative and reform wings of the Party were reconciled, but conflict would soon arise again.
Dec. '84 Publication of Deng's book *Building Socialism with Chinese Characteristics*	Coming a year and a half after the publication (in Chinese) of his *Selected Works*, this collection of speeches and remarks aimed at clarifying socialist reform goals. It confirmed Deng's determination to push ahead with "reform and opening-up" and provided ideological backing for reformers such as Hu Yaobang and Zhao Ziyang. (The expression "with Chinese characteristics" – part of the title of Deng's book – would from then on be used to emphasize the unique nature of China's economic reforms. Several speeches in the book were included in later editions of Deng's *Selected Works*.)
'85 Patent Law enacted	Recognizing the importance for economic development of protecting intellectual property rights, the new law established – for the first time – a national patent registration system. That same year China joined the "Paris Convention for the Protection of Industrial Property", which was supplemented by the "Patent Cooperation Treaty" of '94. When China joined the WTO in '01, it also became a member of TRIPS (a WTO-linked agreement on "Trade-Related Aspects of Intellectual Property Rights"). China's Patent Law was amended several times, most recently in '09.

Date(s) or period	*Explanation*
'85 (1) Publication of the World Bank's second economic report on China and completion of China's own (follow-up) *China 2000* study (2) Publication of a *Conceptual Framework for an Overall Economic Restructuring Plan* by Wu Jinglian et al.	(1) Unlike the 1st WB report, *Socialist Economic Development*, which was primarily *backward-looking*, the 2nd report: *Long-term Development Issues and Options*, prepared at the personal request of Deng Xiaoping, was *forward-looking*. It concluded that China's target of quadrupling GDP by the end of the century was feasible, subject to certain conditions. The report was read by senior leaders and had significant influence on reform policy making in China. At about the same time, China's own follow-up *China 2000* study by Ma Hong became available. Both reports stressed the need for greater emphasis on service sector development. (2) Under the leadership of Wu Jinglian, a *comprehensive* economic restructuring plan was prepared by a team of Chinese economists working for SCRES. The following year ('86) this report became the basis for a detailed reform *implementation* plan aimed at introducing – contrary to the conclusion of the 2nd Moganshan conference of '84 – *comprehensive and rapid* price reform and ending "dual-track" pricing (the negative aspects of which were considered to outweigh positive ones). The *implementation* plan also envisaged that central planning would become unnecessary. However, Wu Jinglian's *implementation plan* was shelved by PM Zhao Ziyang at the end of '86 for political reasons and replaced by relatively modest fiscal reforms for SOEs. (Apparently, conservative opposition to the idea of comprehensive and aggressive market reforms was still very strong at that time.)
Feb. '85 Extension of the "dual-track" pricing system	Although terminating the "dual-track" pricing system had been recommended by Wu Jinglian, the State Council, following a recommendation of the 2nd Moganshan conference (Sept. '84), *extended* the system to industrial SOEs, with the objective to promote SOE commercialization.
2–7 Sept. '85 Bashan Lun (boat) conference	At the suggestion of PM Zhao Ziyang and senior SCRES staff, the World Bank organized a five-day conference for some 70 Chinese officials and economists and prominent foreign economists on a Yangtze River cruise ship (named "Bashan") to discuss macro-economic management and international experience in integrating central planning and markets. The famous economists János Kornai (Hungarian), Wlodzimierz Brus (Polish), James Tobin (American Nobel Laureate), Sir Alec Cairncross (Scottish), the presidents of the central banks of West Germany and France and several other prominent international economists were among the foreign experts. They interacted with prominent Chinese economists such as Xue Muqiao, Liu Guoguang, Gao Shangquan, Zhao Renwei and Ma Hong (as well as some younger ones such as Lou Jiwei, Zhou Xiaochuan and Guo Shuqing) during the cruise. (This boat conference is regarded in China as a turning point in economic reform policy making and in macro-economic management.) Many of the Chinese officials and economists who participated, including all of those mentioned above, played significant roles in the design and/or implementation of China's economic reforms. There are

(*Continued*)

(Continued)

Date(s) or period	*Explanation*
	probably no foreign economists who had a bigger impact on economic reforms in China than Kornai and Brus. Kornai's book *Economics of Shortage, a critique of socialist economics*, first published in '80, was translated into Chinese after the Bashan Lun conference and became a best seller in China. (lun = cruise)
Sept. '85 7th Five Year Plan ('86–'90) endorsed by the Politburo	The plan (reflecting the priorities for economic reform of PM Zhao Ziyang and his deputy, Tian Jiyun) was *comprehensive* in nature. It included micro and macro policy as well as institutional reforms. An outline for this plan had been developed by Wu Jinglian and others in their report: *Conceptual Framework for an Overall Economic Restructuring Plan*, which had become available earlier in '85. The 7th FYP aimed, inter alia, at rapidly developing the non-state economy (which then accounted for 1/3 of China's GDP), e.g., by opening additional zones for foreign investment. The plan was officially approved by the NPC in March '86. (In his annual Work Report for the NPC at that time, PM Zhao thanked foreign experts, specifically those from the World Bank, for their contributions to the 7th FYP.)
March '86 Launch of 863 Program (Beginning of various government programs to promote the absorption of foreign technologies, study abroad and the recruitment of foreign experts and teachers)	With the support of Deng Xiaoping, the Government adopted a program to promote (with subsidies and administrative measures) the acquisition of foreign technologies and indigenous innovation. The program, proposed by a group of Chinese engineers, was named "863" (third month of the year '86) for its timing. It became the start of series of policies over the next several decades aimed at promoting technological development and indigenous innovation, culminating in the *China Manufacturing 2025* program of May '15. (The 863 Program was followed that same year by two similar, World Bank-supported, programs called "Spark" and "Torch" aimed at promoting rural- and SME-based technology development. It was also followed by various government-sponsored scholarship programs to enable Chinese students to study at prestigious foreign universities and (a decade later) by the "973 Program" to facilitate the recruitment of highly trained overseas Chinese and foreign experts. At the end of '08, in the wake of the global financial crisis, China launched the so called "Thousand Talents" Program aimed at promoting the recruitment by Chinese universities of expert foreign teachers in various sciences and the return to China of highly trained Chinese students.
April '86 (1) "Program Office" set up by Zhao Ziyang to accelerate, coordinate and professionalize economic reform policies (2) WFOE Law	PM Zhao Ziyang created a "Program Office" staffed by prominent economists (incl. Gao Shangquan, An Zhiwen, Wu Jinglian, et al.) to map out a detailed reform *implementation plan*. Being concerned about resource allocation distortions and rent-seeking behavior generated by the "dual-track" pricing system, the Program Office recommended ending that system and giving priority to *comprehensive* and *rapid* price (and wage) reforms, combined with coordinated fiscal, banking and trade policy reforms based on Wu Jinglian's report of '85: *Conceptual*

Date(s) or period	*Explanation*
	Framework for an Overall Economic Restructuring Plan. The *implementation* plan was initially accepted by PM Zhao Ziyang and other reform-minded Party leaders, but later shelved (because of opposition from conservative Party leaders, who were more comfortable with "planning" and feared that aggressive price reform would fuel inflation). The *implementation* plan was replaced by relatively modest SOE- and fiscal reforms a few months later). (2) On 12 April NPC adopted the "Law on Wholly Foreign-Owned Enterprises" (WFOE Law), supplementing the EJV Law of '79, making 100% foreign ownership of certain kinds of enterprises possible.
Sept.–Nov. '86 In four "talks", Deng Xiaoping called again for *political reform*	Deng Xiaoping called again for *political reform*, because (in his words) "without political reforms it will be difficult to reform our economic structure". The basis for Deng's repeated calls for *political reform* was pragmatic (non-ideological). He also wanted to distinguish China's political system from that of the USSR, which he distrusted. Specifically, he stressed the need to: 1. Avoid "bureaucracy" and excessive concentration of power; 2. Avoid lifetime tenure in leading positions; 3. Eliminating surviving "feudal" influences; 4. Separate Party leadership from government administration; 5. Separate government administration from SOE management. Deng's calls for *political reform* never reflected any doubt on his part about (or commitment to) a centrally important, exclusive role for the CPC in China's economy. His repeated calls for separating Government and Party in managing the economy were apparently resisted by other (more conservative) Party leaders and never fully implemented.
'86 (1) Labor contracting system for SOEs launched (2) Bankruptcy Law (3) Unemployment insurance initiated	(1) Under a State Council regulation, SOEs were permitted (for the first time), to hire new workers on the basis of fixed term contracts. This was the beginning of the end of China's "iron-rice-bowl" system under which public sector workers (and their dependents) were guaranteed lifetime employment and social security (including pension) by the state. (2) The Bankruptcy Law made it possible (also for the first time) for SOEs to close under legal bankruptcy procedures. The Law designated the company's workers and pensioners as priority creditors. (The Law was revised in '07, mainly to bring the rights of *financial* creditors in line with international practice.) (3) Recognizing that the "iron rice bowl" system (which had ensured employment and social security for all since '56) would eventually have to disappear, unemployment insurance was introduced. This government-sponsored scheme was more fully developed in the late '90s (after the 3rd Plenum of the 15th CC in May '98).

(*Continued*)

(Continued)

Date(s) or period	Explanation
Oct. '86 (1) First experiment with rural pensions (2) Arden House conference in New York	(1) The Ministry of Civil Affairs launched a scheme to provide voluntary rural pension insurance in relatively developed rural areas. This, and similar experiments in later years, failed, essentially because of high administration costs and low participation rates. (2) This was a very important 3-day conference in New York State (financed by the Ford- and Rockefeller Foundations) to discuss many aspects of China's economic reforms. Some 32 scholars (16 from China and 16 from various US and European universities and the World Bank) participated. The Chinese delegation included Wu Jinglian, Zhou Xiaochuan, Zhao Renwei and 13 others; the international delegation included Bruce Reynolds (who edited a book on this conference), Irma Adelman, Barry Naughton, Bela Balassa, T.N. Srinivasan, Gregory Chow and ten others). Along with the Moganshan conferences of '82 and '84, the Bashan Lun (boat) conference of '85 and the Dalian conference of '93, the Arden House conference of '86 offered important opportunities for Chinese reform economists to interact with foreign economic experts and China scholars. (Over the years, there were numerous other conferences and workshops, sponsored by various foreign and Chinese agencies, for Chinese economists and officials to exchange views with foreign experts and for foreigners to ascertain how economic reforms in China were progressing.)
Dec. '86 New SOE reforms	Dissatisfied with the results of earlier approaches to SOE reform, the State Council (still under PM Zhao Ziyang) decided to strengthen SOE managerial autonomy and to tighten their fiscal responsibilities to protect government budget revenues. When Wu Jinglian's reform *implementation* plan was shelved earlier in '86, SOE reform moved central stage in China's evolving economic reform strategy.
Late '86–early '87 Anti- "bourgeois liberalization" campaign	Party conservatives (this time led by Peng Zhen) conducted a campaign against what they perceived as a dangerous relaxation of Marxist-socialist principles. The campaign was extended to economic reforms and reformers. This was probably a major factor underlying PM Zhao Ziyang's decision of late '86 to shelve Wu Jinglian's plan for the *implementation* of *comprehensive* and *rapid* price reforms and to give priority to more limited micro-economic reforms instead. The campaign was also a factor in the forced resignation of Hu Yaobang in Jan. '87.
16 Jan. '87 Party Secretary Hu Yaobang forced to resign	Hu, a key reformer – held responsible by conservative Party elders for anti-government/pro-democracy student demonstrations in many cities in Dec. '86 – was forced to resign. PM Zhao Ziyang was then made acting General Secretary of the Party, a position in which he was confirmed at the 13th Party Congress in Oct. '87. He was replaced by Li Peng as acting PM. (Li was confirmed as PM in March '88.)

Date(s) or period	*Explanation*
April '87 BOCOM and CITIC re-constituted	BOCOM (Bank of Communications, in Shanghai) and CITIC (China International Trust and Investment Corporation, in Beijing) were re-constituted on the basis of semi-private initiatives to promote *private domestic and foreign investment* in China. (BOCOM had been originally established in 1908. A more limited version of CITIC had been in existence since '79.)
Oct. '87 (1) 13th Party Congress ('87–'92) (2) Deng Xiaoping retires	(1) Under the leadership of Zhao Ziyang, who was then confirmed as General Secretary of the Party, the Congress formally approved a *comprehensive* reform plan aimed at establishing a "Socialist Planned Commodity Economy" (a term that had been used at the 3rd Plenum of the 12th CC in Oct. '84). Importantly, this Congress agreed to develop the private sector as a key part of China's economy. The "operating principle" of the approach to reform and development adopted by this Congress was that the "state would *regulate* the market, while the market would *guide* the enterprises in their business decisions". The Congress considered *political reform*, as had been recommended by Deng Xiaoping on several occasions, but made no real changes. (2) The 13th Party Congress was a triumph for the reform wing of the Party. Feeling secure that China was on the right reform path, Deng Xiaoping announced his retirement from the CC and the Politburo SC, encouraging other older leaders to step down also (to make room for "younger blood".) Chen Yun (who favored a less important role for the market than Deng), Li Xiannian and about 90 other senior leaders followed Deng's example. However, Deng Xiaoping stayed on as chairman of the CMC and continued to be recognized as China's "paramount" leader.
March '88 7th NPC	In line with the decision of the 13th Party Congress to promote private sector development, the NPC amended China's Constitution by adding the following provision: "The state permits the private sector of the economy to exist and develop within the limits prescribed by law. The private sector of the economy is a complement to the socialist public economy." (By the end of '88, China had 90,000 registered private companies, employing 1.64 MN people).
Summer '88 Aggressive price reform strategy adopted	Following years of heated, but inconclusive debate among economists and Party leaders on how and how quickly to reform the pricing system, a debate that continued at the annual CPC leadership summer retreat at Beidahe (a seaside resort on Bohai Bay in Hebei), the Politburo (urged by Deng Xiaoping) ordered SPC to significantly accelerate price (and wage) liberalization. This decision unexpectedly contributed to the withdrawal of bank deposits and to panic buying by the general public, which fueled inflation. (Inflation was already high then because of the relatively loose monetary policy that had been in place following a recession in '86.) High inflation reduced support for additional reforms and (together with corruption) became the object of popular protests in Beijing's Tiananmen Square and in other cities in the first half of '89. .

(*Continued*)

(Continued)

Date(s) or period	*Explanation*
'89 Publication of *From Marx to the Market: Socialism in Search of an Economic System* by Wlodzimierz Brus and Kazimierz Laski (Polish economists living in exile in London)	Probably because Brus was well-known and highly respected in circles of Chinese reformers, this book, which repudiated the author's earlier embrace of "market socialism" (central planning with state-determined equilibrium prices based on "scientific" estimates of supply and demand), had a significant influence in China. From then on, many Chinese economists rejected "market socialism" as a basis for their country's economic reform strategy and turned their attention to Western market economies instead. (Much earlier, China's Sun Yefang and Austria's Friedrich Hayek, approaching the subject from different angles, had come to the same conclusion about "market socialism" as Brus and Laski in their '89 book.)
15 April '89 Hu Yaobang dies	The day after his death, students assembled in Tiananmen Square in Beijing to pay tribute to Hu Yaobang, a highly respected reformer and former General Secretary of the CPC. These gatherings triggered popular protests against corruption and high inflation, which ended peacefully. But the student demonstrations continued, becoming very large and increasingly political (pro-democracy) in nature, culminating in a hunger strike. After many weeks, the demonstrations were violently suppressed under Martial Law by the PLA on 3–4 June. Similar protests in many other cities, including Shanghai, ended peacefully.
4 June '89 Tiananmen Square Massacre – followed by new challenges to reform	After this traumatic event, involving the killing and wounding of hundreds of student demonstrators, there was a political backlash against market-oriented reforms (led by Deng Liqun, Wang Rhenzi and others). Zhao Ziyang was purged and placed under house arrest, only 2.5 years after Hu Yaobang, the previous reformist General Secretary of the Party, had been forced to resign. Some conservative Party leaders wanted to reverse earlier market reforms (e.g., by abolishing private farming under the HRS and returning to collective farming.) Although this anti-reform movement gained no traction, it signaled deep divisions within the Party (and among technocrats). Some reform policy components of the 7th FYP ('86–'90) were suspended. It wasn't until early '92 that the Party regained its footing under the leadership of Deng Xiaoping, who (though retired from most official positions) remained China's "paramount" leader. (In the meantime, the 8th FYP ('91–'95), which was essentially and extension of the 7th FYP, was approved by the NPC in March '91.
9 June '89 Deng Xiaoping speech	Addressing (Martial Law) PLA soldiers five days after the Tiananmen "disturbances", Deng stressed that China should not depart from the reform direction set at the 3rd Plenum of the 11th CC in Dec. '78, but implement the "combination of planned economy and market adjustment", as decided by the 3rd Plenum of the 12th CC in Nov. '84.
23–24 June '89 4th Plenum of the 13th CPC CC. Jiang Zemin succeeds Zhao Ziyang as General Secretary of the CPC	At this Plenum Zhao Ziyang was officially dismissed as General Secretary of the Party and replaced by Jiang Zemin. The latter had served as Shanghai's Party Secretary ('87–'88) and would serve as top national leader until the 16th Party Congress in the Fall of '02, when Hu Jintao succeeded him.

Date(s) or period	*Explanation*
'89 and '91 The fall of the Berlin Wall and the collapse of the USSR affected China deeply	These momentous developments had enormous influence in China. That China's reformers ultimately prevailed in the internal debates after the political "disturbances" of '89, owes much to the fact that many of them ascribed the collapse of the USSR to *late* and *inadequate* economic reforms there. An illustration of the effect on China of the USSR's collapse is a 3-day seminar in late '91 – after the failed coup in Moscow – at which the new General Secretary of the CPC Jiang Zemin questioned a group of 20 Chinese economists about reasons for the USSR's demise and capitalism's apparent resilience. These meetings contributed to preparations for the 14th Party Congress in Oct. '92.
5 July '90 High-level meeting of economists with the Politburo's Standing Committee	At the request of the Politburo's SC, leading economists met with their members to discuss causes of the high inflation of the late '80s and the political "disturbances" of '89. The majority opinion was that market-oriented reforms had gone too far and that the Party had not been faithful to Deng Xiaoping's four "Cardinal Principles". But some economists (notably Xue Muqiao, Liu Guoguang, Wu Jinglian and some younger SCRES and DRC economists) argued the opposite. They maintained that a planned economy could not be combined with "market regulation" and that the correct way to proceed, was to *deepen* market-oriented reforms. Xue Muqiao wrote a letter to CPC General Secretary Jiang Zemin to explain why. (Deng Xiaoping sided with the reformers, which decided the outcome of this important meeting.)
Dec. '90–July '91 Shanghai and Shenzhen stock exchanges officially opened	Unofficial share issues and OTC securities trading had started as early as '80 (in Shenyang). In the mid-to late '80s, many Chinese cities, including Shanghai, Shenzhen, Beijing, Shenyang and Wuhan, had small, unofficial, unregulated informal securities markets. The Shanghai and Shenzhen stock exchanges were officially opened with Deng's reluctant support ("if it doesn't work out, we can always close them."). The Shanghai stock exchange (where share trading had originally started in 1866, was officially reopened on 19 Dec.'90 (after having been closed since '49); the Shenzhen stock exchange was officially opened on 3 July '91 (four years after its unofficial start in '87). Initially, both exchanges were supervised by the local Governments and listed SOEs only. There was a major difference between government-owned *non-tradable shares* (usually around 75% of the total share issue) and freely *tradable* (minority) shares, held by the Chinese public and non-state agents. RMB-denominated "A" shares could only be purchased by Chinese and "B" shares were for foreigners (denominated in US$ in Shanghai and in HK$ in Shenzhen). To fight share price depression, the B-share market was opened to Chinese nationals on 19 Feb. '01. In '05, the distinction between tradable and non-tradable shares was modified (by strengthening the rights of minority shareholders). The Shanghai and Shenzhen exchanges trade stocks as well as debt securities; Shanghai is the principal market for government bonds and listed SOEs (including state banks). Corporate bonds are traded on both exchanges and on the OTC bond market. Shenzhen opened a special SME Board in '03 and a NASDAQ-type Board for high-tech start-ups ("ChiNext") in '09.

(*Continued*)

(Continued)

Date(s) or period	*Explanation*
May '93 End of grain rationing	The end of coupon-based grain rationing marked the end of all food rationing (which had been introduced in '53 as part of the 1st FYP). It was a nationally celebrated event of great political and psychological importance; it was interpreted as proof that China's "reform and opening-up" policies had been successful.
June '93 (1) Dalian Conference (2) Publication of a joint article by Wu Jinglian and Zhou Xiaochuan "A Comprehensive Design for the Near- and Medium-Term Reform of the Economic System" in *Gaige* (reform) magazine	(1) The purpose of this conference, held in Dalian, Liaoning (attended by representatives of various government agencies, CASS, World Bank, IMF, esteemed international economists/China experts such as Nicholas Stern, Lawrence Lau, Nicholas Lardy, Athar Hussain, Cyril Lin, Christopher Allsop and the 83-year-old Li Kwoh Ting from Taiwan (a former Finance Minister, known as the "father of Taiwan's economic miracle")), was to identify factors responsible for the high inflation in China at the time and what to do about it. The economy had begun to "overheat" after Deng's "Southern Tour" in early '92, and there was disagreement within the government about causes and about possible remedies. (The Dalian conference followed a similar conference at Harvard early in '93 with the same attendees (except Li). The main conclusion of the Dalian conference (namely that the "overheating" was due to excessive, credit-financed investment) was reported to Vice PM Zhu Rongji (China's "economic czar") and Jiang Zemin. Zhu agreed with the conference's conclusion and, with the help of his unofficial inner circle of economic advisors (including, inter alia, Guo Shuqing, Lou Jiwei and Wu Xiaoling), prepared a 16-point macro-economic stabilization plan, which was made public a few weeks later. (The World Bank published a special report on the Dalian conference in '94. It was edited by three conference participants: Peter Harrold, E. C. Hwa and Lou Jiwei. After the Bashan Lun conference of '85, the Dalian conference was probably the most important in the history of economic policy making in China since the start of market-oriented reforms in the late '70s.) (2) This 9.5-page joint article was first published (in Chinese) in *Gaige* (reform) magazine and reprinted in a Chinese book on economic reform in '96. The article had great influence on Zhu Rongji (who succeeded Li Peng as PM in March '98) and on actual reform policy making from then on. The article built on a book the two authors had published in '88, *The Integrated design of China's Economic Reform* (not available in English).
July '93 16-point macro-economic stabilization package	After the Politburo had approved the package of policy measures aimed at reducing inflation (based on Dalian conference conclusions), Zhu Rongji led the implementation effort, which included, inter alia: (1) recentralizing government control over the financial system (which started immediately), (2) reforming China's fiscal and exchange rate systems (which was done on 1 Jan. '94) and (3) indexing bank deposit rates to inflation (done immediately). This package of reform measures marked a huge advance from China's earlier approach to macro-economic management. It contributed significantly to preparations for the 3rd Plenum of the 14th CC in November, which adopted a

Date(s) or period	*Explanation*
	comprehensive micro-, macro-, and institutional reform plan. The policy package of July, together with the 3rd Plenum of Nov. and subsequent reform measures, succeeded in bringing inflation under control a few years later ("soft landing") and set the economy on the most comprehensive reform path since the late '70s.
11–14 Nov. '93 3rd Plenum of the 14th CC of the CPC	This, another critically important 3rd Plenum adopted the "Decision on Issues of Building a Socialist Market Economy", including 50 sub-decisions aimed at building a "Modern Enterprise System", enhancing foreign economic relations, promoting private SMEs, deepening fiscal, legal and financial system reforms and at transforming the social security system. This Plenum confirmed the Party's commitment to market-oriented reforms and the promotion of a mixed public/private economy in which "public ownership" would still be "primary". Because of the comprehensive nature of its "Decision . . ." this 3rd Plenum set China's reform agenda for the rest of the '90s and beyond. It was the most important Plenum since the 3rd Plenum of Dec. '78. The key document of the 3rd Plenum of Nov. '93, "Decision on Issues of Building a Socialist Market Economy", was drafted by a team of 25 technocrats/economists (including Liu Guoguang, Gao Shangquan, Zhou Xiaochuan, Wang Mengkui, Li Jiange and 20 others) under the leadership of Wen Jiabao, who was then an alternate member of the Politburo and who would later serve as PM under President Hu Jintao ('03–'13).
24 Nov.'93 Publication in the *People's Daily* of the World Bank's first Quarterly Economic Report on China	This report, prepared by the WB's resident mission in China, was published (in Chinese) in the *People's Daily* at the request of Vice PM Zhu Rongji. The report noted that inflation was still a major problem and that it would be premature to relax the macro-stabilization program of July.
1 Jan. '94 Package of macro-economic and institutional reform measures following the 16-point macro-stabilization program of July '93	Key components of this important package were: (1) Unification of China's multiple exchange rate system (at the then prevailing free-market rate of RMB8.7 per USD) and introduction of a "market-driven, managed float" exchange rate system, as had been recommended by members of Zhu Rongji's unofficial inner circle of Chinese advisors; (2) Creation of an IRS-type Central Government tax agency (for the first time in China's history) and introduction of a major program of fiscal reforms. This "revenue sharing system" (as it was called), aimed at improving fiscal buoyancy and at channeling a larger share of total revenues to the Central Government for redistribution to poor provinces; (3) Creation of a modern, dual-rate, national VAT system and a national personal income tax system (based or progressive rates and automatic payroll deductions); (4) Termination of FX "swap" markets, the FX "retention system" and the FEC (a special currency for foreigners in China, which had been introduced in April '80;

(*Continued*)

(Continued)

Date(s) or period	*Explanation*
	(5) Permitting the privatization of small SOEs (over 72,000) and local-Government-owned TVEs (over 0.5 MN); (6) Ending the "dual-track" pricing system; (7) Facilitating the reform of state-owned commercial banks through the creation of "policy banks". (This package of measures, most of which had been recommended by Wu Jinglian and Zhou Xiaochuan in their joint article of June '93, created a new macro-economic control system centered on the market-based allocation of resources.)
'94 Establishment of Shanghai Interbank Foreign Exchange market and three "Policy Banks"	To enable implementation of the decision (of 1 Jan. '94) to unify China's multiple XR system and to introduce a unified, "market-driven", managed float system instead, a market for forex trading between banks was created in Shanghai. To facilitate the reform of state-owned commercial banks, three policy banks: the CDB, ADB and China Exim Bank (Chexim), were created during '94. (The creation of "policy banks" had also been recommended by Wu Jinglian and Zhou Xiaochuan in their influential joint article of June '93).
'94–'95 (1) Budget Law (2) Company Law (3) Commercial Banking Law (4) Central Bank Law	(1) One of the main features of this first Budget Law was the prohibition of government borrowing from the central bank (except for short-term liquidity management), thus laying the groundwork for building a market for government bonds. The new law became effective on 1 Jan. '95 and was amended in Aug. '14. (2) This law set minimum capital requirements for new companies and defined various forms of corporate ownership, including LLCs and joint stock companies. It made possible the legal incorporation of SOEs as well as share sales to non-state agents. The law was revised in '99, '05 and '13. The most recent revision sharply lowered minimum capital requirements for starting a new business. (3) and (4) Some of the main features of these two related laws, both promulgated in '95, were: (a) PBoC is *not* an *independent* central bank but is answerable to the State Council; (b) The Commercial Banking Law codified regular fractional reserve banking, but, in line with America's Glass-Steagall Act of '33, the original '95 Law barred commercial banks from engaging in investment banking- and insurance business. However, "universal banking" later emerged in the form of financial holding companies engaging in a broader range of financial business. (Both laws were amended and modernized in '03.)
31 July'95 CICC established	China's first investment bank was a JV of Morgan Stanley, CCB and two smaller Chinese financial institutions. The establishment of China International Capital Corporation represented a financial sector development of great importance. CICC engages in investment banking, securities issues and trading, investment management and other financial services, primarily for institutional clients. Its first CEO was Edwin Lim, the World Bank's first res. rep. in China ('85–'91), then on a leave of absence from the World Bank.

Date(s) or period	*Explanation*
Sept. '95 5th Plenum of the 14th CC	This Plenum reaffirmed the Government's strategy to privatize small SOEs (and TVEs), using the slogan "grasp the large ones and let go of the small ones". To reduce the scope for "asset stripping" (transferring the best assets of SOEs to the private sector, while leaving the state with poor assets and debt), management buy-outs were banned.
March '96 9th FYP ('96–'00) approved by the NPC	The 9th FYP aimed especially at increasing economic *efficiency*. (This was the first indication that China's top economic managers were developing doubts about the sustainability of China's investment-driven growth model.)
Sept. '96 PBoC joins Bank for International Settlements	By joining BIS, the Swiss-based "central bankers' central bank" (created in '30, during the Depression) China committed itself to adopting international loan-risk classification and bank capital adequacy standards in the future. It was a critical step helping China prepare for later domestic bank reforms. (In '09, China joined the rule-setting, BIS-sponsored "Basel Committee on Banking Supervision").
Late '96 "Several Theoretical and Policy Issues for Upholding the Dominant Role of Public Ownership"	Party conservatives lashed out again; a group of prominent conservative Chinese economists published an influential report criticizing the government for allowing the non-state economy to become very important. In their view, "socialism" required that SOEs remain dominant in the economy; they warned that China would go the same way as Gorbachev's USSR if China did not restore economic dominance of the state.
1 Dec. '96 China complies with Article 8 of the IMF Charter	This meant that China's currency had become fully convertible for *current account* transactions, as had been recommended by Wu Jinglian and Zhou Xiaochuan in their joint article of June '93. China then announced that it aimed at achieving full currency convertibility (including an open capital account) by the end of the century. However, it was frustrated in achieving this objective by the Asian financial crisis that started in Thailand on 2 July '97. No new target date for achieving full currency convertibility was set, but it is understood to remain the objective of China's top financial system managers/reformers.
'97 (1) Monetary Policy Committee (2) Publication of the World Bank's seven-volume "China 2020" economic report	(1) In light of the growing size and complexity of China's economy and financial system, the State Council established a Monetary Policy Committee to advise PBoC, as had been recommended by Wu Jinglian and Zhou Xiaochuan in their joint article of June '93. (2) This major new economic report was reviewed by and discussed with the Chinese Government. It had considerable influence on the formulation of macro-economic and sectoral policies.
19 Feb. '97 Deng Xiaoping dies	At the official memorial service a few weeks later, CPC General Secretary Jiang Zemin reminded the audience of Deng's calls for *political reform*.
March '97 Launch of 973 program	This was a government-sponsored program to attract foreign experts, including overseas Chinese, to teach at Chinese universities and work at Chinese R&D centers.

(*Continued*)

(Continued)

Date(s) or period	*Explanation*
1 July '97 Return of Hong Kong to China	After 146 years of British rule, this was an event of great economic and political importance. It marked the continuation (under different political and legal circumstances) of a very constructive economic relationship between HK (then named "Special Administrative Region" (SAR) and mainland China. Soon after the political transition, especially after China joined the WTO (Dec. '01), HK became the most important source of FDI in China, as many of its industries migrated to neighboring Guangdong to take advantage of cheaper labor and lower production costs in general. HK continued to serve as a transit center for part of the mainland's trade with the rest of the world and as a source of professional services, mainland staff training and policy advice. Merchandise trade between HK and mainland China remained extremely important. In later years, mainland tourism to and investment in HK became very important for the continued growth of HK's economy. Furthermore, HK became the first major offshore RMB center after China launched its RMB internationalization policy in '09. The model for political reunification between HK and mainland China (named "One Country-Two systems" by Deng Xiaoping) was also used for the return of Macau (which had been under Portuguese rule over 400 years), in '99.
2 July '97 Start of the Asian financial crisis (AFC)	This major financial, banking and social crisis, which started in Thailand, quickly blew over to Malaysia, Indonesia and most other countries in Southeast and East Asia. Although the crisis affected China only mildly – mainly through reduced exports –, it was nonetheless a "wake-up call" for the leadership in Beijing. To protect the Chinese economy against the slowdown and deflation that resulted from the AFC, the Central Government launched a fiscal stimulus program (in '98), which lasted until '01. In addition, China embarked on more aggressive, reform policies in other areas, including: (1) new SME promotion- and SOE reform policies, (2) massive urban housing privatization (started in '99), (3) NPL-clean-up and bank reforms (also started in '99) and (4) removal of export restrictions on non-state firms. However, China did *not* devalue its currency, as had been widely expected. A few weeks after South Korea became engulfed by the AFC, China tied the RMB more closely to the USD (Dec. '97), so that harmful competitive devaluations in the region could be avoided and a stable RMB could serve as "anchor" for other regional currencies. (This XR measure, which was applauded by the US and other Western powers, helped the Asia region overcome the AFC more quickly than otherwise would have been possible. China kept the RMB/USD XR fixed until 21 July '05).
12–18 Sept. '97 15th Party Congress ('97–'02)	At the opening session of this Party Congress, General Secretary Jiang Zemin called for the establishment of a "sound market system" based on a well-defined ownership structure (dominated by the state, but including many other forms of ownership). Jiang's statement stressed the need for "readjusting the state

Date(s) or period	*Explanation*
	sector" by allowing the state to withdraw from some sectors, while increasing its market share in others. Jiang also mentioned the importance of developing the non-state economy in a "communist country ruled by law". The PLA was ordered to divest its commercial holdings. The Congress also called for "political reform to expand socialist democracy…", but there was no specific follow-up. (The Congress ignored the report of late '96 by prominent conservative Chinese economist, who had argued that reforms had gone too far in promoting the non-state economy.)
June '98 Founding of CE50 (Chinese Economists 50 Forum)	This informal Forum (renamed the Chang'an Forum in '01), comprising some 50 leading Chinese economists, played an important role in the interaction between Chinese economists and government officials responsible for economic policy making and implementation. Forum members include senior government officials with professional economics training, such as, e.g., Liu He (principal economic advisor to President Xi Jinping), Lou Jiwei (Finance Minister until Nov. '16), Zhou Xiaochuan (governor of PBoC) and Yi Gang (deputy governor of PBoC). CE50 also interacts frequently with foreign experts. In '08, CE50 and Sina Finance, a major financial services company, reached a cooperation agreement, renaming the Forum Sina Chang'an Forum. (On 20 July '16 Wu Jinglian delivered a major speech for this Forum on structural economic reform.)
Oct. '98 The Central Government forces closure of the bankrupt Guangdong International Trust and Investment Corporation	After the Central Government, under the leadership of PM Zhu Rongji, refused to step in and "save" it, the company (GITIC, one of China's largest financial SOEs at the time, owned by the Guangdong Provincial Government), defaulted on its external bond obligation and filed for bankruptcy (in Jan '99). Zhu Rongji's decision was supported by Wang Qishan, then vice governor of Guangdong. GITIC's demise signaled to the world and to domestic financial institutions that Beijing was taking the reform of China's financial system seriously and that the Central Government would not automatically guarantee the liabilities of SOEs, as had been widely assumed by foreign creditors. The decision to let GITIC fail was a watershed event in financial sector management and in China's relations with external creditors.
Nov. '98 (1) Reorganization of China's central banking system (2) Establishment to China Insurance Regulatory Commission (CIRC)	(1) PBoC, which used to have numerous small branch offices all over China (typically under the de-facto control of local Governments), was reorganized into nine large regional offices, each covering several provinces. This new central bank model, which resembled the US Federal Reserve system in some ways, had been recommended by Wu Jinglian and Zhou Xiaochuan in their joint article of June '93. (2) That same month, CIRC was established (spun off from PBoC) as a separate agency.

(*Continued*)

(Continued)

Date(s) or period	*Explanation*
'99–'05 Period of most intensive reform of state banks and SOEs	Starting with a modest initial recapitalization of RMB270bn in '98 (financed from excess bank reserves with PBoC), all state commercial banks underwent major internal reforms in the following years. They were audited according to international standards, legally incorporated under China's Company Law, gradually recapitalized from various foreign and domestic sources (including official FX reserves) and listed on the Shanghai and HK stock exchanges. However, the state retained majority ownership of those listed banks. During this period of intensive economic reforms (incl. the imposition of serious budget constraints on SOEs), some 25 mn SOE workers were laid off or took "early retirement". The Central Government reorganized itself and trimmed its workforce significantly. (Although total public sector employment contracted by over 40 mn during this period, national unemployment barely increased, as China's rapidly growing private sector absorbed most former public sector workers.)
1 July '99 Securities Law	Almost 10 years after the Shanghai and Shenzhen stock exchanges opened for business (under local Government control), this new law finally defined the rules for listing and de-listing, information disclosure requirements and share trading. Earlier (from around '93), formal responsibility for the supervision of China's stock exchanges had shifted from local Governments to CSRC, but this agency did not become fully effective until '02. (The Securities law was amended in '04 and in '05.)
'99 Four Asset Management Companies (AMCs) established	This was a key step in the process of state bank reform and recapitalization. The four (state-owned) AMCs (also called "bad banks") started the process of NPL clean-up by taking over RMB 1.4BN (at face value) from state banks.
'99–'03 Urban housing privatization	To relieve SOEs of a major financial burden (namely, the provision of housing for their employees), protect the economy against fall-out from the AFC (by stimulating domestic demand) and promote private construction industries, the State Council (under PM Zhu Rongji) decided to transfer ownership of almost all urban housing units to occupants (at artificially low prices, because there was no mortgage market at that time and cash wages were still very low). (Some efforts to promote private homeownership had started in the early '90s but had never amounted to much.) Implementation of this new, massive, privatization program was left to local Governments. The program transformed China's economy by creating much private wealth, accelerating urbanization, creating a huge (private) domestic construction industry, increasing labor mobility and (later) contributing to *speculative* house buying and -construction. (The wholesale privatization of urban housing had been recommended by Wu Jinglian and Zhou Xiaochuan in their joint article of June '93).

Date(s) or period	*Explanation*
25 Feb. 2000 Jiang Zemin launches the "Three Represents"	This ideological innovation had significant political, social and economic implications. By opening CPC membership and top Party positions to private entrepreneurs, capitalists, managers and professional elites, Jiang Zemin aimed at turning the Party into a *universal* party. Mao's CPC had been a party of and for workers, peasants and soldiers (the proletariat), united in class struggle against the economic elite (the *bourgeoisie*). Jiang wanted to promote the development of a "harmonious" middle-class society, while relegating Mao's imperative of class struggle to history. (If Marx had foreseen the emergence of a middle class, his ideas on the inevitability of class struggle and socialist revolution might not have emerged.) Although Jiang Zemin and his successor Hu Jintao aimed at promoting a "harmonious" society, for various reasons, serious social tensions continued after the concept of "Three Represents" was formally adopted at the 16th Party Congress in Nov. '02.
1 Aug. '00 National Social Security Fund established	NSSF was initially established to compensate for a fundamental shortcoming in the pension system reforms of '96 and '97, which aimed at providing government-mandated pension benefits for all urban workers (state and non-state). A key feature of the new ("defined contribution") pension system (first introduced in '96) was *funded individual accounts* to finance a large part of pension rights under the new system. However, the government had failed to set aside funds to cover the "implicit pension debt" (pension rights earned under the old pension system) when it changed over to the new pension system. Consequently, the new system soon ran into serious cash-flow problems, and most *individual accounts* in the new system remained unfunded ("empty") because current contributions were needed to finance "old" pension obligations. The NSSF – funded by fiscal contributions and the transfer of state assets) was meant to solve that problem.
Sept. '00 UN Summit set Millennium Development Goals	The Summit established major social and environmental development targets (Millennium Development Goals, MDGs) to be achieved by '15. China took the Summit very seriously and used the MDGs to formulate a range of domestic social policies aimed at, e.g. poverty reduction, improving mother and child health care, achieving universal primary education, gender equality and reducing the incidence of major diseases. (By the end of 2015, China had made more progress toward achieving social MDGs than any other major developing country.)
Nov. '00 Start of a campaign to reduce "rent seeking"	While Zhu Rongji was PM, the Party became very concerned about growing corruption. The Central Commission for Discipline Inspection (created by the 3rd Plenum of Dec. '78) began a campaign to eradicate corruption "at its roots" by streamlining the pervasive administrative licensing system, which existed at all levels of government.

(*Continued*)

(Continued)

Date(s) or period	*Explanation*
March '01 10th FYP ('01–'05) approved by the NPC	While reaffirming the *efficiency* objectives of the 9th FYP, the 10th FYP emphasized the need for "structural economic adjustments" and industrial "upgrading" through improved science and technology and reduced pollution. The priorities of this FYP indicated increased awareness of the need to change China's growth model for long-term sustainability.
11 Dec. '01 China joins WTO	The Accession Protocol required the removal of export subsidies and further reductions in trade tariffs and non-tariff trade barriers. It also required the opening of certain service sectors (including banking and life insurance) to foreign investors over a 5-year adjustment period and the removal of restrictions on domestic sales by foreign-invested enterprises (FIEs). FIEs would also be afforded "national treatment" in most other areas. Of its own volition, China widened the scope for WOFEs (WFOEs). As part of Deng's earlier "reform and opening-up" strategy, China had already significantly lowered trade barriers and investment restrictions in manufacturing sectors prior to WTO accession and had already reformed its earlier system of state trading monopolies. But China was (and is) still largely closed to foreign investment in many service industries and had retained selected local content requirements for FIEs. China agreed to China-specific WTO "safeguards" (for 7 years) and to be treated as a "non-market economy" (for 15 years) for the application of anti-dumping laws of WTO member countries. (During the following 5 years, China introduced or amended thousands of laws and regulations to comply with WTO requirements.)
8-16 Nov. '02 16th Party Congress (Nov. '02–Oct. '07)	This Congress incorporated Jiang Zemin's theory of the "Three Represents" (first presented in Feb. '00) into the CPC's Constitution and elected Hu Jintao as the new Party General Secretary (succeeding Jiang Zemin). The Congress stressed the importance of giving full market access to non-state enterprises and private capital. It also reasserted the need to develop a "communist political democracy ruled by law" and to improve "political civilization" through political reform.
'02–'07 Introduction of major social policy initiatives aimed at improving rural living conditions	During this period, the government of President Hu Jintao and PM Wen Jiabao introduced several major institutional/policy initiatives aimed at improving economic conditions in rural China, including free primary education, removal of agricultural taxes, minimum income support and basic health insurance for rural families. (Some of these benefits were later extended to urban families as well.)
5 Dec. '02 Hu Jintao speech	On the occasion of the 20th anniversary of China's '82 national Constitution, Hu delivered a speech confirming the Party's commitment to establish a "socialist market economy" under rule of law, based on the national Constitution.

Date(s) or period	*Explanation*
1 Jan. '03 Government Procurement Law	China's first public procurement law, approved by the NPC in June '02, became effective on 1 Jan. '03. Under this law, purchases by government agencies should generally be limited to domestically made goods. Partly because of this law, it has not been possible for China so far to join the WTO's Government Procurement Agreement (GPA), as it had promised to do when it joined the WTO as a full member in Dec. '01.
1 March '03 (1) CBRC and SASAC established (2) NDRC established	(1) Following-up on the opening session of the 16th Party Congress of Nov. '02, the NPC created: (1) CBRC to take over day-to-day banking supervision from PBoC and (2) SASAC (State-owned Assets Supervision and Administration Commission) to exercise SOE ownership rights on behalf of the state and improve the performance of the 185 non-financial, Central-Government-owned SOEs (mostly listed holding companies in energy, manufacturing, transportation and telecommunications) that were initially assigned to it. Following this model, many local Governments created their own SASACs. Mainly as a result of mergers, the number of companies held by central-SASAC at the end of '16 had been reduced to 102. (SASAC has not solved structural SOE problems, such as asymmetric incentives and a tendency to overleverage and create excess capacity.) CBRC was only partially successful in controlling risky "shadow banking" that emerged from around '11, but a new top manager of CBRC (appointed early '17) is pursuing more aggressive supervision in this regard. (The total number of SOEs, including financial sector enterprises and all subsidiaries, at the end of '15 was reported to be 155,000, about one-third of which (including some very large holding companies) was owned by the Central Government. (2) The State Commission for Restructuring the Economic System (SCRES), created in '82, was merged with SDPC (SPC until '98) to form the "National Development and Reform Commission". NDRC is a powerful Central Government agency (with offices at lower-level governments) to guide the nation's development/reform efforts and macro-economic policies. (NDRC is also responsible for setting many industrial and other standards.)
11–14 Oct. ' 03 3rd Plenum of the 16th CC of the CPC	This Plenum acknowledged that there were still many problems in China's "preliminary socialist market economy" due to "incomplete" transition. It adopted the "Decision on a Number of Issues Concerning the Improvement of the Socialist Market Economy" aimed at accelerating market reforms (especially SOE governance reforms and enforcement of "rules-based" competition) as the best way to solve remaining system problems. While SASAC and CBRC had been created earlier that year to improve the performance of large financial and non-financial SOEs, NDRC was expected to improve the planning- and policy

(*Continued*)

(Continued)

Date(s) or period	*Explanation*
	preparation process. While explicitly recognizing growing social and environmental problems, as well as resource constraints, the Plenum called for a more "balanced" development strategy. It also called for greater reliance on private investment and *hukou* reform to facilitate rapid and orderly urbanization. The Plenum marked a major change in official thinking on long-term economic development and identified "new directions" that would be fleshed out in the 11th FYP ('06–'11) and beyond. (However, the *implementation* of difficult and controversial economic reforms slowed in the following years, which may have contributed to the development of special interest groups and "rent-seeking" behavior in the public sector of the economy.)
March '04 Constitutional Amendment recognizing the importance of private enterprise	After earlier revisions of the '82 national Constitution (in '88, '93 and '99), the NPC adopted further changes, including confirmation that private property has the same legal status as state property. (In Oct. '07, the NPC approved China's first "Property Rights Law".)
'05–'10 Active promotion of private enterprise	During this period, the State Council issued several new directives aimed at encouraging, supporting and guiding private sector development. However, de-facto market-entry restrictions on private businesses remained in many areas and, realizing that state power remained pervasive in large segments of the economy, many private enterprises began to "collude" with government as part of "normal" business practice, thus reinforcing an emerging culture of rent-seeking and corruption.
21 July '05 RMB de-linked from USD	The fixed XR regime, which had been in place since Dec. '97 (following the collapse of South Korea's economy during the AFC), ended. China effectively revived the "managed float" system it had introduced on 1 Jan. '94. (The RMB/USD XR appreciated very little in the next 18 months, but significantly in the following years.)
10 Dec. '05 Publication of Liu Guoguang's article "Some Issues on Economic Teaching and Research"	At the age of 82, the famous economist Liu Guoguang, who had been one of the architects of China's early market-oriented economic reforms in the late '70s and '80s and a vice president of CASS, caused a stir in circles of Chinese economists, by expressing deep concern that Western neo-liberal economics had become mainstream in China and that Marxist economics had been marginalized. He urged the Ministry of Education to remove non-Marxist university presidents, deans and directors of education from their positions and recommended that all "sea turtle" economists (Chinese graduates returning from overseas training) should be re-educated in Marxism before being allowed to teach at Chinese schools. The article was based on a speech Liu had given upon being awarded the "China Economics Award for Outstanding Contribution" in July '05. In subsequent op-eds and interviews, Liu clarified that he was impressed by many serious social and economic problems that had developed in China since the introduction of market reforms (including widespread corruption, extreme income and wealth inequality, marketization of power, environmental degradation, high rates of

Date(s) or period	*Explanation*
	coal mining accidents etc.). He didn't blame market economics per se, but market failures and distortions, which, in a "socialist market economy", should have been corrected by the state. He concluded that China had placed too much emphasis on markets and too little on socialism. In his opinion, the Chinese state had become too weak to correct market failures. He attacked economic neo-liberalism as dangerous and historically alien to China. Liu's speech and subsequent article, had no practical follow-up in China at the time, but, 8 years later, were echoed by the Government of President Xi Jinping (CPC General Secretary since the 18th Party Congress in the Fall of '12), in warnings against the use of Western textbooks at Chinese universities.
Jan. '06 Introduction of "Indigenous Innovation" policy by the State Council	As part of its preparations for the 11th FYP ('06–'10), the State Council (under PM Wen Jiabao) introduced a "National Medium and Long-Term Plan for the Development of Science and Technology (2006–2020)", or MLP. This initiative was aimed at promoting the creation of China's own intellectual property and proprietary product lines by "enhancing original innovation through co-innovation and re-innovation based on the assimilation of imported technologies". The MLP aimed at turning China into a technology powerhouse by '20 and a global technology leader by '50.
March '06 11th FYP ('06–'10) adopted by the NPC	This FYP made a commitment to changing China's *growth model* from dependency on domestic investment and *external* demand, to *domestic* consumer demand and service sector development. These plan objectives were frustrated by the global financial crisis of '08/'09 to which China responded with a massive stimulus program (mainly based on credit expansion), much of which took the form of increased investment by local Governments in infrastructure and real estate.
16 March '07 Property Rights Law passed by NPC	After seven years of preparatory work, the NPC passed China's first Property Rights Law to provide better protection for private property rights. The Law became effective on 1 Oct. '07, the 58th anniversary of the PRC. It was a breakthrough in legal system development. It signaled that reformers favoring private-sector development had prevailed over conservatives, who continued to argue for a stronger role of the state in the economy. (Private property rights could apply to all kinds of assets, except land).
April '07 Broadcast by CCTV of its 12-episode TV documentary on *The Rise of Great Nations*	This historic TV broadcast was the result of a project by (state-owned) China Central TV aimed at educating the Chinese people on how, in the past, other countries had become "Great Nations". CCTV employed numerous economic experts and historians around the world for interviews underpinning this 12-episode documentary. The countries covered (sequentially) in this unique series, starting around the year 1500, were Portugal, Spain, Holland, Great Britain, France, Germany, Japan, Russia and the US. The narrative focused on economic, technical and financial dimensions of national journeys to "greatness". The TV series is believed to have had considerable influence on China's economic policy makers in the following years.

(*Continued*)

(Continued)

Date(s) or period	*Explanation*
15–21 Oct. '07 17th Party Congress (Oct. '07–Nov. '12) endorses Property Rights Law	This Congress reiterated the need for the state to provide *equal* protection of property rights, regardless of the identity of the owner and to ensure fair competition between state and non-state enterprises (creating a "level playing field"). Unfortunately, practical follow-up to this principle was limited; rent-seeking behavior and corruption intensified, while the power of special interest groups ("vested" interests) increased.
'07–'08 Anti-Monopoly Law (AML)	This critical piece of legislation, which had been under preparation since '94, was approved by the NPC on 8 Aug. '07 and became effective on 1 Aug. '08. It was meant to protect China against the development of avoidable monopolies. In practice, the AML was often used against non-state enterprises (especially FIEs). In the following years, many FIEs complained about de-facto AML-inspired discrimination against them.
9 Nov. '08 Stimulus Program launched	In response to the *global financial crisis* that followed the collapse of Lehman Brothers in the US in Sept. '08, China launched a huge stimulus program to protect its economy against fall-out from the GFC. Most of the additional purchasing power created by this program came from bank credit and (unplanned) shadow banking. China's stimulus program became the largest, in both absolute and relative terms, in the world. (The GFC contributed to a sharp reduction in China's appreciation for the US as a successful economic model to follow.)
Dec. '08 Launch of the "Thousand Talents" Program	In the wake of the GFC, the government launched a new program to attract highly experienced and highly trained foreign experts and teachers, including overseas Chinese, to Chinese universities and R&D centers, with the help of subsidies and incentive programs. The program echoed the "973 program" of March '97.
23 March '09 China's proposal for International Monetary System reform	About six months after the collapse of Lehman Brothers in the US and just before the G-20 meeting in London of 2 April, Zhou Xiaochuan, China's central bank governor posted a proposal on PBoC's website for IMS reform. Based on the "Triffin Dilemma", the proposal (to broaden the base of the SDR and turn it into a premier global reserve asset, as well as a transaction currency) was well received in major EM and continental European countries but ignored by the US, which has de-facto veto power over such proposals.
July '09 Start of pro-active RMB internationalization policies	When it became clear that PBoC's proposal for IMS reform was not going to be acted upon by the international community (essentially because the US ignored it), China initiated a set of pro-active RMB internationalization policies (essentially supplementing and intensifying earlier such policies). Hong Kong became the first offshore RMB center, many additional currency swap agreements with other central banks were negotiated, selected Chinese trading companies were authorized to pay or invoice in RMB and Chinese banks were encouraged to help finance outward FDI with RMB loans.

Date(s) or period	*Explanation*
Oct. '10 Policy on Strategic Emerging Industries (SEI) announced – a new industrial policy	The State Council issued a policy document: "Decision on Accelerating the Development of Strategic Emerging Industries", including: (1) Energy-efficient and environmental technologies; (2) Next-generation IT; (3) Biotechnology; (4) High-end equipment manufacturing; (5) New energy sources; (6) New materials; (7) New energy vehicles. The new policy signaled that government agencies at all levels of government must support SEI development through regulatory interventions.
March '11 (1) 12th FYP ('12–'16) adopted by the 22nd NPC (2) Start of property tax experiments in Shanghai and Chongqing	(1) This FYP was essentially a repeat of the preceding plan, the structural economic reform objectives of which had been frustrated by China's response to the GFC. By the end of the 11th FYP, no progress toward "economic rebalancing" had been made, but other economic problems, including overleveraging and excess capacity in mining and heavy industries, had developed or intensified. (2) Shanghai and Chongqing were selected for property tax pilot programs. Since many local Governments experienced serious revenue shortfalls, while land values (on which much of their local fiscal revenues depended) were expected to fall in light of the Central Government's efforts to kill an emerging real estate bubble, the introduction of property taxes seemed the best solution. However, there was much opposition to this idea. Experiments in the two cities were very limited in scope and there was no follow-up at the national level for more than 5 years, when the property tax debate heated up again.
8–12 Oct. '12 18th Party Congress (Nov. '12–Fall '17)	Xi Jinping was elected General Secretary of the CPC, replacing Hu Jintao. Xi pledged to continue the economic reforms and started a major campaign against corruption. (The Congress adopted a new Party Constitution, which in its preamble says: "The realization of communism is the highest ideal and ultimate goal of the Party", echoing language in the preamble of the CPC's '56 Constitution: "The aim of the Party is the achievement of socialism and communism in China".)
'13 (1) Launch of the 12th FYP ('12–'16) (2) Publication of *China 2030*, a major economic report produced jointly by the World Bank and the DRC of the State Council	(1) The main objective of this FYP (which had been approved by the NPC on 11 March) was to "rebalance" the economy and to avoid the "middle income trap". The rebalancing objective had also been at the center of the preceding FYP ('07–'11), but that plan was interrupted by the GFC of '08/'09, which led China to put the 11th FYP aside in favor of a massive, multi-year stimulus program, starting Nov. '08. (2) This was the first major economic report produced *jointly* by the World Bank and the State Council's DRC. Its focused mainly on the need for economic restructuring to avoid the so- called "middle income trap". The report was reviewed and discussed at the highest levels in the government.

(*Continued*)

(Continued)

Date(s) or period	*Explanation*
April '13 Communiqué on the current state of the ideological sphere (Document No. 9)	This document (an earlier version of which had been issued in July '12, during the Hu Jintao/Wen Jiabao administration, was issued by the CPC's General Office *for internal circulation*. After it was leaked to and published by *Mingjing* (a US-based Chinese language magazine) in Sept. '13, it caused consternation in Western countries, as the document seemed to signal a significant departure from earlier Party-sanctioned "reform and opening-up" policies and justify (on ideological grounds) a crackdown on Chinese human rights lawyers, certain media outlets, liberal academics and other independent thinkers. The document warned against the following seven "mistaken" ideas: (1) Promoting Western constitutional democracy (including separation of powers, multi-party system, general elections, independent judiciary, nationalized armies and other characteristics). (2) Promoting "universal values" in an attempt to weaken the theoretical foundation of the CPC's leadership. (3) Promoting civil society in an attempt to dismantle the CPC's social foundation. (4) Promoting neo-liberalism, attempting to change China's basic economic system. (5) Promoting freedom of the press, challenging the principle that the media and the publishing system should be subject to CPC discipline. (6) Promoting historical nihilism, undermining the history of the CPC and the New China. (7) Questioning "reform and opening-up" and the socialist nature of socialism with Chinese characteristics. Since this was one of the first Party documents circulated after the election of Xi Jinping as CPC General Secretary, many "China-watchers" abroad worried that it effectively marked the end of Deng Xiaoping's "reform and opening-up" policies and a return to dogmatic Marxist policies. In fact, China continued many of the earlier economic reform policies, especially in the financial arena, and 6 months later, the "Decision" of the 3rd Plenum of the 18th CC in Nov. '13 pointed in a different policy direction than Doc. No. 9. Nonetheless, Doc. No. 9, even though it was apparently not released for circulation outside inner-Party circles, appeared to signal a change in Party priorities from market-oriented economic reform to the restauration of CPC power, prestige and ideological purity under a nationalistic banner. It also signaled a change in foreign policy with potentially serious consequences for China's relations with the rest of the world. (There are unconfirmed reports that Doc. No. 9 was withdrawn after it caused strongly negative international reactions.)

Date(s) or period	*Explanation*
July '13 End of government control of lending (interest) rates	In line with an earlier announced plan to gradually liberalize interest rates (and financial sector policies in general), PBoC removed all remaining restrictions (mainly a mandatory *minimum rate*, or *floor*) on lending rates charged by financial institutions. (The *ceiling* on deposit rates was removed in Oct. '15.)
9–12 Nov. '13 3rd Plenum of the 18th CC	This was another very important 3rd Plenum. Its "Decision" was to "deepen comprehensive economic reforms" through the implementation of some 60 sub-decisions. Some of the most important were: (1) To set up a *Central Leading Team for comprehensively deepening reform;* (2) To allow the market to play a "decisive" role in the allocation of resources; (3) To retain for the state a leading role in the economy; (4) To gradually reform and eventually abolish the *hukou* system; (5) To abolish the "reform-through-labor" system of re-education; (6) To relax the "one-child policy" (by allowing two children per family); (7) To intensify SOE reform. The potential conflict between objectives 2 and 3 is believed to underlie subsequent economic problems. Earlier economic policies that embedded potential conflict between economic and political objectives were the "Indigenous Innovation" policy of Jan. '06 and the SEI policy of Oct. '10. Rent-seeking behavior and corruption seem to have increased after this 3rd Plenum, perhaps because of the growing power of vested interests and the apparent slowdown in reform momentum. (Doc. No. 9 of April '13 was not mentioned in the "Decision" of the Plenum.)
Early '14 Publication of *Urban China. Toward Efficient, Inclusive, and Sustainable Urbanization*	This was the second major economic report produced jointly by the World Bank and the State Council's DRC. It focused on a wide range of institutional, financial, demographic, infrastructure and social issues related to urbanization. It contributed to the formulation of China's long-term urbanization strategy. Like the *China 2030* report of '13, it relied heavily on international experience.
Aug. '14 Budget Amendment Act	The main objective of this amendment was to make it possible for Provincial Governments to borrow in their own name by selling bonds. *Direct* borrowing by local Governments was prohibited under the original Budget Law of '94/'95. However, many local Governments had borrowed *indirectly* through front companies (often using local-Government-owned land as collateral) to finance local infrastructure and real estate projects. Under the new budget policy, local Governments could issue bonds and use the proceeds to pay off short-maturity/high-cost bank debt to lighten their debt service burden. The law was also aimed at promoting the development of domestic capital markets.

(*Continued*)

(Continued)

Date(s) or period	*Explanation*
March '15 Private entrepreneurship encouraged	In his (annual) *Work Report* for the NPC, PM Li Keqiang encouraged university graduates unable to find well-paying jobs, to start their own companies. He referred to "mass-entrepreneurship" as the best hope for China's economy in the long run.
May '15 Launch of "Made in China 2025" industrial policy	A State Council circular was issued, outlining a major long-term policy initiative aimed at upgrading Chinese industry and at capturing a larger share of the value added in international manufacturing chains. This new industrial policy built on the "Indigenous Innovation" policy of Jan. '06 and the SEI policy of Oct. '10. It is consistent with various government-sponsored efforts to absorb foreign technologies and attract foreign experts, including overseas Chinese, to Chinese universities and R&D centers (such as the "Thousand Talents" Program of '08, and the 863 and 973 programs of '86 and '97).) The new policy aims at protecting China's international competitiveness in light of rising domestic wages and other cost increases. It promotes "smart" and "green" manufacturing based on domestic innovation through increased government-sponsored and corporate R&D, improved Internet use, rising domestic content, better protection of intellectual property, targeted financial support and fiscal incentives. The circular identified 10 priority sectors: (1) next-generation IT; (2) high-end numerical control machinery and robotics; (3) aerospace and aviation equipment; (4) high-tech maritime equipment and vessels; (5) advanced rail equipment; (6) energy-saving and electric vehicles; (7) electrical equipment; (8) agricultural machinery and equipment; (9) new materials; (10) biopharmaceuticals and high-performance medical devices. (Fundamental, as yet unanswered, questions raised by this new industrial policy are how it relates to the "Decision" of the 3rd Plenum of Nov. '13 to allow market forces to play a "decisive role" in resource allocation and the future role of FDI in China's industrial development.)
July '15 Further opening of the capital account	Foreign central banks, international financial organizations and SWFs were given direct access to China's Interbank Bond Market, a significant step toward opening the capital account to global capital markets.
10 Aug. '15 Change in exchange rate policy	PBoC announced that the starting RMB/USD XR for next day trading would from then on be the previous day's closing rate (instead of any rate within that range, at its discretion). The immediate consequence of this market-oriented change in the mechanism for setting the XR was a 1.9% devaluation. (Financial markets misinterpreted this as the beginning of a major slide in the RMB's international value, which contributed to sharp declines of domestic share values and major capital outflows.)

Date(s) or period	*Explanation*
Sept. '15 Guiding opinions on the restructuring and reorganization of Central Government SOEs	The State Council announced a plan to accelerate SOE reform by: "cleaning-up and arranging for the exit" of some poorly performing SOEs; restructuring and consolidating some other SOEs through mergers; and promoting the development of other SOEs.
Oct. '15 End of Government control of deposit (interest) rates	Removal of the *ceiling* on deposit rates completed the government's plan to gradually remove interest rate restrictions. It was an extremely important financial reform. Lending rate restrictions had been gradually relaxed earlier and finally removed in '13.
30 Nov. '15 IMF Board decides to include RMB in its SRD basket	At its 5-yearly review of SDR valuation, the IMF's Executive Board voted to include the RMB in the basket and to adjust the currency weights in the basket (effective 1 Oct. '16). In the new basket of 5 currencies, the RMB was assigned a weight of 10.92%, compared to 40.73% for the USD, 30.93% for the euro, 8.33% for the Japanese yen and 8.09% for the British pound. Though practical consequences of this IMF decision were limited, it was politically very important for China. (One potentially important effect was/is that, from 1 Oct. '16, the RMB can be used in financial transactions between the IMF and its member countries.)
Dec. '15 Annual Central Work Committee (of the Party) meeting on the economy	Faced with slowing growth (partly due to slowing external demand), high and rapidly rising leverage in many parts of the economy (especially local Governments and SOEs), the meeting decided to tackle pressing excess capacity problems in basic industries through "supply side" reforms. This was understood to mean that SASAC would engineer more mergers between SOEs and require greater supply adjustments from enterprises with excess capacity, while the Central Government would avoid further "demand side" stimulus. To avoid severe regional economic imbalances, "supply side" SOE reform was formulated with that undesirable outcome in mind.
Feb. '16 Further opening of the capital account	Following the opening of China's Interbank Bond Market (CIBM) to foreign central banks, international financial organizations and SWFs on 15 Feb. '15, the CIBM was opened to international investors in general. This was a significant measure to further open China's capital account to global capital markets.
April '16 Publication (in English) of *Whither China? Restarting the Reform Agenda* by Wu Jinglian and Ma Guochuan	This important book, in the form of a dialogue between Wu Jinglian (one of China's most experienced and distinguished economist) and Ma Guochuan (Chief Commentator of Caijing Business Magazine), takes stock of China's reform efforts since the late 1970s and concludes that badly needed *structural* reforms, including the establishment of a genuine rule-of-law system, had been lagging since the early '00s, that state interventions in the economy had remained very strong and that there was an obvious trend toward "crony capitalism". The book warned of economic stagnation, unless vigorous market reforms

(*Continued*)

(Continued)

Date(s) or period	*Explanation*
	were resumed and serious *political reforms* were implemented. The authors do not specify, however, what they mean by "political reform". (The title of this book, *Whither China?* is the same as the first section of Mao's famous essay "On New Democracy" of '40. Concerns about the emergence of powerful interest groups seeking to influence the Government and crony capitalism, had also been expressed by Prof. Yao Yang of Peking University in an article in *Foreign Affairs* magazine in 2010.)
28 April '16 Foreign NGO Law	This controversial law (which became effective 1 Jan. '17) defines the legal framework for the operation of foreign NGOs in China and shifts responsibility for the registration and supervision of those NGOs from the Ministry of Civil Affairs to the Ministry of Public Security. Domestic NGOs remain the responsibility of the Ministry of Civil Affairs. The law is having a depressing effect on foreign NGO activities in China.
9 May '16 Interview in the *People's Daily* with a "person of authority"	This important interview with an unidentified "person of authority" (probably a senior official speaking on behalf of President Xi Jinping) cautioned against increasing leverage to solve structural economic problems. The interview stressed the risks of financial and currency instability associated with high leverage. Its prominent publication in the *People's Daily* suggested that there was disagreement within the leadership on how to deal with falling growth and poor SOE performance.
31 May '16 SOE Party Committees to take control over all major SOE management decisions	SASAC announced that all major SOE decisions related to national macro-economic policy and national security (incl. key personnel decisions), would from then on be subject to prior approval by the company's internal Party Committee. This announcement seemed to indicate a tightening of Party control over SOEs and a prioritization of Party mandates over business interests. There was no indication that China's Company Law would be amended in accordance with the new policy.
20 July '16 Wu Jinglian's speech on structural economic reform	The famous economist Wu Jinglian spoke at the Sina Chang'an Forum on the theme "what is structural reform and why is it so important?" To promote "reform and innovation", he said, we must first establish a consensus on reform objectives and priorities. He argued that supply-side structural economic reforms had to be combined with efforts to deepen market reforms, which could be done, e.g., through the introduction of a "negative list" to broaden foreign investor access to Chinese markets. Financial reforms should be deepened and the state should withdraw from direct SOE controls. Generally, Wu emphasized the need to promote genuinely competitive markets and cautioned against reliance on state-sponsored "industrial policy". That same month, the State Council announced a "guiding opinion" on structural economic reform that in some significant ways differed from Wu Jinglian's advice.

Date(s) or period	*Explanation*
July '16 Guiding opinion on the restructuring and reorganization of Central Government SOEs (2)	Following its "Guiding opinions…on central Government SOEs" of Sept. '15, the State Council announced that it would fortify a group of central SOEs through mergers. This was widely understood to mean that SOE reform would from then on rely in particular on mergers (as distinct from efforts to improve efficiency within SOEs), with the objective to create a group of world-scale SOEs in key industries such as ocean shipping, electronics, steel and non-ferrous metals, building materials, nuclear and other power equipment, rail equipment and food trading. Foreign acquisitions are part of this strategy. (This new policy announcement reinforced the impression created by the "Made in China 2025" policy of May '15 and the earlier SEI policy (Oct. '10) that the government is increasingly relying on "industrial policy" to achieve its industrial development objectives, despite the 3rd Plenum decision of 13 Nov. to rely on the market as the decisive factor in resource allocation.)
16 Aug. '16 Opening of direct link between Hong Kong and Shenzhen stock exchanges	As part of its policy to gradually open China's capital account, the State Council announced that later in '16, a direct link between the HK and Shenzhen stock exchanges would be opened. In '14, a direct connection between the HK and Shanghai stock exchanges had been established, with limits on the volume of daily transactions and aggregate amounts. As from 1 Jan. '17, when the direct link between the HK and Shenzhen stock exchanges (including ChiNext) became effective, aggregate limits on direct foreign purchases of Chinese A shares by foreigners (through HK) were lifted, though daily transaction limits will continue to be apply.
21 Aug. '16 Social organizations are required to include CPC representative(s) in their management	A joint CC/State Council regulation required all "social organizations" in China, including domestic and foreign NGOs, to include Party representatives in the management of their operations. This regulation, together with the Foreign NGO Law of 28 April '16 and the SASAC announcement on SOE management of 31 May '16, suggested that the Party is determined to exercise greater control over the economy and society. This new regulation seemed to run counter to Deng Xiaoping's efforts to increase the distance between the Party and Government on the one hand and between government administration and SOE management on the other.
Oct. '16 Property tax debate heats up again	The limited scope property tax experiments started in Shanghai and Chongqing in '11, finally succeeded in rekindling serious debate on the introduction of a national property tax. If implemented, this would be the most important fiscal reform in China since '94.
Nov. '16 Land policy reform aimed at encouraging large-scale "corporate farming"	Under this new policy, village committees were authorized to lease large blocks of agricultural land to private corporate investors for large-scale farming in exchange for an annual fee. This new policy followed an earlier ('08) land policy change under which individual peasants were permitted to lease their land (land-user rights) to other farmers with the objective to thus promote more efficient, larger-scale farming. Results of the earlier ('08) policy change had been disappointing in that regard.

(*Continued*)

(Continued)

Date(s) or period	*Explanation*
5 Dec. '16 Opening of direct share trading link between the Hong Kong and Shenzhen stock exchanges	An announcement that this would be done had already been made on 16 Aug.
Dec. '16 New capital account restrictions introduced	PBoC introduced new capital account restrictions, especially on lending and M&A abroad by Chinese companies. The new restrictions were prompted by unusually large outflows of Chinese capital in '16 and the fear that such flows might become even larger in '17. Though earlier measures to open the CIBM to foreign investors and create direct links between the HK and domestic stock exchanges were not affected, the new restrictions ran counter to the government's policy to gradually open the country's capital account and may slow, or possibly reverse, RMB internationalization.

Note

1 This chronological survey is necessarily highly selective. It was pieced together from a variety of sources, including English-language publications (both Chinese and non-Chinese in origin), personal communications with China experts around the world, and recollections from the time I served as Chief of the World Bank's Resident Mission in China ('93–'97). It inevitably reflects my judgment on what was important in the evolution of economic policy making. Although the focus of this chronology is economic policy making, actual economic developments are sometimes mentioned to clarify the context of policy making. Most published sources used are included in the Bibliography at the end of this book. One of the most important sources is the ten-volume series *Chinese Economists on Economic Reform* edited by the DRC Foundation in Beijing, comprising selected works by Xue Muqiao, Yu Guangyuan, Du Runsheng, Ma Hong, Wang Mengkui, Chen Xiwen, Guo Shuqing, Lou Jiwei, Zhou Xiaochuan and Li Jiange, published by Routledge, 2011–2016. This English-language series is based on a 15-volume Chinese-language series published by the DRC Foundation in 2008 to commemorate the 30th anniversary of the 3rd Plenum of the 11th CC of the CPC in Dec. '78, which is generally considered the start of China's market-oriented economic reforms. Among the many other published sources used, six were particularly important: Joseph Fewsmith (1994); Wu Jinglian (2005); Wu Jinglian and Ma Guochuan (2016); and Barry Naughton (1995, 2007, 2013). Many other source references are included in the Annotated chronology. Quotations in English from Chinese documents are based on official translations.

1 Puzzles and surprises

Many have written on the evolution of China's economic policies since the PRC was established in 1949. Most of my comments in this chapter will be "old hat" to those who are familiar with the story. At the risk of revealing my own ignorance, I summarize below what puzzled and surprised me most when I studied it. Some of the puzzles have a plausible answer; others remain puzzles, at least for me.

> *Puzzle 1*. Why did Mao unexpectedly "propose" on 24 September 1952 that the transition to socialism should start immediately and be accelerated?

In his 1940 essay "On New Democracy", Mao envisaged that the transition to socialism would take "quite a long time" and should not start immediately with the establishment of the "New Democratic Society" (i.e., the start of communist rule). He then also thought that, after the transition to socialism had started, capitalism and socialism would co-exist for a long time. This relaxed approach to socialist transition was confirmed by the Central Committee at its 2nd and 3rd Plenums (of the 7th Party's Congress) in March 1949 and June 1950. Then, unexpectedly, only 27 months later, during a meeting of the Central Committee on 24 September 1952, Mao "proposed" that starting the transition to socialism could not wait and had to be implemented more quickly than originally intended.[1] Why did he apparently change his mind, and what were the implications of this change in transition strategy? There is no clear answer, but it is obvious that the change had significant consequences; it led to the rapid collectivization of agriculture already during the 1st Five-Year Plan (1953–1958), conflicts between Mao and other senior Party leaders (e.g., Liu Shaoqi and Deng Zihui) and, ultimately, to the disastrous Great Leap Forward (1958–1960) and the Cultural Revolution (1966–1976). The most probable solution for this puzzle is that there were several causes, including:

(1) In the early 1950s, when the USSR and Stalin were Mao's role models, it is possible that Mao, impressed by Stalin's book *Economic Problems of Socialism in the USSR*,[2] felt compelled to avoid problems identified by Stalin.
(2) It is also possible that Mao wanted to impress Stalin, who had expressed concern that the new communist government in Beijing might slide off in the direction of Yugoslav-type socialism, placing too much emphasis on democracy and nationalism.

(3) Since the PRC's involvement in the Korean War had extended the Cold War to China, it is possible that Mao had given up hope for constructive relations with the US and decided to put all his "eggs" in the basket of rapid transition to socialism.

(4) Financial pressures: the 1st Five-Year Plan (1953–1958), then being prepared with Soviet technical assistance, gave priority to rapid industrialization (only part of which could be funded from Soviet loans), required additional domestic financial resources. It is possible that Mao and his economic advisors concluded that the best way to mobilize the extra financial resources, was to extract them from agriculture through collectivization. The fact that around that same time a decision was made to unify the government's system for procuring and selling grain, lends weight to this financial/fiscal explanation for Mao's "proposal".

Puzzle 2. Why didn't China move to a liberal market economy model immediately after the 3rd Plenum of December 1978, as Russia tried to do after the collapse of the USSR in the early 1990s?

The most plausible answer is that *radical* change of the economic system wasn't on anybody's mind in China in the late 1970s. Political leaders, including Deng Xiaoping, only supported *gradual* change that would not threaten political and social stability. There were no foreign advisors in China at that time who might have pushed for radical change (as was the case in Moscow when the USSR collapsed in 1990/91.) Leading Chinese politicians and economists in the late 1970s firmly believed in the innate superiority of socialism over capitalism – they were united in their fear that capitalism might return if they liberalized too quickly. The theories of Marx and Engels on the internal contradictions of capitalism and the inevitability of its collapse (and those of Lenin on the dynamic relationship between capitalism and imperialism) carried significant weight in China for a long time, even after Mao's death and the arrest of the "Gang of Four" (1976). In late 1978, there was no pressing political need in China for radical system change as there was in Moscow when the USSR fell apart; the CPC was firmly in charge. The highest priority was to *stabilize* the economy and society after the ravages of the Cultural Revolution. Initial economic system changes in China under Deng Xiaoping were in fact quite moderate. Nobody in the leadership argued for giving up central planning or public ownership of the means of production. However, it had become politically acceptable to sharply reduce the military budget, to introduce markets on the margin of the economic system and to tolerate social inequality based on differences in skill and effort.

Puzzle 3. Why was transition to "mature communism", as understood by Marx and Engels, apparently not considered feasible or desirable in China?

This is one of the greatest puzzles of all. The probable reason why full communism, as understood by Marx,[3] was apparently thought to be unattainable in

China, already in Mao's days (although nobody said so publicly), was the realization that it was not practical (or even desirable) to bring *all* means of production under public ownership and eliminate the need for exchange through markets. Unlike the means of *industrial* production (all of which had been nationalized at the time of the 8th Party Congress in September 1956), *agricultural* land was operated by collective farms (later Communes) for the benefit of their members. Collective farms were not owned by "the whole of the people" (a term used to indicate everybody, or the state representing everybody), as theoretically required under Marxist communism. As long as there were separate agricultural collectives or Communes, there was a need for market exchange, not only between towns and agricultural production centers, but also among towns and agricultural production centers. In other words, market exchange could not be avoided and some prices would inevitably be market-determined, which meant that "mature communism" as understood by Marx and Engels, couldn't be achieved. (Without explicitly saying so, Stalin had come to the same conclusion in his *Economic Problems of Socialism in the USSR*.)

Although the record is not clear on this, Mao is believed to have aimed at transitioning to some form of communism when he launched the Great Leap Forward in 1958. If transition to Marxist communism was in fact Mao's ultimate goal, we shall probably never know how he intended to move from an agricultural system based on separate production units (collective farms or Communes) to a system based on collective ownership of *all* agricultural land.[4] As is well-known, the Chinese economy virtually collapsed as a result of the Great Leap Forward; hence, Mao could not have moved to full Marxist communism, even if he had wanted to. Could it be that Mao and his followers never really aimed at establishing full communism, but used the term as a symbol of paradise? This puzzle will probably remain unresolved.

Puzzle 4. Why does the CPC Constitution (adopted by the 18th Party Congress in November 2012) in its preamble say: "The realization of communism is the highest ideal and ultimate goal of the Party"?[5]

The language echoes the preamble of the CPC's Constitution adopted by the 8th Party Congress in September 1956: "The aim of the Party is to achieve socialism and communism in China". If "mature communism", based on collective ownership of all means of production and the absence of markets, is practically unattainable, it is puzzling why the CPC officially aims at achieving an unrealistic goal. Could it be that the term "communism" is used by the CPC not as a practical goal, but as a symbol of an undefined, vague ideal? Communism as promoted by Marx and Engels in the 19th century was essentially a "Western" ideology.[6] It is not part of China's ancient cultural or political history.

Puzzle 5. What did Deng Xiaoping mean by his repeated calls in the 1980s for *political reform*, and why was his recommendation never fully implemented?

Deng called for *political reform* on at least a half-dozen occasions during the 1980s, starting on 18 August 1980, less than two years after the historic 3rd Plenum of December 1978. What he had in mind was the need to: (1) separate the roles of Party and Government in managing the economy and (2) separate government administration from SOE management. Deng's motivation for his *political reform* recommendation was to strengthen China's economy, not to limit the Party's power. He never fully achieved his *political reform* objectives.[7] In the late 1980s, PM Zhao Ziyang tried several times to change domestic governance systems in the direction recommended by Deng but never made much progress, because opposition among Party conservatives was too strong.

> *Puzzle 6*. If the land reforms of 1949–1952 gave property rights to the peasants who were assigned plots, were those rights legally formalized (e.g., through cadastral registration)? What happened to peasant rights when the gradual move toward collectivization in agriculture started in 1953?

It is often assumed that peasants who received agricultural land during the early land reforms became the legal owners of that land, but the facts are not clear. Some sources suggest that all agricultural land in China became state property soon after the PRC's establishment on 1 October 1949. There is no evidence that a new cadastral registration system was developed in the early 1950s or that compensation was paid to the original landowners. Peasants, who soon after the initial land reforms were encouraged to merge their farms into (voluntary) cooperatives, followed a little later by (involuntary) "higher cooperatives" (collectives), didn't receive compensation either.

> *Puzzle 7*. what motivated Mao to launch the Great Leap Forward (in 1958)?

The Great Leap Forward was launched by Mao the 2nd Session of the 8th Party Congress in May 1958. He used the term "General Line for Socialist Construction" to label his new initiative. Although Mao did not see it that way, it was a very risky initiative. The GLF triggered disastrous economic and social consequences, including one of the largest famines in history. The GLF also led to growing "distance" between Mao and other senior leaders, including deputy Party Chairman Liu Shaoqi, PM Zhou Enlai, Deng Xiaoping and Chen Yun. The split between Mao and senior colleagues was essentially over economic policy, but there were deeper political disagreements. One of Mao's known objectives in launching the GLF was for China to quickly become an economic superpower by outpacing Britain (e.g., in steel production) and the US, thus demonstrating that his approach to socialist transformation was superior to that of the USSR. There may have been other objectives, but those aren't as clear. There are indications in written communications from Mao to fellow Party leaders in late 1958, that he intended the GLF to be a "bridge" between socialism and communism. According to the first Session of the 8th Party Congress in September 1956, socialism had then been achieved. Since in Marxist theory, socialism is a transitional stage to communism, it is conceivable that Mao forced all agricultural collectives into (a much smaller number of) huge Communes (as part of the GLF), to facilitate and accelerate China's transition to communism (however defined). Some of Mao's written comments at the first Zhengzhou meeting of late 1958 suggest that this may indeed have been his motivation for launching the GLF.

Puzzle 8. Mao may not always have been as powerful as he is usually thought to have been.

There were several indications that Mao did not always get what he wanted or acted "defensively". Two illustrations are:

(1) With the support of Chen Yun, Mao wanted to "cool down" the GLF at the first Zhengzhou meeting (2–10 November 1958) and adopt more realistic output targets for key commodities such as steel and grain. However, for reasons that aren't obvious,[8] the original (unrealistic) output targets for the GLF were not revised.

(2) Following the second Zhengzhou meeting (late February/early March 1959) to discuss theoretical issues and review the GLF, at which agreement in principle was reached to reduce the size of agricultural Communes and to make the smaller "Production Brigade" the basic accounting unit, a meeting of economists was held in Shanghai in April to discuss theoretical issues and possible reasons for the poor economic results of the GLF. The meeting was attended by, inter alia, Xue Muqiao and Sun Yefang, both of whom were highly respected technocrats. With regard to the GLF, the main conclusion of the meeting was that the problems were due to *tensions in the relationship between plan and market in a socialist economy*. Since he had already agreed to reduce the size of Communes and to make (the smaller) Production Brigades the basic unit of account in agriculture (instead of the larger Communes), why did Mao squash further discussion of the Shanghai meeting's fundamental conclusion at the Lushan Party meeting a few months later? Was this a sign of weakness on Mao's part?

Puzzle 9. Did Xue Muqiao, one of China's most influential and revered economists, genuinely change his ideas on the best way to pursue economic development in China, or was he a political turncoat?

There is a puzzling contrast between Xue Muqiao's 1959 and 1979 books on socialist transformation. In 1959, during the Great Leap Forward, when many of the Leap's economic and social problems were already known to the urban elite, Xue published a book (co-authored by two other Chinese economists), which explained and praised Mao's economic policies, without a critical note. The book must have pleased Mao; it was translated and published the next year in many languages by China's Foreign Languages Press.[9] Twenty years later, in 1979, when Mao was dead and Deng Xiaoping had become "paramount" leader,

Xue published another book: *China's Socialist Economy*, which was very critical of Mao's "rushed" transition to socialism and the GLF. His 1979 book became required reading for Party cadres and was very influential. It advocated a model for socialist development that included systematic application of market principles and managerial independence for SOEs. Hence the puzzle: did Xue, like many others during the Mao era, bend with prevailing political winds, or did he genuinely believe what he wrote in 1959 and changed his mind later?

A further twist to this puzzle: in April 1959, Xue participated in a meeting of economists in Shanghai to discuss theoretical issues and possible reasons for the GLF's poor economic results. With regard to the GLF, the meeting concluded, as already mentioned under puzzle 8, that the fundamental reason for its economic failure was *tensions in the relationship between plan and market in a socialist economy.*[10] If Xue agreed with that conclusion, why didn't he raise the issue in his 1959 book: *The Socialist Transformation of the National Economy in China?* Was he under pressure from the Party or colleagues to write that book? The answer to the puzzle is almost certainly that Xue, like so many others, was constrained by the political realities of the time and never fully believed what he published in 1959. He was not a political "turncoat".

> *Puzzle 10.* Why was Hu Qiaomu, Mao's right hand man and a conservative, appointed as the CASS's first president when it was created in May 1977?

Hu Qiaomu had been Mao's personal assistant for many years and was known as a "conservative". However, in May 1977 (after Mao's death and the arrest of the "Gang of Four"), when the CASS was established as a government think-tank to help prepare reformist economic policies, Hu was appointed as its first president.[11] In July 1978 (as president of CASS), he submitted an influential report to the State Council, *Act in Accordance with Economic Laws; Step Up the Four Modernizations*, which became one of the pillars of the historic 3rd Plenum of December '78. Was Hu Qiaomu given the prestigious CASS position to placate him or had he become a supporter of drastic economic reform? A possible explanation lies in the fact that Hu Qiaomu was known not only as a political conservative but also as a powerful, independent intellectual. He was a plausible candidate for the CASS presidency, because his conservatism credentials were well established, while he was trusted thinker, who then recognized that certain market-oriented economic reforms were necessary. (In 1983, Ma Hong became Hu's successor as CASS president and when the post became vacant again in 1985, Hu became the CASS' "honorary president".)

> *Puzzle 11.* Deng Xiaoping's relationship with Mao Zedong. Why did Deng agree to manage Mao's vicious anti-rightists' campaign in the late 1950s?

Deng was an early ally and admirer of Mao and didn't begin to distance himself from some of his economic policies until the Great Leap Forward was launched in 1958. Both had participated in the Long March (1934–35) and they had fought together in the revolution. Moreover, as regional Party leader for southwestern China (until 1952), Deng had overseen PLA efforts to expel remaining Nationalist forces from that region, after the PRC was established in 1949. In light of Deng's known reservations about the GLF, it is puzzling that he continued to serve as Mao's principal agent in suppressing dissent in 1958 and 1959, during the anti-rightist campaign. Did even Deng fall victim to the "Mao cult" at that time?

Puzzle 12. Why did PM Zhao Ziyang need so many reform-oriented think-tanks?

After the China Academy of Social Sciences had been established in May 1977 – less than a year after Mao's death – PM Zhao created the System Reform Office (May 1980), which soon thereafter (1982) was enlarged to become the State Commission for Restructuring the Economic System (SCRES), reporting to him, as head of the State Council. In 1981, Zhao created the Development Research Centre (DRC), also reporting to the State Council. A few years later (in 1986) he set up a small brain-trust of prominent reform economists in his own front office (called "Program Office") to coordinate economic reform efforts. From these apparently overlapping institutional initiatives, it seems that PM Zhao felt a need for all the intellectual support on economic reform he could get. On behalf of "paramount" leader Deng Xiaoping, Zhao was in charge of leading China's unprecedented economic reforms and handling frequent challenges from more conservative Party leaders. But were all those government-sponsored think-tanks really needed?

Puzzle 13. The relationship between Chen Yun and Mao Zedong.

At the 8th Party Congress in September 1956, Chen made a very important speech, which was (implicitly) critical of Mao's policy to accelerate "socialist transformation". Chen also argued that the Party should leave room for a free-market component for small private enterprises in China's socialist, centrally planned economy. Although Chen's speech is believed to have been seen and approved by Mao beforehand, there was no follow-up to Chen's free-market recommendations. Mao was apparently tolerant of Chen's divergent views; while he punished others who had reservations, such as, e.g., Sun Yefang and Gu Zhun, he protected Chen Yun.

Surprise 1. The extent to which initial economic reforms in the late '70s were influenced by the need to create jobs for the millions of people (especially youth) returning to the cities from the countryside after the Cultural Revolution had ended.

To reduce the risk of social instability, there was a compelling need for job creation in urban areas after the Cultural Revolution. One of the first and most important reform measures in the late 1970s was to legitimize and facilitate street vending and other labor-intensive retail trading. Most of the millions of people returning to the cities after the Cultural Revolution, had been forced by the Party to undergo "re-education" through labor in rural areas. If it hadn't been for the special efforts to create job opportunities in urban areas for these people, Deng Xiaoping's economic reforms might not have been as successful as they were.

Surprise 2. The historic 3rd Plenum of December '78 did indeed accelerate the return to private farming (under the household responsibility system – HRS), but in the Plenum's Communiqué and other official statements, the Party continued to emphasize the need for collective farming.

The 3rd Plenum of December 1978 did not mark a clean break with collective farming in China, as many Western observers (mistakenly) believe. Although "sideline" production on small individual plots was allowed, it took the Party almost two years (until a Politburo meeting on 27 September 1980) to publicly acknowledge that private farming had in fact returned in much of China and to endorse the principle that farmers can "choose their own method of production". In some parts of rural China, under order from local political leaders, collective farming continued much longer. It wasn't until January 1982 that the Politburo formally approved the household (contract) responsibility system and formally authorized local governments to dissolve agricultural Communes if they wished. (Most Communes had already been dissolved by then.)

Surprise 3. It puzzled and surprised me to see that several of the most famous Chinese reform economists (such as, e.g., Xue Muqiao, Liu Guoguang and Yu Guangyuan, all devoted Marxists who were utterly convinced of the superiority of socialism over capitalism, nonetheless frequently referred to economic conditions in "advanced capitalist countries" to illustrate how backward China was and how much catching up it had to do. Social conditions in advanced capitalist countries were often pictured as horrible – confirming the theories of Marx and Engels – but economic achievements were generally admired.

Surprise 4. Similarly, it puzzled and surprised me to see the extent to which theories by Marx, Engels and Lenin about the future of capitalism were uncritically accepted as dogma, even in the late 1970s and early 1980s, after the Party had officially adopted Deng Xiaoping's "reform and opening-up" strategy.

Surprise 5. I was surprised to see the extent to which East European countries and economists influenced economic thinking in China after the Cultural Revolution had ended.

Although China's economic development in the 1990s followed a pattern similar to the model of East Asian "miracle economies", when market-oriented reforms started in the late 1970s, Chinese officials and economists were especially interested in studying the economic experience of fellow-socialist countries in eastern Europe. There were many missions to Hungary, Poland, Romania and Yugoslavia to study their experience with central planning and government-controlled pricing. Although the Chinese were disappointed to find that none of those east European economies were truly "socialist", they didn't drop eastern Europe as a model until Wlodzimierz Brus and Kazimierz Laski (two Polish economists living in exile in London) published a book in 1989 that clearly demonstrated the shortcomings of socialism and the socialist economic model. The Hungarian economist János Kornai (who taught at Harvard from 1986–2002) was probably the most influential foreign economist in China during the 1980s. His 1980 book *The Economics of Shortage* (a critique of socialist economic policies) was translated and became a best-seller in China. (In his interactions with Chinese counterparts, Kornai always emphasized the importance of "hard budget" constraints on SOEs.)

Surprise 6. The importance of Gu Mu's study mission to Western Europe in May/June 1978.

When – after Mao's death and the arrest of the "Gang of Four" in 1976 – many Party elders were ready to acknowledge that China had fallen far behind the rest of the world in economic development, many missions were sent abroad to study international economic and political conditions. The best known of those missions were Deng Xiaoping's visits to Japan, Singapore and other Asian miracle economies in 1978 and missions by Chinese economists to various east European socialist economies. The most influential study mission in the late 1970s, however, was the one led by Vice PM Gu Mu to France, Switzerland, West Germany, Denmark and Belgium in May/June 1978. Mission members were surprised to find that those countries had achieved a high level of technical, economic and social development and that they were not about to collapse, despite being capitalist. The mission had expected to find much unemployment, crime, deprivation and instability in accordance with prevailing Marxist theories about capitalism. The Gu Mu mission suggested that China had much to learn from western Europe and recommended that China's ban on borrowing capital from the West should be lifted. The State Council accepted most of Gu Mu's recommendations and in July 1978 permitted borrowing from the West for economic modernization. That decision, along with the establishment of Special Economic Zones, underpinned the "opening-up" part of Deng Xiaoping's "reform and opening-up" strategy adopted by the 3rd Plenum of December 1978. China's decision to seek membership in the Bretton Woods organizations institutions was another important part of the strategy.

Surprise 7. The Chinese communists, who were relatively inexperienced in economic matters when the CPC was gaining strength in the 1930s and '40s, were more effective in suppressing inflation in areas they controlled than Chiang Kaishek's more experienced Nationalist Government.

If Chiang Kaishek had been able to control hyperinflation during the civil war, it would have been much harder for the communists to prevail in that conflict. I was surprised to see how much importance the communists attached to financial stability and how effective they were in fighting inflation before the establishment of the PRC in 1949. Already in 1932, they introduced their own currency and their own central bank in the Jiangxi Soviet.[12] In December 1948, the People's Bank of China (PBoC), which later became China's central bank, was established in Shijiazhuan, Hebei based on a merger of three regional banks. PBoC then issued a new currency, the renminbi, to redress hyperinflation in northeastern China through currency substitution and other measures. When this turned out successfully, PBoC was moved to Beijing in 1949, when the city was under CPC/PLA control, and instructed to repeat the currency substitution nationwide after the PRC was established on 1 October. Whilst most historians typically focused on the political and military achievements of the CPC, I found that the financial history, including a surprising degree of fiscal conservatism and appreciation of the importance of financial stability, deserves more attention.

Surprise 8. The extent to which debate among Chinese reform economists (after the arrest of the "Gang of Four") was dominated by the question whether it was permitted under socialism to pay people "according to work performed".

While some prominent Chinese economists favored it, the "Gang of Four" was strictly opposed to the principle of *distribution according to work*. They strongly favored the communist principle of *distribution according to need*, because China was "on a path to communism". In 1977, after Mao's death and the arrest of the "Gang of Four", many conferences, attended by hundreds of economists and officials, were devoted to this question. Deng Xiaoping finally put an end to these debates by authorizing an article in the People's Daily of 5 May 1978, which reconciled "socialism" with the principle of *distribution according to work*. Until then, there was no issue that more animated debate among Chinese economists and government officials. Once the controversy had been laid to rest (thanks to Deng's intervention), the road was clear to officially tolerate a degree of social inequality and to introduce market principles and incentives aimed at raising the performance of workers and enterprises. Official acceptance of the principle *distribution according to work* was probably the most important ideological breakthrough in the late 1970s.

Surprise 9. The extent to which China relied on its own thinkers and think-tanks for analysis and advice to shape the direction and content of economic reforms from the late 1970s.

From my own work experience, I was aware of the important role the World Bank played in helping the government think through and shape its economic reform strategy (through studies, conferences and technical assistance embedded in projects). But, examining the record, I was surprised to find that the reform policy process, from the late 1970s, was in fact primarily driven by the analytical work and advice of China's own economists and officials. Perhaps the main reason underlying the World Bank's relative effectiveness in China was (and is) the government's determination and ability to guide the bank's activities and assess the quality of its advice. In the interaction between the bank and the government, the Chinese were always "in the driver's seat" and assumed full responsibility for their own decisions. When things went wrong, they didn't blame foreign advisors, but went back to the drawing board to make corrections. Since the start of China's market-oriented reforms in the late 1970s, numerous Chinese books, reports and articles about reform strategy have been written. Perhaps the single most influential article was "A Comprehensive Design for the Near- and Medium-Term of the Economic System" by Wu Jinglian and Zhou Xiaochuan, published (in Chinese) in Gaige magazine, June 1993; this article was reproduced in English in *Wu Jinglian. A Voice of Reform in China*, edited by Barry Naughton, the MIT Press, 2013.

Surprise 10. The importance of coining the term "socialist market economy" in 1992 to describe the kind of economic system China wanted to establish.

I was surprised to learn how important this had been in the evolution of China's reforms. In the West, we normally don't attach a lot of importance to names; we ask rhetorically: "what's in a name?" By contrast, in China the name of a person, thing or concept is typically very important; a name has real meaning. For example, one of the more important contributions Jiang Zemin made to China's reform efforts when he was the Party's General Secretary (1989–2002) was to give a name to the goal of those efforts. In his opening speech for the 14th Party Congress, on 12 October 1992, he said: "Now that we have gained a deeper understanding of market forces in practice, we should state explicitly that the objective of economic reform is to establish a SOCIALIST MARKET ECONOMY that will further liberate and expand productive forces". The speech was met with thunderous applause. Even Deng Xiaoping, who was 88 and had retired from official functions, applauded Jiang's speech in front of his TV set at home.[13] The new term, which had been proposed by Wu Jinglian a year earlier, replaced SOCIALIST PLANNED COMMODITY ECONOMY, a name that had been given to the goal of China's reform efforts by the 3rd Plenum of the 12th Central Committee of the CPC, in 1984. The new term, which has not been changed since, kept the designation "socialist" but dropped "planned", while replacing "commodity economy" (which had USSR connotations) with "market economy" (which sounded more modern). Sometimes, the Chinese add "with Chinese characteristics" to SOCIALIST MARKET ECONOMY to underline China's unique circumstances and methods.

Surprise 11. I was surprised to find that much of China's economic history during the Mao era remains cloudy more than 40 years after his death.

Surprise 12. I was surprised to find that leading Chinese reform economists consider Gu Zhun, a philosopher/economist and historian (who was trained as an accountant and who died in 1974), the "father" of China's market reforms. Gu, who is relatively unknown in the West, was probably the most outspoken Chinese critic of Mao's economic policies in the 1950s and an early advocate of market-oriented and political reform.

Notes

1 Some sources put Mao's decision to accelerate China's transition to socialism in 1955, when he presented his report "On the Cooperative Transformation of Agriculture" to the Party.

2 The book appeared in a Chinese translation in 1952. It included comments by Stalin on a draft textbook on Marxist political economy, which was discussed at a conference in Moscow in November 1951. (The book, with editorial notes, was also published in English (in the US) that same year.) Since the Moscow conference was closely followed in China, it is possible that an early Chinese translation was available to Mao before September 1952.

3 Although there are different definitions of "communism", for Marx it meant that all means of production, including land and capital, would be publicly owned, that each person would be paid according to his/her needs and that there would be no needs for markets. The CPC's Constitution does not define socialism or communism.

4 The only option would have been to bring all agricultural land under one massive, state-owned farming organization, which must have looked not only impractical, but also undesirable, even to Mao.

5 The same phrase appears in the first paragraph of the preamble ("General Program") of the amended CPC Constitution adopted by the 19th Party Congress, October 2017.

6 I was reminded of this by Martin Wolf in an interview with Wang Yang of the FT's Shanghai office on 8 June 2017. A video of this interview was published by the FT's China edition.

7 Deng, a powerful political leader, had to content with fellow Party leaders, some of whom were more conservative than he was.

8 Presumably, other senior Party leaders were more conservative and/or more dogmatic than Mao was.

9 Xue Muqiao, Su Hsing and Lin Tse-Li. *The Socialist Transformation of the National Economy in China*. Foreign Languages Press, Peking, 1960.

10 The 1959 Shanghai economics meeting seems to have been the first occasion during the GLF at which high-profile Chinese economists publicly expressed reservations about China's socialist economic model of that time.

11 When the CASS was established, the Institute of Economics of the already existing CAS was transferred to it. Since the Institute, under the leadership of Sun Yefang, had become a center of critical thinking on socialist economic policies, the CASS became a very important source of advice on how reorient China's development strategy.

12 When the communists were forced to leave the Jiangxi Soviet in 1934 and started what later became known as the "Long March", currency reserves and equipment of this central bank were taken along. For more details on this episode, see: James Stent (2017, pp. 66–67).

13 Hu Shuli, Huo Kan and Yang Zheyu. "Setting Economic Reform in Stone, China's Way." *Caixin Online*, January 2013, Part I.

2 Evolution of economic policy making

The Mao Zedong years

The factors driving economic policy making in China have changed dramatically since the CPC began to think about *national* economic management (well before the PRC was established in 1949). During the Mao years (from before 1949 to his death in 1976), Marxist theory was the main driving force, though the perceived need for financial stability and related fiscal conservatism, played a major role. The theories of Marx and Engels had enormous influence in China long after the start of market-oriented reforms. Ideological considerations based on those theories remained important in the 1980s, but pragmatism began to prevail as Deng Xiaoping prioritized economic development over political objectives.

It is probable that the CPC leadership began to think about national economic management when it established USSR-style "Soviets" in the early 1930s in areas liberated by the PLA in eastern China. Beyond a few general ideas, however, it is not clear what kind of economic model the leaders then had in mind. They shared an almost axiomatic belief in the correctness of Marxist and Leninist historical perspectives and a strong distrust of capitalism. Their economic policy making was aimed at ending "feudalism" in rural China and at establishing a national *socialist* economic system. Though mainly driven by ideological considerations, early communist leaders were keenly aware of the importance of financial stability, which required fiscal prudence and control over money supply, when possible. The communists' first central (and commercial) bank was established in late 1931 in the Jiangxi Soviet, before Mao Zedong was confirmed as top Party leader. The bank was managed by Mao's younger brother Mao Zemin and equipped with a mint (to make silver coins) and a printing press to produce paper money.

When the communists had to abandon the Jiangxi Soviet in October 1934, they took the central bank's money, equipment and key staff with them on, what would later be called the "Long March".[1] After the Zunyi meeting in January 1935 (at which time Mao Zedong was confirmed as Party leader), it was decided that carrying the bank any further was not practical. All communist paper money, minting and printing equipment was then destroyed. A new economic and financial system was set up in Ya'nan in northern Shaanxi after the Long March. Mao Zemin then served as the CPC's Economy Minister for northwestern China, though only part of the northwest was under communist control.[2]

The history of economic policy making by the CPC in Ya'nan is not as well known as that of northeastern China after the PLA had established effective control over that area. Chen Yun was the communists' principle economic officer in the northeast, before the PRC was established. An important development was the establishment of the People's Bank of China (PBoC) in Shijiazhuan (December 1948) through the merger of three regional banks. It issued a new currency, the renminbi to fight hyperinflation through currency substitution and other means.[3] For example, PBoC introduced a system of bank deposit accounts the value of which was linked to a basket of basic consumer goods (rice, cotton cloth, cooking oil and coal). PBoC was moved to Beijing in early 1949, when the city had been secured for the CPC by the PLA.

After establishment of the PRC (1 October 1949), PBoC introduced the renminbi nationally, also through currency substitution. The fact that the new PRC Government was able to tame high inflation relatively quickly (through currency substitution, fiscal prudence and other means) was one of the main factors explaining the rapid growth of popular support for the CPC in urban areas, where most people were initially skeptical of the communists.

Mao's essay "On New Democracy" (1940) explained his plan for a mixed capitalist/socialist economy and transition to socialism over a "quite a long" period after the anticipated defeat of the Japanese occupiers and political victory of the CPC over Chiang Kaishek's KMT. These ideas guided economic policy making for a while after 1949. But, for reasons that aren't entirely clear, less than three years later, Mao indicated[4] that he found it necessary to start the transition to socialism immediately and to make the transition at an accelerated pace. As explained below, the collectivization of agriculture started during the 1st Five-Year Plan (1953–1958). Remaining private industrial and commercial firms were required to form joint venture partnerships with state-owned firms (many of which were inherited from the Chiang Kaishek Government), to be nationalized later. The new government's policy regarding private financial institutions was different. Already in 1951, PBoC absorbed remaining commercial banks with positive net-worth, while those with negative net-worth were simply closed. The Shanghai stock exchange was closed and other financial institutions were closed or nationalized. From 1952 until 1979, PBoC was the only financial institution in China (except that PBoC was a department of the Ministry of Finance from 1969 until January 1978).

During the first few years of the PRC, management of the economy and formulation of economic policies was the responsibility of the Central Economic and Finance Commission headed by Chen Yun. A State Economic Commission, Planning Commission, Statistical Bureau and Price Commission were added in 1952, and a ministerial State Council (Cabinet) was created in late 1953. From then on, the State Council and its agencies became the main institutions responsible for economic management and policy formulation. But, important policy initiatives had to be approved by the Party, as remains the case today.

In agriculture, the mainstay of China's economy for decades after the PRC was established, the initial policy attention of the new government was focused on land reform – the distribution of arable land owned by landlords to poor and landless peasants. When the initial land reform was completed (1952), in an effort to increase agricultural productivity, Mao encouraged peasants to form voluntary "mutual-aid" teams (cooperatives). This policy soon morphed into the forced establishment of larger, "higher cooperative" (collective) farms. No compensation was paid to landlords who lost their land as part of the initial land reforms – many were tortured or killed. Peasants who were forced to merge their farms into collectives, didn't receive compensation either. Apparently, the state became owner of all land in China as part of the early economic reforms under Mao Zedong. The reorganization of agriculture included the establishment of large state farms in northeastern and western China. In 1958, as part of the Great Leap Forward, collective farms were merged into a much smaller number of huge agricultural Communes.

Mao's plan for agricultural development was presented to the Party in his report *On the Cooperative Transformation of Agriculture* of July 1955. The Party's top agricultural officer Deng Zihui and his deputy Du Runsheng (who later became one of most important economic reform economists under Deng Xiaoping) objected to Mao's collectivization policies, but were overruled. They and other Party leaders were distraught by the fact that Mao ignored the first national Constitution (1954), which guaranteed "*the right of peasants to own land and other means of production*".

Like Mao's agricultural collectivization policies of the early and mid-1950s, the dismissal of Gu Zhun as director of Shanghai's Financial and Taxation Bureaus in 1952, was another indication that Mao wanted to accelerate China's socialist transformation. Since Shanghai was the Central Government's most important source of fiscal revenues, Gu Zhun occupied positions of great importance for the whole nation; the trouble was that Gu believed strongly in the co-existence of socialism and capitalism, something Mao had apparently already given up on in 1952. Gu Zhun later joined the Institute of Economics of the China Academy of Sciences (CAS) headed by Sun Yefang, where he met several other economists who later became active reformers under Deng Xiaoping, including Xue Muqiao, Liu Guoguang, Du Runsheng, Wu Jinglian and Dong Fureng. During the "let a hundred flowers bloom and a hundred schools of thought contend" campaign of 1957, Sun Yefang and Gu Zhun were the only Chinese economists who publicly expressed reservations about Mao's socialist economic policies. Like Deng Zihui, they both suffered for their ideas during the anti-rightists' campaign that followed the "let a hundred flowers bloom . . ." campaign and again during the Cultural Revolution.

The first known meeting of Chinese economists where the poor economic results of the Great Leap Forward were discussed[5] took place in Shanghai in April 1959 – after the Second Zhengzhou meeting[6]. The Shanghai meeting concluded that the GLF problems were due to *tensions in the relationship between plan and market in a socialist economy*. By the standards of those days, this was a remarkably critical, honest conclusion. In normal times, it might have led to drastic policy change, but in fact, there was no follow-up, except that GLF was effectively terminated more than a year later. The economists meeting in Shanghai, April 1959, was attended, inter alia, by two of China's most famous economists at that time: Sun Yefang and Xue Muqiao. That Sun Yefang had reservations about the GLF, and Mao's economic policies in general, was well known, but that Xue Muqiao apparently agreed with the conference's main conclusion, was a surprise to me. That same year (1959), on the occasion of the 10th anniversary of the PRC, Xue published a book (with two co-authors), which explained and praised Mao's socialist transformation policies without reservations.[7]

Professional economists did not play an important role in economic policy making in China until after Mao's death (9 September 1976) and the arrest of the "Gang of Four" four weeks later. In the early 1960s, key politicians such as Liu Shaoqi, Chen Yun, Zhou Enlai and Deng Xiaoping supported a relaxation of agricultural collectivization and a return to private farming (under the so-called "household (contract) responsibility system", HRS)[8] in some areas – professional economists had no say in these matters at that time. However, during the Cultural Revolution that followed, the market-oriented economic rehabilitation policies of the early 1960s were rolled back, and mandatory *collective* farming (on communal farms that were much smaller than during the GLF) was fully restored.

Looking back at the Mao Zedong years with the benefit of hindsight, it is hard to imagine that management of China's economy could have been worse. We should remember, however, that Mao also did wonderful things for China; apart from reuniting the country, he restored a sense of national pride, greatly improved women's rights, basic health care and primary education, ended opium abuse, simplified Chinese characters, developed pinyin and promoted its use for teaching purposes.

The Deng Xiaoping years

The arrest of the "Gang of Four" on 6 October 1976 – with the permission of Mao's successor Hua Guofeng, only four weeks after Mao's death – marked the effective end of the Cultural Revolution (CR) and the beginning of what is today known as China's "reform era". The nation breathed a sigh of relief when the nightmare of the CR was finally over. People everywhere began to express themselves more freely and economists began to debate openly how to restore and develop the economy. It was a cacophony of different opinions, some of which were still heavily influenced by Marxist theory. If it hadn't been for Deng Xiaoping, a chaotic situation might have developed. Fortunately, Mao's chosen successor Hua Guofeng, who lacked a vision for economic development different from Mao's,[9] was persuaded by Chen Yun and others to rehabilitate Deng Xiaoping[10] to help guide economic reform. After Deng was rehabilitated by the Party in July 1977, the cacophony began to calm down and a new vision for economic development began to emerge, culminating in the Central Party Work Conference of November/December 1978 followed by the historic 3rd Plenum of the 11th Central Committee of the CPC, 18–22 December 1978.

Hua Guofeng's permission for the arrest of the "Gang of Four" in October 1976 and the rehabilitation of Deng Xiaoping the following year represent his greatest contributions to China's economic development. However, as Deng (and Chen Yun) recognized the folly of Hua's 10-Year Development Plan and his lack of meaningful leadership after Mao's death, his influence in the Party soon began to shrink. At the instigation of Deng Xiaoping, he was replaced as Party chairman by Hu Yaobang in June 1981.

Meanwhile, Deng was the effective "paramount" Party leader and arbiter of (sometimes bitter) ideological disputes among economists and officials over the practical meaning for China of Marx's "law of value",[11] the question whether workers in a socialist system should be paid according to their contribution or according to their needs[12] and the appropriate "balance" between "planning" and reliance on market forces. There was also much discussion on the meaning of "ownership" and the need for ownership reform. Deng encouraged economists and officials to learn from the experience other countries, which led to numerous study missions abroad, especially to socialist countries in Eastern Europe and invitations to foreign experts to share their knowledge in China. Deng visited Japan, Singapore and several other Asian countries, and persuaded the international community to accept the PRC instead of the ROC (Taiwan), as China's representative in the Bretton Woods institutions (IMF and World Bank). Membership in these institutions gave China access to relatively inexpensive capital and a large pool of knowledge on development around the world, which China used very effectively.[13]

Deng Xiaoping's genius was that he combined a clear vision of economic modernization with great persuasive powers and practical policy insights. After his political rehabilitation in 1977, his greatest contribution to China's modernization and development was his insistence on independent, non-ideological thinking by fellow Party members, while emphasizing that economic policy making had to be based on empirical information. He relegated "class struggle" to the past and put economic development ahead of other Party objectives. It was more than a breath of fresh air; it marked the end of China's international isolation and the beginning of economic "reform and opening-up", a set of goals and policies that has guided economic policy making long after Deng's death in 1997. He was totally opposed to "personality cult" and voluntarily stepped down from most official positions in 1987.[14] This made "collective leadership", a critical change in governance, possible. When the Tiananmen disaster of 1989 led to temporary paralysis in the Party on the direction of reform policy, he stepped in and, once again, when he was already in his late 80s, provided decisive leadership with his so called "Southern Tour" of early 1992, committing the Party to an ambitious reform agenda.

It is impossible to disentangle economics and politics in China. This is especially true for the period of early reforms under Deng Xiaoping in the late 1970s and early 1980s. For example, a small but important decision by Deng in early 1978 was to lift PBoC out of the Ministry of Finance, thus restoring it as a separate agency. After the 3rd Plenum of December 1978, with the encouragement of Chen Yun, Du Runsheng and others, Deng quietly promoted the break-up of agricultural

Communes and a return to private farming under the HRS. He did so despite official policy, which then still mandated collective farming. Deng persuaded fellow leaders to accept a new way of thinking about development and relations with the outside world. By not denouncing Mao Zedong, he avoided a potentially destabilizing break with the past. He and US President Jimmy Carter masterminded the normalization of bilateral US-China relations on 1 January 1979, a development of great economic and political significance for both countries and for the whole world. Further illustrations of the Party's decision to open the economy were the adoption in 1979 of a Joint Venture Law (the first major piece of legislation approved by the National People's Congress, China's legislature, after the 3rd Plenum of December 1978) and the establishment of Special Economic Zones (starting in 1980). Both measures were aimed at attracting foreign investment and learning from abroad.

Deng was not a micro-manager; he liked to delegate. For example, he relied heavily on PM Zhao Ziyang to manage the economy and formulate economic reform policies. (After the forced resignation of Hu Yaobang in January 1987, Zhao became the Party's new General Secretary, initially on an "acting" basis.) In the political and institutional environment created by Deng, professional economists thrived; they were taken seriously for the first time since the PRC was established. After Mao's "ideological prison" had been closed, independent, critical thinking was encouraged, which is one of Deng's greatest contributions to China's reforms. Otherwise, Deng was a Leninist, in the sense that he strongly believed in the supremacy of the Party and its control over the economy and the military.

One of the main centers for new economic thinking (created in May 1977, after the CR had ended) was the CASS. It inherited the Institute of Economics of the China Academy of Sciences, CAS (which continued as an agency focused on "hard" sciences after the CASS had been created). The Institute had been a center of (suppressed) opposition to Mao's socialist economic policies in the 1950s under its leader Sun Yefang. At various points in time, the Institute employed Liu Guoguang, Xue Muqiao, Du Runsheng, Gu Zhun, Wu Jinglian and Dong Fureng, economists who all became very influential thinkers about economic management during the reform era. Their thinking was initially influenced by the need to create employment opportunities for the millions of (mostly young) people, who, after the CR had ended came to the cities from rural areas, where they had been sent for "re-education". This led to a revival of street vending and retail trade in general.

The objectives of Deng-led "reform and opening-up" policies were to promote productivity growth in agriculture and attract foreign investment in manufacturing (e.g., through the establishment of Special Economic Zones). However, there was no comprehensive reform plan or model. The economist Du Runsheng, who, as deputy of Deng Zihui in the early 1950s, had been opposed to Mao's aggressive agricultural collectivization policies, played a key role in providing an economic rationale for the break-up of Communes and a return to private farming. But, as became clear during the 3rd Plenum of December 1978 and the Central Party Work Conference that preceded it, not all political leaders were ready for such radical policy change. According to the official Communiqué of the Plenum, the Central

Committee insisted on the continuation of collective farming, though "sideline" production on small private plots (on collectively owned land) was permitted. Meanwhile, more progressive Party leaders, such as Deng Xiaoping and Chen Yun, had become convinced of the need to restore economic incentives for individual farmers and hence to break up the Communes.

What happened in practice illustrates the political confusion and disagreement among Party leaders that characterized the early reform years. Despite the 3rd Plenum's official Communiqué, private farming (under the HRS) did in fact return quite quickly in some parts of rural China,[15] though not in areas controlled by conservative political leaders, who favored collective farming for ideological reasons.

Incremental, ad hoc and partial economic reforms, mainly in rural China, continued for several years until the 3rd Plenum of the 12th Central Committee of the CPC (October 1984) provided an overall framework of agreed objectives and methods. That Plenum's "Decision on Restructuring the Economic System" made the reform agenda more comprehensive in nature and gave a name to the kind of economic model China was trying to establish: Socialist Planned Commodity Economy. The name implied that building a socialist economic system would continue to be the overall goal, to be pursued through a combination of planning and reliance on market forces.[16] It is no surprise, therefore, that much of the writing by professional economists around that time focused on issues that were then still controversial, such as the practical meaning of Marx's "law of value" and the appropriate balance between plan and market. Politicians struggled with the same issues. Some (such as, e.g. Chen Yun) favored greater reliance on planning, while others (e.g. PM Zhao Ziyang) preferred greater reliance on market forces. The economist Xue Muqiao published a textbook in 1979 on how to build a "socialist economy" in which acceptance of the reality of market forces under socialism, was a central theme.[17] Gradually, over the next decades, the relative importance of planning declined and its nature changed, from the allocation of resources to setting objectives and priorities ("perspective planning").

As the 1980s progressed, debates among reformers began to center on narrower issues, such as, e.g., how much managerial independence to give to SOEs and local governments, how SOEs should be taxed, whether SOEs should be permitted to go bankrupt, which prices should be determined by the market and which should be set by government planners, should "dual-track" pricing[18] be permitted etc.

Zhao Ziyang, as PM and later General Secretary of the Party (from 1987, until he was purged and placed under house arrest at the time of the Tiananmen disaster of June 1989), did much to promote the professionalization of national economic management and the formulation of a *comprehensive* economic reform strategy. He welcomed the opinions and advice of foreign experts. He created the System Reform Office[19] in 1980 (which in 1982 became the State Commission for Restructuring the Economic System [SCRES]) and the Development Research Centre (DRC) in 1981. Both think-tanks reported to the State Council and played central roles in formulating reform strategies and policies. SCRES was merged with the State Development and Planning Commission (SDPC) to form the powerful National Development and Reform Commission (NDRC) in 2003. The DRC still exists today and continues to play a key role in crafting reform policies, sometimes in collaboration with the World Bank.

Chen Yun, the first manager of China's economy after the PRC was established (as head of the initial Central Economic and Finance Commission) and main architect of China's economic recovery in the early 1960s (after Mao's disastrous GLF), was one of Deng's most important partners in the late 1970s and early 1980s. It wasn't until the mid-1980s that Chen Yun began to worry that Deng's reforms were too liberal and developed his famous "bird cage" theory.[20] Chen Yun, one of China's great leaders of the 20th century, who had been on Mao's political "right" for most of the 1950s and 1960s, moved to Deng's "left" in 1984.

In the mid-1980s, a group of economists working for PM Zhao Ziyang, under the leadership of Wu Jinglian, began to argue for a more *comprehensive* approach to economic reform. They felt that the initial ad hoc, incremental and partial reforms should be replaced by an overall, integral reform plan, covering all aspects of the economy, including accelerated price liberalization and abolition of the "dual-track" pricing system (which they saw as a source of economic distortions and corruption). They also argued for comprehensive fiscal and financial system reforms, labor market and SOE reforms as well as building a modern social security system and liberalizing foreign trade and investments. They strongly promoted the idea that China should join the GATT[21] (of which China became an "observer" in 1982), accelerate the "opening-up" process and promote private sector development. To promote SOE reform, they argued that China should introduce a bankruptcy law (which happened in 1986) and gradually break-up the "iron rice bowl" employment/social security system by permitting the hiring of "contract workers". Social security reform initially focused on the "pooling" of SOE pensions in urban areas.

The 13th Party Congress (October 1987) marked a significant breakthrough toward greater reliance on market forces, a *comprehensive* approach to formulating reform strategy and the promotion of private sector development. Deng, who was content with the results of the 13th Party Congress, then decided to retire from official positions (except the Central Military Commission) and encouraged other older leaders to do the same to make room for "new blood".

Many of China's efforts to integrate and accelerate economic reforms were shelved after the Tiananmen disaster of 1989, when disagreements within the Party on the direction of reform intensified. However, economic reform did not come to a standstill, as is often argued – witness, e.g., the decision to open stock exchanges in Shanghai and Shenzhen (1990/91) and to develop Pudong (1991). Nonetheless, there was considerable confusion and a significant slowdown in the pace of reforms. It wasn't until Deng Xiaoping (who had retired from most official functions in 1987 but was still revered as "paramount leader"), traveled to southern China in early 1992 to urge the resumption and intensification of economic reforms, that the Party reunited behind his "reform and opening-up" policies and reform momentum returned. (It was the second time that Deng provided critical leadership to the Party and the nation[22] – the first time was in the late 1970s.) In June 1993, Wu Jinglian and Zhou Xiaochuan published a joint article: "A Comprehensive

Design for the Near- and Medium-Term Reform of the Economic System", which became a blueprint for many of the most important economic policy reforms and related institutional changes during the 1990s.

The Zhu Rongji years

At the end of 1991, Zhu moved to Beijing as deputy PM under Li Peng with special responsibilities for the economy. Jiang Zemin was then the Party's General Secretary. Before his promotion to the Central Government in Beijing, Zhu was mayor and Party chief of Shanghai, where he had earned a reputation as an effective leader and problem solver, precisely what was needed in Beijing in the wake of the Tiananmen disaster. He soon became known as China's "economic czar".

At the end of 1992, under the leadership of Jiang Zemin, the 14th Party Congress confirmed the Party's commitment to economic reform and labeled the reform objective as establishing a SOCIALIST MARKET ECONOMY. This name change was significant. The previous label for China's reform objective had been SOCIALIST PLANNED COMMODITY ECONOMY.[23] In the new label, the reference to planning was dropped and "commodity" economy became "market" economy.[24]

As result of the significant public and private investment wave that followed Deng's Southern Tour in early 1992, inflation soon became a serious problem. It was a major challenge for the Party and Zhu Rongji as its economic manager. The inflation problem was the subject of a several international conferences in 1992 and 1993 involving the IMF, World Bank, several of China's major think-tanks and individual experts. Zhu Rongji paid personal attention to the final and most important of those conferences, which was held in Dalian.[25] Zhu accepted the conference's conclusion that the inflation was primarily due to excessive credit-financed investment. He persuaded fellow leaders that China urgently needed a package of macro-economic policy (and associated institutional) reforms to stabilize the economy. The announcement and implementation of this package (starting July 1993, one month after the publication of the joint article by Wu Jinglian and Zhou Xiaochuan mentioned above) marked the start of modern macro-economic management in post-Mao China, starting with a controversial recentralization of financial controls.

Later in 1993, at the 3rd Plenum of the 14th Central Committee of the CPC in November, the Party consolidated the July reforms and took them to a higher level. The Plenum "decision" included a *comprehensive* plan for modernizing China's enterprise system, involving legal, fiscal, financial and many other systematic reforms. The Plenum marked the start of a decade of very intensive reforms under the leadership of Zhu Rongji (with the support of Jiang Zemin). On 1 January 1994, the fiscal system was drastically reformed and the multiple exchange rate system, which had been in use since the 1980s, was unified (as recommended by Wu Jinglian and Zhou Xiaochuan in their joint article of June 1993). Soon thereafter, Zhu, who often relied for technical advice on a group of young Chinese economists,[26] started serious banking and SOE reforms, including the adoption of a Commercial Banking Law and a Central Banking Law. Early bank reforms under Zhu's leadership also involved the forced closure of many International Trust and Investment Companies (ITICs), usually subsidiaries of state-owned commercial banks that had developed as "shadow banks" in the early 1990s, in response to tighter credit controls.

Financial and SOE reforms were intensified significantly in response to the Asian financial crisis of 1997/98, and Zhu allowed one of the largest state-owned financial institutions, the Guangdong International Trust and Investment Corporation (GITIC) to go bankrupt in 1998 when it defaulted on external debt obligations. Under Zhu's leadership, China made special efforts to expedite WTO entry negotiations.

One of the most consequential reform decisions taken by Zhu Rongji in 1998, after he had succeeded Li Peng as PM, was to transfer ownership of residential housing units in urban areas (then still almost entirely publicly owned), from SOEs and other public agencies, to occupants. Since there was no mortgage industry in China at that time, while cash wages were very low and few families had financial assets, transfer prices had to be kept artificially low. The resulting housing ownership transfer, implemented by local governments, was probably the largest privatization in history and the largest wealth transfer from the public sector to private citizens (because of artificially low transfer prices). The policy was aimed at:

(1) removing the large financial burden on SOEs of providing and maintaining employee housing (with the objective to make them more internationally competitive in preparation for WTO membership);
(2) creating a large source of domestic demand for home improvement (to compensate for the expected decline in external demand);[27]
(3) promoting the emergence of a large private construction industry;
(4) increasing labor mobility (to improve overall economic efficiency.)

Implementation of this massive housing privatization project was essentially completed by 2003. It was as, if not more, important for China's economic development as the re-introduction of private farming (under the HRS) in the late 1970s and early 1980s.

Meanwhile, Zhu Rongji also intensified SOE reform (through privatization, mergers, closures and many other measures) especially after he became PM in 1998. Management buy-outs were discontinued, after it became clear that such transactions often led to "asset stripping" – leaving the previous public owner with poor quality assets and debt, while the new private owners kept the best assets for themselves.

Between 1998 and 2003, economic reforms in China were at a peak. The world has probably never seen more intensive national structural economic reforms in such a short time frame. All developments at that time, including China's eventual entry into the WTO in December 2001, suggested that the country was in the process of becoming a "market economy", as Western partners were hoping and expecting. China's economic reforms were going forward full speed under Zhu's leadership. For example, due to intensive SOE reforms between 1998–2003, total employment in state-owned units in urban areas fell by more than 20 million,[28] but unemployment didn't rise, because rapidly growing private-sector expansion compensated for the loss of public sector jobs.

In April 1999, PM Zhu visited the White House in Washington, DC with the intention to complete WTO entry negotiations, which had been dragging on for many years. But he was rebuffed by President Bill Clinton, who didn't think the time was right for such a deal. A month later, during the "Kosovo War" a US (NATO) war plane accidentally bombed the Chinese Embassy in Beograd, killing three people. This "accident",[29] together with Zhu Rongji's ill-fated visit to the White House in April, was feared (in the West) to have killed China's interest in joining the WTO. But China's determination to join was very strong, and negotiations were resumed later that year.

Zhu also intensified banking reforms after he became PM. He accelerated the process of fully accounting for non-performing loans (NPLs) on the balance sheets of state banks and bank recapitalization. Prior to the listing of state banks on domestic and Hong Kong stock exchanges, large foreign banks were invited to buy a strategic minority share in those banks. The entire process took about a decade and was completed under Zhu's successor as PM, Wen Jiabao. It was the largest banking reform in history and one of the most successful. Before the end of the first decade of the 21st century, China's state commercial banks were all recapitalized and listed, a process that had been started by Zhu.

The Hu Jintao–Wen Jiabao years

Economic reforms under the government of President Hu Jintao and PM Wen Jiabao (2003–2013) initially followed the same pattern as under the predecessor government of Jiang Zemin and Zhu Rongji, but soon began to embrace different priorities. In the first half of their 10-year period, the Hu/Wen government focused in particular on improving living conditions and promoting development in rural areas, through infrastructure investments (especially in western China), the introduction of free primary education (which was later extended to urban areas), basic health insurance, a minimum income program for rural areas and the removal of agricultural taxes. Instead of continuing intensive (and often painful) SOE reforms, the new government focused on the promotion of "indigenous innovation" and the formulation of "industrial policy".[30]

During the second half of the Hu/Wen government, the top economic priority became changing China's growth model by reducing dependence on public investment and external demand, promoting domestic consumer demand, and service sector development. Unfortunately, soon after "economic rebalancing" had become the central focus of economic reform policies, China was hit by the global financial crisis of 2008/9. The resulting fall in export orders led to numerous lay-offs (mainly of migrant labor in manufacturing and construction in urban areas). The government responded to the crisis with a massive stimulus program, most of which was to be financed through credit expansion. The program was effective in quickly restoring growth momentum and full employment, but "economic rebalancing" was put on the back-burner. It generated major structural economic problems (including real estate over-building and land speculation, over-leveraging by local governments and corporations, large-scale (risky) shadow banking and significant excess capacity in many industries). These structural economic problems were still plaguing China at the end of the first 5 years of the follow-up government of President Xi Jinping and PM Li Keqiang.

Although impossible to prove, it seems likely that the relatively slow pace of fundamental economic reforms during the Hu/Wen government contributed to a worsening of corruption and to a misallocation of capital.

The Xi Jinping–Li Keqiang years

At the 3rd Plenum of the 18th Central Committee of the CPC in November 2013, Xi Jinping and Li Keqiang confirmed the Party's commitment to the economic reforms started under Deng Xiaoping in the late 1970s and the "economic rebalancing" objectives of the preceding Hu/Wen government. The Communiqué of the Plenum stated, inter alia, that:

(1) reforms would be "comprehensively deepened";
(2) the market would have a "decisive" role in allocating resources; and
(3) the "dominant role of the public ownership system" and the "leading role of the state-owned economy" would persist.

Although the question of how possible conflict between the second and third objectives mentioned above would be resolved was not addressed, the Plenum indicated that the reform process set in motion by Deng Xiaoping in the late 1970s, including SOE reform, would continue. However, the governance style and actual economic policy making by the Xi/Li government so far suggests that the third objective (continued state control over the economy) was assigned priority over the second (reliance on the market as the "decisive" factor in resource allocation). On the political side, apart from corruption fighting, President Xi seems to give priority to the restoration of Party power and national prestige over economic reform. On the economic side, he seems to rely more on state-directed "industrial policy"[31] than on the liberalization of market forces.

Meanwhile, the private sector of China's economy continues to expand, both absolutely and relatively, but direct and indirect Party influence on private-sector behavior is increasing. Altogether, it is not entirely clear where the new government is leading the economy. It is possible that "public opinion" in China may yet push economic policy in a more liberal direction, but the opposite may also happen. Although state control over the economy is expanding, "economic rebalancing", as defined by the 11th, 12th and 13th Five-Year Plans, is slowly progressing.

There seems to be controversy in China over the future of the financial system. Financial sector managers appear to be aiming at further domestic financial liberalization and international integration, but there is concern that those objectives may conflict with other Party priorities. Two indications of possible conflict are: (1) ill-considered, state-led interventions in the stock markets in mid-2016 and (2) the imposition of additional capital controls in late 2016 and early 2017 to reduce capital outflows. Unless the trend toward financial sector liberalization and international integration of China's financial markets is resumed decisively, the reform of China's financial system may stall or regress.

The emphasis on state-directed "industrial policy" in domestic economic policy making by the Xi/Li Government is mirrored externally in the huge "Belt and Road Initiative", or BRI.[32] President Xi first presented his vision for promoting economic development in participating countries in Eurasia, Africa and the Middle East (including China itself) through China-led infrastructure development, in a speech at Nazarbayev University in Astana, Kazakhstan, October 2013. A month later, just before the 3rd Plenum of the 18th Central Committee of the CPC, in a speech in Indonesia, he announced that China would establish an Asian Infrastructure Investment Bank and invited other countries to join. These two Chinese initiatives are related, but separate. Both have since taken shape. The AIIB started operations in 2015 and is now a multilateral development bank with 57 member countries, based in Beijing. It is focused on infrastructure development, especially in Asia, but, in principle, anywhere. A parallel initiative (originally proposed by India in 2012, but endorsed by the other four BRICS countries, Brazil, China, Russia and South Africa) was establishing the so-called "New Development Bank" (NDB) which is headquartered in Shanghai, for the financing of infrastructure and sustainable development projects in BRICS countries. It started operations at the end of 2016. A parallel BRICS initiative was to establish an IMF-style "Contingent Reserve Arrangement" (CRA) for emergency liquidity (balance of payments) support to member countries.

AIIB, NDB and CRA are important new multilateral financial institutions, but China's BRI (or OBOR) is emerging as a far larger program of (mostly infrastructure) development projects aimed at promoting development in and "connectivity" between markets in over 60 participating countries. China has tentatively pledged $1 trillion financing over 10 years through AIIB and various national financial institutions, such as the newly created Silk Road Fund and existing financial institution, including China Development Bank, China Export-Import Bank and state-controlled commercial banks. In May 2017, several hundred BRI (OBOR) contracts were signed, and major projects (in Pakistan, Laos, Turkey, Sri Lanka, Indonesia and China) were already under implementation.

BRI (or OBOR)[33] represents a new approach to international development cooperation and new thinking about China's place in the world. It stresses the importance of infrastructure, "economic corridors" and "connectivity" between markets. China is at the center of this initiative as a place to buy and sell, as well as secure financing, technical know-how and construction capability. In the eyes of some critics, BRI (or OBOR) represents Deng Xiaoping's "opening-up" strategy in reverse: Deng encouraged China to open up to the rest of the world for China's economic benefit. The Xi/Li government is asking other countries to open up to China for their economic benefit.

Whereas one can only hope that BRI (or OBOR) will be a successful model for international economic cooperation and development, it is hard to suppress the concern that it will be seen by the Xi/Li government as an alternative to the domestic economic reforms envisaged by the 3rd Plenum of November 2013. If that were to happen, BRI may become a burden on China, instead of a source of long-term development.

Notes

1 Stent (2017, pp. 66–67).
2 An indication of limited communist control in the northwest is that Mao Zemin was arrested by a warlord in Xinjiang and executed (1943) when he refused to denounce communism.
3 Much of the early history of currencies issued by the CPC in China is explained in PBoC's currency museum in Beijing.
4 At a Central Committee meeting on 24 September 1952.
5 Fewsmith (1994, p. 62). (The main purpose of this meeting was to discuss theoretical issues concerning the functioning of a socialist economy.)
6 See Annotated chronology, late Feb./early March '59.
7 Xue Muqiao, Su Hsing and Lin Tse-Li. *The Socialist Transformation of the National Economy in China*. Published in English by Foreign Languages Press, Beijing, 1960.
8 Under this system, individual farmers were permitted to sell their output in excess of assigned plan quota at free-market prices. The HRS system was at the heart of China's agricultural revival in the late 1970s and early 1980s under Deng Xiaoping.
9 One of the first things Hua, Mao's direct successor, did after becoming the Party's chairman in 1976 was to instruct his officials to develop a 10-Year Development Plan aimed at Soviet-style "heavy" industrialization. The Plan was formally approved by the National People's Congress in February 1978 but never implemented, thanks to Deng Xiaoping's interventions.
10 Deng was generally recognized as a powerful, visionary political leader, but he was under house arrest when chaos threatened to develop in late 1976 and early 1977. He had been relieved of his official functions (and placed under house arrest) by the "Gang of Four" in April 1976, following anti-government student demonstrations in Tiananmen Square in Beijing, which he was accused (by the "Gang") of having organized. (The demonstrations were related to the death of PM Zhou Enlai in January of that year, when Deng was deputy PM.)
11 "Law of value", a concept developed by Karl Marx, sometimes referred to as "rule of value", is a frequently used term in early Chinese reform literature. Literally, the "law" (or rule) means that in a socialist economy, goods and services should be exchanged at prices proportionate to the amount of standard labor inputs. The "law" also referred to the conclusion of Stalin (in his *Economic Problems of Socialism in the USSR*) and other socialist leaders that spontaneous market forces of supply and demand should not be ignored in a planned socialist economy. Already in the 1950s under Mao Zedong, when this point was still controversial in China, prominent economists and philosophers such as Sun Yefang and Gu Zhun, emphasized the importance of this "law". Xue Muqiao made it a central theme in his *China's Socialist Economy* textbook of 1979, which became required reading for Party cadres. For a discussion of the "law of value", see, e.g., Fung (1982) and Fewsmith (1994), pp. 62, 94).

12 This was a highly controversial issue in China in the late 1970s, until Deng Xiaoping authorized the publication of an article in the *People's Daily* of 5 May 1978, which argued that paying people according to their contribution is consistent with socialism. This opened the way to the systematic use of incentives to promote economic efficiency and a tolerance for inequality based on unequal skills or effort.
13 See Chapter 5 on China's entry into the World Bank.
14 Deng retained his chairmanship of the Central Military Commission until 1989.
15 A spontaneous breakup of agricultural Communes and return to private farming (under the HRS) had been occurring in Anhui and Sichuan since early 1978, with the support of provincial Party leaders.
16 The term "commodity economy" meant about the same as "market economy", but was preferred in China at that time; it was commonly used by economists and politicians in Russia and socialist Eastern Europe.
17 An English language version of this book was published by Foreign Languages Press in 1981.
18 This referred to the practice (originally developed for the (contract) HRS in agriculture in the early 1960s) of simultaneously having a government-controlled price for the contract, plan or quota part of output and a market-determined price for the rest.
19 In 1982, the System Reform Office was expanded to form the State Commission for Restructuring the Economic System (SCRES).
20 Chen Yun compared the economy to a bird in a cage, the dimensions of which could be adjusted by the government to give the bird more or less freedom to move around.
21 General Agreement on Tariffs and Trade of 1947, predecessor of the WTO, which came into existence on 1 January 1995.
22 Deng's so-called Southern Tour also made a deep impression on overseas Chinese in Hong Kong, Taiwan and elsewhere. They regained confidence in China's reform and modernization efforts and began to invest more in mainland China, while visits to ancestral homes in the country became popular. In the US (and the West in general) Deng's Southern Tour went largely unnoticed – the US and many countries imposed sanctions on China following "Tiananmen", while many held Deng personally responsible for the massacre.
23 This term had been agreed at the 3rd Plenum of the 12th CC of the CPC in October 1984 and was still used at the 13th Party Congress in October 1987.
24 The term "commodity economy", then used in the USSR to indicate that there was still a need for markets to exchange commodities because "mature communism" had not yet been achieved, was replaced by "market economy", signaling a more Western orientation in economic reform.
25 The Dalian conference in June 1993 was attended by Li Kwoh Ting, economic advisor to the president of Taiwan and a former economy minister (popularly known as the "father" of Taiwan's economic miracle). Li had been brought to the mainland as a World Bank consultant for the conference at Jiang Zemin's request. The Dalian conference was also attended by Lawrence Lau, a Taiwanese professor of economics at Stanford University who had been an informal economic advisor to Zhu Rongji. After the conference, Li Kwoh Ting met privately with senior Chinese leaders.
26 In the mid-1990s, this "inner group" comprised Zhou Xiaochuan, Lou Jiwei, Guo Shuqing and Li Jiange. Wu Jinglian was their informal intellectual leader, and Wang Qishan often participated in the discussions.
27 The expectation was that private home owners/occupants would take better care of the property than the previous public-sector owners.
28 China Statistical Yearbook 2004, table 5–4.
29 Few Chinese believed that the bombing was accidental.
30 The term "industrial policy" in this context refers to government efforts to promote the development of certain types of industries or enterprises and research through various incentives and/or public investment.
31 An indication of this is the launch of the government's "Made in China 2025" initiative in May 2015. This initiative, which built on the previous government's "Indigenous Innovation" policy of January 2006 and the "Strategic Emerging Industries" policy of

October 2010, aims at upgrading Chinese industry and at capturing a larger share of value added in international manufacturing chains. The government circular announcing the "Made in China 2025" initiative identified 10 priority sectors. For more detail, see Annotated chronology, May 2015.

32 The official name for President Xi's Belt and Road Initiative is "Silk Road Economic Belt and 21st Century Maritime Silk Road", an abbreviated version of which is "One Belt, One Road", or OBOR.

33 China's BRI (or OBOR) is sometimes compared to the US-financed Marshall Plan after WWII, but it is potentially much larger in financial terms and involving many more countries in a larger geographic area.

3 Architects of China's market-oriented economic reforms

Introduction

The main architect of China's economic reforms from the late 1970s was undoubtedly Deng Xiaoping, a politician and statesman who was strongly interested in economic development. Deng tried to start some fundamental reforms already in 1975 but was sidelined by the "Gang of Four" for political reasons.[1] After Mao Zedong's death (September 1976), the arrest of the "Gang of Four" (October 1976) and his political rehabilitation (July 1977), Deng resumed his reform efforts, culminating in the historic 3rd Plenum of the 11th Central Committee of the CPC in December 1978. For all practical purposes, Deng was Mao's successor as Party leader, but it took several years before Mao's official successor, Hua Guofeng, was replaced, not by Deng, but by Deng's protégé, Hu Yaobang.[2] Another very senior politician who weighed in heavily in favor of (cautious) market-oriented reforms from the late 1970s was Chen Yun. Chapter 4 is devoted to him.

Unlike Mao, Deng relied heavily on professional economists to advise him on economic policies and associated institutional development. He often solicited advice, but the political climate changed so much under his leadership that it could also be provided unasked. Over the years, hundreds of Chinese economists and other technocrats contributed to the process of economic modernization and reform. In this chapter, I include brief sketches on 20 of them; most of them also feature in the Annotated chronology and in other chapters. It is, unfortunately, not possible to do justice in this book to all their contributions or to many other Chinese economists who also contributed to economic policy making. The brief sketches on individual economists below are inevitably incomplete and reflect my own biases.

Perhaps the most important general conclusion of this chapter is that the importance of ideological considerations in economic policy making sharply declined under Deng. But they did not disappear altogether. For well over a decade after the start of market-oriented economic reforms in the late 1970s, there were major disagreements between "conservatives" and "reformers" on the appropriate balance between proactive "planning" and passive reliance on "regulation by the market" and other issues. Initially, there were many technocrats and politicians who believed that regulation by markets was only appropriate for small-scale "sideline" agricultural products and some consumer goods. There was also controversy over the appropriate pace of price liberalization and the need for ownership reform. Uncertainty about ultimate reform goals and conflict between economic and political objectives returned under President Xi Jinping.

It is indicative of the shift from ideological thinking during the Mao years to pragmatic thinking under Deng Xiaoping, that citations from Marx or Engels, still common in Chinese economic literature of the 1980s, almost disappeared in later work. However, after the start of market reforms in the late 1970s, opinions among economists and officials about the appropriate balance between plan and market, the extent and pace of price liberalization, the role of private enterprise and many other issues shifted only gradually. Ideological considerations continued to be important for some leaders, but ceased to play a major role from around 1993, when Zhu Rongji had established himself as leader of the reform effort (with the full support of Party General Secretary Jiang Zemin). However, there was hardly ever a consensus on what next to do or on the ultimate goal of reform.

The best way to organize this chapter, I thought, was to divide the 20 selected reform economists into three age categories: (1) the older generation of deceased or retired economists, who were already active before the establishment of the PRC in 1949 and, generally, had little formal education; (2) a middle group of economists who were professionally active only after 1949, especially after the start of Deng's reforms, and had mixed educational backgrounds and (3) the younger generation of economists who became involved only after the start of Deng's reforms and tend to be highly educated, often including training abroad.

The selection of people in each group is inevitably somewhat arbitrary; coverage of the younger generation of economists in this chapter is especially incomplete. Some important "younger generation" economists not included in this chapter, due to lack of space, are: Wang Qishan, Liu He, Chen Yuan, Chen Xingtai, Liu Mingkang, Yu Yongding, Qin Xiao, Qiang Yingyi, Xu Shanda, Hu Angang, Wang Tongsan, Chi Fulin, Zhang Weiying, Mao Yushi, Hu Zuliu (Fred Hu), Fan Gang, Huang Yiping, Li Daokui (David Li), Wu Xiaoling, Zhu Min, Yi Gang, Hu Biliang, Fang Xinghai, Ma Jun, Xiao Geng, the Malaysian/Chinese economist Andrew Sheng (who, in various executive and academic positions in Hong Kong and the mainland, contributed significantly to economic policy making in modern China) and the Taiwanese economist Lawrence Lau (who was a professor at Stanford University and an advisor to Zhu Rongji in the 1990s).

A. *The older generation*

1. *Xue Muqiao (1904–2005)*[3]

I agree with Wu Jinglian that Xue (who died in 2005, when he was almost 101) was the most important Chinese economist of the 20th century.[4] He was already involved in economic policy making and management before the establishment of the PRC in 1949 and after 1949 under Mao. He then became one of the principal architects of market reforms under Deng Xiaoping. The evolution of Xue's thinking on how to develop a "socialist economy" mirrors Deng's. Xue remains well remembered and highly respected in China today.

During the almost seven decades that he was professionally active, Party leaders such as Mao Zedong, Zhou Enlai, Chen Yun, Deng Xiaoping, Li Xiannan, Hu Yaobang, Zhao Ziyang, Jiang Zemin and Zhu Rongji all took Xue's opinions on how to manage China's economy seriously. But economic development did not always mean the same thing in Xue's lifetime. From the establishment of the PRC until Mao's death in 1976, it essentially meant establishing a "socialist economic system" in a poor, rural economy with little industry. After the historic 3rd Plenum of the 11th Central Committee of the CPC in December 1978, it meant promoting economic growth and improving standards of living and as rapidly as possible, without giving up the CPC's monopoly on political power. Xue's penultimate essay on economic development was in the form of a letter to the Standing Committee of the Politburo in 1990 (about a year after the Tiananmen disaster of 1989, when Party leaders were deeply divided on the direction of economic reform) urging the Party to intensify market reforms.

Xue came from a relatively poor rural family in southern Jiangsu. He received little formal education and, like several other older generation economists, was essentially self-taught. He joined the CPC in 1927, the same year he was arrested during Chiang Kaishek's bloody crackdown on communists. During his three years in jail following that arrest, he read many books on political economy, including works by Marx and Engels. As a young man, he believed strongly in their theories. While he apparently became less interested in Marxism later in life, he remained convinced that "the socialist system is the best political and economic system for social justice and common prosperity".[5]

Xue witnessed dramatic changes in China during the century he lived; as a young teenager, he participated in the May 4th protest movement against the West in 1919 (after the Chinese delegation to the Versailles Peace Treaty negotiations returned empty-handed and humiliated by the transfer of German possessions in Shandong to Japan).[6] During the Cultural Revolution, Xue was accused of being a "capitalist roader"[7] and forced to undergo "re-education" through labor on a farm.

During China's civil war (1945–1949), Xue's economic expertise was used by the Party to fight inflation. As an economic theorist, he had concluded that in an inflationary environment, stable money drives out unstable money and used this principle to help introduce a new currency in areas liberated by the PLA. He also promoted the idea that the Party should control money supply and key prices in those areas.[8]

Xue served in senior government positions under both Mao Zedong and Deng Xiaoping. For example, in the early 1950s, he was Secretary General of the PRC's initial Central Economic and Finance Commission (under Chen Yun) and Director of the National Commodity Price Commission. In those functions, he had a major role in drafting China's 1st Five-Year Plan.[9] In the mid-1950s, he was head of a "Planning System Discussion Group" which had been asked by the Party to define the scope and methods of central planning. Xue was then in favor of partially replacing mandatory planning by "reference planning" and relying on "the market" for the supply and pricing of non-essential consumer goods. After Mao's disastrous Great Leap Forward had been discontinued in the Fall of 1960, Xue helped Chen Yun and Zhou Enlai design an interim "Adjustment Plan" to rehabilitate the economy. During the early 1980s he served as Director General of the State Statistical Bureau, chief advisor to the State Commission for Restructuring the Economic System (SCRES) under PM Zhao Ziyang and head of the sub-group on economic reform under Chen Yun's Finance and Economic Commission, established by the State Council in early 1979.

For me (author of this book), two intriguing questions about Xue Muqiao as a reform economist are: (1) *when* did he change his mind on the best approach to establish a socialist economic system (by relying more on markets and less on planning)? and (2) did he ever change his mind regarding Marx's prediction that capitalism would inevitably lead to anarchy and collapse? Although he was inclined to take markets seriously, during the Mao years, he wrote several essays analyzing and applauding Marxist-Leninist economic policies; in 1959, during the Great Leap Forward, he (and two co-authors) published a book, *Socialist Transformation of China's National Economy*,[10] which explained and praised Mao's efforts to establish a socialist economic system based on collectivized agriculture and state ownership of all important means of production; his earlier preference for relying on "the market" for supplying and pricing non-essential consumer goods was not expressed in this book. Why did Xue Muqiao publish a book in 1959 that so uncritically supported Mao's "socialist transformation"? Was he under pressure to publish something he may not have fully believed in? Twenty years later, after Mao's death, Xue published another book: *China's Socialist Economy*[11] in which he criticized Mao's "rush" to collectivize agriculture in the 1950s, while arguing that certain economic laws, such as the "law of value", applied as much to a socialist economy as to a capitalist one. The book advocated greater reliance on "regulation of the economy by markets", material incentives, competition, decentralization, managerial independence for SOEs and acceptance of diverse forms of ownership, including private ownership. The book became *required* reading for Party cadres.[12] Three more Chinese editions of the book appeared in 1981, 1986 and 1987.

It appears that Xue Muqiao changed his mind on the merits of Mao's approach to economic development and "socialist construction" during the Cultural Revolution when he was forced to undergo "re-education" and work on a farm. In those years, he wrote several drafts of a text book on socialist economic development, which could then not be published for political reasons. Publication of *China's Socialist Economy* in 1979 (his *magnum opus*), became possible after Deng Xiaoping had become de-facto "paramount" leader of the Party in 1978. The book is a revised version of his earlier, unpublished draft textbook. According to his daughter Xiaohe,[13] Xue had long believed that China should embrace market economics but was held back by the conflict between Party discipline and expressing his own opinion.

In April 1977, when Deng Xiaoping was still under house arrest, Xue wrote him and Li Xiannan (then Vice Chairman of the Party and chief economic advisor to Mao's successor Hua Guofeng) a letter pointing out that the severe economic imbalances that had developed during the Great Leap Forward and the Cultural Revolution, required urgent correction. The letter attracted much attention in circles of Party leaders and convinced most of them that drastic changes in economic policy were indeed needed. The following year (1978), Xue Muqiao made another important contribution to new thinking about economic development by co-authoring Hu Qiaomu's report to the State Council of July *Act in Accordance with Economic Laws; Set up the Four Modernizations*.[14]

Xue's last essay (written in 1992, when he was 88) sums up the evolution of his thinking about economic development in China from the early 1950s through the breakup of the USSR in 1991. He saw China's great economic progress since the early 1980s as affirmation of his believe in the merits of a mixed socialist/capitalist economic system. The best way to derive full benefit from a socialist economic system, he argued in his later years, is to combine it with essential elements of capitalism, to create a "planned market economy". Xue remained faithful to socialist ideals throughout his professional life, but his belief in Marxist theory seems to have gradually evaporated.

In March 2005, four months before his death, Xue was among the first Chinese economists to receive the government-sponsored "China Economics Award for Outstanding Contribution".[15] He turned down a proposal by his students to start a "Xue Muqiao economics prize", as he did not want to compete with Sun Yefang, in whose name a prestigious economics prize had already been established. Xue was a great reformer and a generous person.

2. *Sun Yefang (1908–1983)*[16]

Although Sun died at a younger age (75) and was a less prolific writer than Xue Muqiao, he had almost as much influence on economic thinking and policy making in China during and after the Mao era. Soon after Sun's death in 1983, a group of Chinese economists founded the "Sun Yefang Economic Science Foundation", which awards prizes for research in economics, to Chinese economists in government or academia every two years. These awards have become very prestigious in China. Recipients of the prize include PM Li Keqiang, central bank governor Zhou Xiaochuan, Li Jiange (3x), Chen Xiwen, Chen Qingtai, Wu Xiaoling, Wu Jinglian (5x), Guo Shuqing, Lou Jiwei, Wang Mengkui, Lin Yifu, Wang Yan (2x), Liu Shijin and several others who are less well known internationally.

Both Xue and Sun were born in Jiangsu, but Sun came from a relatively wealthy family. He received higher education (at the Sun Yat-sen University in Moscow). Like Xue, he was keenly interested in "political economy". Both were active CPC members well before the PRC was established in 1949 and held senior government positions under both Mao Zedong and Deng Xiaoping. As distant cousins and lifelong friends,[17] they knew each other well. They both served as economic advisors to PM Zhao Ziyang in the early 1980s.

Both published important books on economic strategy and reform in 1979. While Xue published *China's Socialist Economy*, Sun published *Some Theoretical*

Issues in Socialist Economies (a collection of 20 essays written from 1956–1978) in which he raised critical questions about the functioning and efficiency of China's planned socialist economy. Both books recommended ways to improve the efficiency of China's economy and growth and their analyses cover the same basic issues, but Sun's essays were more academic and theoretical in nature. He used mathematical tools to prove his points; Xue's writing was more "down-to-earth". Both argued for greater managerial independence for SOEs, stressing that *ownership* and *management* of SOEs were separate things. Both believed in the ideals of socialism, but Xue was more inclined to stress the need for economic system reform (e.g., greater reliance on "regulation by markets", competition, private ownership and private investment), while Sun concentrated on demonstrating how shortcomings in China's centrally planned socialist economy could be corrected without changing the system per se. He focused on the pricing of goods and services provided by the state and on the measurement of SOE performance. Sun was firmly opposed to dogmatic thinking and always insisted on logical reasoning and evidence.[18] Also, he was courageous enough to (obliquely) challenge some of Mao's economic policies in the late 1950s.[19]

The more or less simultaneous publication in 1979 of the two books mentioned above is indicative of the confusion and the conflicting opinions on priorities for economic reform in the late 1970s and early 1980s. Xue and his followers wanted to *change* the system; Sun and his followers concentrated on perfecting the existing system.

Unlike Xue, who remained "silent" during the "Let a hundred flowers bloom and a hundred schools of thought contend" campaign that followed the first Session of the 8th Party Congress (September 1956), Sun, who had just become (acting) director of the Institute of Economics of the China Academy of Science (CAS), politely questioned Mao's policy of requiring farmers to join agricultural collectives and later (during the Great Leap Forward) huge "People's Communes". (The Great Leap had been approved at the 3rd Plenum of the 8th Party Congress in the Fall of 1957.) Sun also argued that Marx's "law of value" (which in his opinion had been misinterpreted by Party ideologues) had to play a role in a socialist economic system.[20] Another prominent Chinese intellectual who expressed similar misgivings about Mao's economic policies around the same time was Gu Zhun

Sun was later criticized by Mao and accused of being the "biggest revisionist". He was imprisoned for his economic ideas during most of the Cultural Revolution (1966–1976) and rehabilitated only after Mao's death. The Party had misunderstood Sun's arguments and falsely accused him of promoting capitalist ideas.

The most important contribution Sun made to economic thinking in China (already in the 1950s) was to provide a theoretical foundation for the optimal pricing of goods and allocation of resources by the planning authorities in a socialist economy, based on his interpretation of the "law of value". In Marx's theory, the "value" of a product is determined by the amount of direct and indirect (standard) labor incorporated in it. Sun, however, pointed out that "value" reflects *relative scarcity*, not necessarily labor input. Yet, he agreed that in a socialist, state-owned economy, it is the responsibility of the government to set important prices. To create incentives for lowering production costs, increasing profits and improving product quality in a socialist economy, he argued, *official* (state-determined) prices had to be based on *standard* labor inputs *across enterprises*, not on enterprise-specific cost data. Similarly, enterprise performance should be measured by profit, not by gross output, as was then common in China. Sun demonstrated that, contrary to Marx's theory, the "law of value" does apply in a planned socialist economy. Sun's ideas on value, pricing and measuring SOE performance in a socialist economy (and other economic issues) would later be used to support arguments in favor of reforming China's socialist economy in the direction of a market-oriented system.

Xue Muqiao agreed with Sun Yefang that economic laws were *economic laws*, regardless of a country's political system.

3. Du Runsheng (1913–2015)[21]

Du was the third oldest of the older generation economic reformers (after Xue Muqiao and Sun Yefang) and the most influential in the areas of agriculture and rural development. He was born in Shanxi and is known in China as the "father of rural reform".[22] He joined the CPC in 1936 and worked with the PLA as a guerilla fighter against the Japanese occupiers. As a recognized expert in agriculture and rural development, he led early land redistribution efforts in liberated areas under CPC control. He also ran the Party's rural land reforms in the south after the PRC's establishment in 1949.

Du studied agricultural economics at Beijing Normal University in the late 1930s. He was very active in the Party in the 1940s before the PRC was established and, like Xue Muqiao and Sun Yefang, held senior government positions under both Mao Zedong and Deng Xiaoping. Because agriculture accounted for over 80% of China's GDP and employment in the early 1950s and still over one-third of GDP when market-oriented reforms started in the late 1970s, Du was at the center of China's economic development for much of his professional life.

After the 3rd Plenum of December 1978, Du was the main architect of China's household (contract) responsibility system (HRS) and its system of land-user rights for individual farmers. These two factors explain much of China's early success in rural reform and agricultural development.[23] Since agriculture was such an important part of China's economy and because China is so big and populous, Du Runsheng was undoubtedly one of the most influential economists in history. Partly as a result of his role in China's economic reforms, hundreds of millions of peasants were able to escape abject poverty.

In the mid-1950s, when he was the second most important government official responsible for agriculture and rural development, Du ran into trouble with Mao. It happened when he sided with his boss Deng Zihui against *forced* collectivization in agriculture. He had supported the formation of *voluntary* cooperatives in the early 1950s, but believed that *forced* collectivization, as per Mao's plan for socialist construction in China (following Stalin's example), would deprive farmers of incentives to work hard and thus lead to reduced productivity. Mao wanted to send Du to a rural labor camp for re-education, but, because his services were badly needed at the center, his "punishment" was delayed. In 1956, he was essentially demoted (to the position of Deputy Secretary General of the China Academy of Sciences, CAS.) He stayed in that position until the start of the Cultural Revolution in 1966. As an "intellectual" and an official who had dared to challenge Mao, he was persecuted and forced to do hard physical labor during much of the Cultural Revolution period (1966-'76). (Deng Zihui was also persecuted during the Cultural Revolution and died in 1972.)

Du's promotion of the HRS in agriculture under Deng Xiaoping was a pragmatic compromise between the need for planning in a socialist economy (with no private ownership of land) and the need for output growth in agriculture. Under the HRS, which required individual farmers to deliver a certain quantity of output at a government-controlled price before they could sell the rest of their production at free market prices, it was possible to have it both ways (plan and market). Therefore, the "contract system" (as the HRS is sometimes called) inevitably involved "dual-track" pricing. This was controversial as it seemed to combine elements of capitalism and socialism in a way that promoted false reporting and other corrupt practices.[24]

Spontaneous de-collectivization in agriculture, with open or tacit support from local political leaders, started in Anhui and Sichuan, before the 3rd Plenum of December 1978. But it took until September 1980 for the Party to accept in principle that farmers should be allowed to choose their own method of production and until January 1982 for the HRS (with "dual-track" pricing) to be officially approved by the Central Committee. At that time, the Party also accepted Du Runsheng's proposal that individual farmers should be given legal land-user rights (initially for 15 years, later extended to 30) to their farm on communally-owned agricultural land.[25] In his capacity as vice chairman of the State Agriculture Commission under Deng Xiaoping, Du campaigned hard for a return to private farming, adoption of the HRS system with "dual-track" pricing and acceptance of land-user rights for individual farmers. To improve farmer incomes, he promoted the integration of crop farming and animal husbandry. He also fought, but unsuccessfully, for the establishment of farmer associations to give farmers a voice in China's political system. He also fought for the relaxation of *hukou* (household registration) restrictions on the movement of rural people to urban areas and their rights as residents after they had settled in an urban area. At the 3rd Plenum of the Central Committee of the CPC in November 2013, the Party decided to reform the *hukou* system in directions Du had recommended earlier.

During the initial reform years (late 1970s and early 1980s), Du, as head of the Government's Agricultural Development Center, submitted frequent reports to the Party on rural development. During those years, he made countless pro-reform speeches all over China and published many articles. In 1983, he was appointed director of the Party's influential Rural Policy Research Office, an acknowledgement of the crucial role he had played in agricultural reforms until then. He continued to play a central role in national economic policy making for agriculture and rural development and wrote many influential articles until a few years before his death in 2015, at age 102. Du was a modest person who always downplayed his contributions to China's agricultural success. His former student Chen Xiwen (a prominent member of China's younger generation of economic reformers discussed below) is Du's successor as the Party's top expert on rural development.

4. Gu Zhun (1915–1974)[26]

Gu Zhun is better known in China as a philosopher and historian than as an economist. He is now recognized as one of the most important thinkers of the Mao era. He was a brilliant and courageous intellectual; an original thinker with a fiercely independent, some say stubborn, mind. Like Sun Yefang, he opposed some of Mao's economic policies in the 1950s. He died (of lung cancer) at the age of 59. Had his health kept up for another decade, he might have emerged as one of the most important Chinese reform economists under Deng Xiaoping. Given the breadth and depth of his interests and academic pursuits, he would be called a "Renaissance Man" in the West. Because of his strong interest in economic development, his deep understanding of the causes of poverty and his belief in liberal democracy, he is sometimes referred to as "China's Amartya Sen".[27]

Gu was the youngest child in a large, relatively poor family of merchants in Shanghai; available information suggests that he received no formal education beyond elementary school and was therefore largely self-taught. At the age of 12, he became an apprentice in a Shanghai accountancy firm, where he studied accountancy and business economics. He was recognized, already then, as a quick learner with an independent mind. He published his first book (a text book on advanced business accounting) at the age of 17. The book caught the attention of Sun Yefang, who was seven years his senior and later became his friend and mentor. Like Sun and other older generation reform economists, Gu started his career as a devoted Marxist. Later in life, he concluded that Marx's theory about the inevitability of capitalism's collapse and Lenin's theory about the links between capitalism and imperialism, were faulty.

Gu joined the CPC in 1935 when it was dangerous to do so, as the Party had been outlawed by the Nationalist government of Chiang Kaishek and was then operating "underground". When the PRC was established in 1949, Gu was one of the CPC's top accounting and finance experts. He was appointed vice director of the Shanghai Financial and Economic Committee and director of its Finance and Taxation Bureaus, which, given the fact that Shanghai was the new republic's principle source of fiscal revenues, were all critically important positions. In 1952, he was fired from these positions, probably for political reasons.[28] A few years later, Gu was offered a research position at the Institute of Economics[29] of the CAS, of which Sun Yefang was then the acting director. It was in that job, during Mao's "let a hundred flowers bloom and a hundred schools of thought contend" campaign, that Gu wrote his famous 1957 essay "On Commercial Production and the Theory of Value under Socialism" (which was implicitly very critical of Mao's economic policies).

The essay earned him great respect among professional colleagues and the ire of the Party.[30] It reflected even bolder thinking on the practical meaning of the "law of value" and the role of markets under socialism than Sun Yefang expressed in his writings around the same time. At the Institute of Economics of the CAS, Gu also met and worked with Zhao Renwei and Wu Jinglian. The latter was 15 years Gu's junior and looks at him as his mentor and the true "father" of China's market reforms. Gu encouraged Wu and Zhao to learn English so that they could study important economic literature and history. At the Institute, which was a breeding ground for early thinking about market-oriented economic reform (while Mao was still alive), Gu Zhun also collaborated with Yu Guangyuan and Liu Guoguang, two other older generation reform economists. Later, Gu became more outspoken in his criticism of Mao's policies. In 1972, he wrote *What Shall We Do After Nora Left?* in which he cautioned against "revolution" and revolutionary change on the ground that it was very difficult to find a path to stability afterwards; it was sharply (though obliquely) critical of Mao economic policies (and a throwback to a famous 1920 Chinese novel by Lu Xun).

In 1958, when the "Great Leap Forward" started, Gu was branded a "Rightist" and expelled from the Party during the anti-rightist campaign. He was twice forced to undergo "re-education" through hard labor in rural camps. In between those hardship periods, back at the CAS' Institute of Economics, he translated Schumpeter's *Capitalism, Socialism and Democracy* and work by the British (Keynesian) economist Joan Robinson into Chinese. He was cruelly persecuted before and during the Cultural Revolution when his wife, who later committed suicide, was forced to divorce him, while his children had to disavow him.

In his later years, Gu became convinced of the need to replace communist idealism in China with practical empiricism and pluralism through political reform. His ideas on the importance of empiricism were similar to those expressed by Deng Xiaoping in his famous speech of 13 December 1978 ("Emancipate the Mind, Seek Truth from Facts and Unite as One in Looking to the Future"), which set the tone for the historic 3rd Plenum later that month.

Gu was very interested in political development. He studied the origins and functioning of democracy in ancient Greece and wrote a series of articles, which were combined in two books, *The Greek City State* and *From Idealism to Empiricism*, that were both published in 1982,[31] eight years after his death, when Deng Xiaoping had changed China's political landscape. Gu thought that the best solution for China was to establish a Constitutional rule-of-law system in a multi-party, liberal democracy. His student and friend Wu Jinglian was the only one present at his death in a Beijing hospital in 1974.

5. *Yu Guangyuan (1915–2013)*[32]

Yu, who had been a senior propaganda official under Mao, became a close collaborator of Deng Xiaoping in the late 1970s and 1980s.[33] He was a co-author of Deng's famous closing speech of 13 December 1978 for the Central Party Work Conference that set the tone for the watershed 3rd Plenum of December 1978 ("Emancipate the Mind, Seek Truth from Facts and Unite as One in Looking to the Future"). He also worked closely with Hu Yaobang (chairman/General Secretary of the CPC, 1981–1987) and Zhao Ziyang (PM 1980–1987 and CPC General Secretary, 1987–1989). Yu agreed with Xue Muqiao that Mao Zedong had unwisely "rushed" China's transition to socialism in the 1950s.[34]

Yu was born in Shanghai in 1915 and received an undergraduate degree in physics from Tsinghua University in 1936. He joined the CPC in 1937 and went to the communist base in Ya'nan, where he became a physics teacher at the local CPC-led university. Like Xue Muqiao and Gu Zhun, he studied "political economy" on his own. In 1961, he published (as editor) a textbook on *Political Economics* which was used by several Chinese universities for years. Despite being a devoted Party member and prominent "intellectual", Yu was accused of "counterrevolutionary revisionism" during the Cultural Revolution and "struggled" against.

He got to know Deng Xiaoping in 1975, when he served as a member of the Political Research Office of the State Council under Deng. Accused by the "Gang of Four" of masterminding the student demonstrations in Tiananmen Square, following the death of Zhou Enlai), Deng lost his job as vice PM in April 1976. When he was rehabilitated in July 1977, Deng invited Yu back into his inner circle. A few months earlier, Yu had been appointed vice president of the newly established China Academy of Social Sciences (CASS), a position he held for almost two decades. Simultaneously, he became the first director of the Economic Research Institute of the State Planning Commission. Earlier, as director of the Party's Central Propaganda Department (under Mao), Yu had been associated with the CAS' Institute of Economics, which was co-administered by his Department and the State Planning Commission.

During the early reform years (late 1970s and early 1980s), Yu was one of the top intellectual leaders weighing policy options and controversial reform issues. He sided with Xue Muqiao, Sun Yefang and Liu Guoguang in arguing that the "law of value" applied as much to a socialist economic system as to capitalism and that markets had to be an important part of a planned socialist economy. The one issue that remained highly controversial, however, was the question of compensation: should workers in a socialist system be paid (1) equally, (2) on the basis of their contribution or (3) on the basis of their needs (as under mature communism)? Several major conferences involving hundreds of economists and officials were organized to discuss this issue in 1977 and 1978. Yu played a key role on all of them.

Yu strongly favored the principle of "distribution according to work" (i.e. paying people on the basis of their contribution). But there was at that time, still considerable opposition against that idea on ideological grounds. The issue was finally settled when Deng Xiaoping authorized the publication of an article in the *People's Daily* of 5 May 1978 explaining why "distribution according to work" was consistent with socialist principles and why it was in China's interest to pay people according to their contribution. It was a very consequential publication. By implication, the *People's Daily* article justified the use of material incentives and therefore also social *inequality*, under socialism. Naturally, acceptance of the use of material incentives under socialism made questions of SOE reform, pricing and social security more urgent. The issue of compensation was central in shaping many initial market-oriented reforms, often under Yu's professional leadership.

Like most older generation architects of market-oriented reforms in China (except Gu Zhun), Yu remained convinced of the fundamental values of Marxism throughout his professional career.

In 1979, not long after the 3rd Plenum of December 1978, Yu became head of a "Theory and Methodology Research Group" (under Chen Yun's Financial and Economic Committee of the State Council) to help guide the economic reform efforts. Dong Fureng was his deputy in this sensitive assignment. The Group dealt with many controversial issues, including the need for "ownership" reform. Based on study tours to several Eastern European socialist countries, Yu concluded that there was room for different kinds of ownership (including private ownership) under socialism. This suited Deng Xiaoping, who needed greater flexibility in masterminding the overall reform effort. Another important contribution Yu made during the early reform years was to draw attention to ecological constraints to rapid economic development. He was the first major figure in the Party to express concern about emerging environmental problems and resource constraints in China.

Though a Marxist at heart, Yu was inclined to liberal economic and political views, sometimes against prevailing Party doctrine. Not long after the June 1989 military crackdown on student-led protests in Tiananmen Square in Beijing, he was reprimanded by the Party for having sided with General Secretary Zhao Ziyang in trying to find a negotiated solution for the disturbances. Despite this political put-down, he remained active as an economic reformer. He published many influential essays in favor of market-oriented reforms in the 1990s and early 2000s, before he finally retired.

Yu was a kind, warm-hearted man, who was loved by many, as his daughter Yu Xiaoqing, a senior World Bank official, will testify.

6. *Liu Guoguang (b. 1923)*[35]

Liu, the most highly educated of the older generation reform economists, did his undergraduate studies in economics, at the National Southwest Associated University in Kunming[36] (before the PRC was established in 1949) and his graduate studies, also in economics, at the Moscow Economics University, where he was assigned by the Party to undertake higher studies in 1951 and from where he graduated in 1955. In between his undergraduate and graduate studies, he taught economics at Nankai University in Tianjin.

After he returned from Moscow, he joined the Institute of Economics of the CAS under (acting) director Sun Yefang. Liu received an honorary doctorate in economics from the Russian Academy of Sciences in 2000 and the "China Economics Award for Outstanding Contributions" in 2005 (along with Xue Muqiao, Ma Hong and Wu Jinglian). Throughout his long career, he was an active Party member; he made several official study tours to eastern Europe and the Russian part of the USSR, and he participated in numerous debates on economic policy making in China.

During the late 1950s, well before the Cultural Revolution, he undertook economic research projects with Sun Yefang at the Institute of Economics of the

CAS[37] in Beijing. Although he was a loyal Party member, he was still forced to do hard labor in rural areas for "re-education", both before and during the Cultural Revolution – presumably because he was an "intellectual".

Liu was a prolific writer. During the 1980s and '90s, he published numerous articles, often co-authored by other Chinese economists, such as Zhao Renwei and Zhang Zhuoyuan, on various aspects of China's economic reform efforts and challenges. Topics that interested him most, included the optimal balance between "planning" and "regulation by markets", the structure of China's economy, ownership diversification, SOE reform, regional inequality, monetary and fiscal policy and the person Deng Xiaoping as a political leader. Many of his articles appeared in major mainland and Hong Kong newspapers and in Party-sponsored Chinese journals such as *Red Flag*. (Much of his written work is available in English – see the Bibliography at the end of this book). He also wrote or co-authored many books on aspects of China's economic reforms. By all accounts, Liu is one of China's most accomplished academic reform economists.

When reading his wide-ranging articles, one question that emerges is, to what extent he moved away from his original conviction that the economic theories of Marx and Engels were correct. He was clearly very supportive of Deng Xiaoping's "reform and opening up" policies aimed at promoting economic development through improved efficiency and increased openness to the outside world. He offered many practical suggestions to support Deng's reform efforts. Yet, deep down, he seems to have remained convinced that Marx's theory about the inevitable collapse of capitalism and the innate superiority of socialism as an economic system, was basically correct.

Liu caused quite a stir in circles of Chinese economists in July 2005 when, in a speech following the ceremony at which he was honored with the "China Economics Award for Outstanding Contribution", he (at age 82) expressed deep concern that Western neoliberal economics had become mainstream in China and that Marxist economics had been marginalized. In a follow-up article published in a Chinese economic research journal in October 2005, he elaborated on this theme and urged the Ministry of Education to remove non-Marxist university presidents, deans and directors of education from their positions. (It was his last published article.) He also recommended that all "sea turtle" economists (those returning from overseas training) should be re-educated in Marxism before being allowed to teach at Chinese schools.

In subsequent op-eds and interviews, Liu explained that he had become very impressed by the many serious social and economic problems that had developed in China since the introduction of market-oriented reforms (including widespread corruption, severe income, wealth and regional inequality, the monetization of power, environmental degradation, high rates of industrial and mining accidents, etc.). He didn't blame market economics per se, but argued that the Chinese state needed more power to deal effectively with widespread market failures and economic distortions associated with market reforms.

Liu concluded that in China's efforts to establish a "socialist market economy", too much emphasis had been placed on markets and too little on socialism. He attacked economic neoliberalism as dangerous for and alien to China. Liu's complaints do not appear to have had much practical follow-up in China at the time he made those comments, but President Xi Jinping (CPC's General Secretary since the 18th Party Congress in the Fall of 2012), warned against the use of Western textbooks in Chinese universities eight years later, perhaps unintentionally echoing Liu's concerns.

7. *Ma Hong (1920–2007)*[38]

Ma was the only other older-generation reform economist from an interior province – both he and Du Runsheng were born in Shanxi. His original surname was Niu (cow in English), but he changed that to Ma (horse) while staying at the communists' revolutionary base in Ya'nan, after he had joined the CPC in 1937, like Yu Guangyuan. He also changed his first name; to Hong (the Chinese character for flood). Ma Hong was professionally active before and after 1949. He became one of China's leading economic policy makers and reformers in the 1980s.

Like Gu Zhun, Ma was from a poor family and had little or no formal education beyond primary school; he started his first job at age 13. In his later teenage years, when he had become an active Party member (and deeply involved in the CPC's struggle against the Japanese occupiers), Ma studied political economy, including works by Marx and Engels, at the Party School of the Central Committee of the CPC in Ya'nan. He served in various local government positions in areas that had been liberated by the PLA in northeast China, both before and after the PRC was established in 1949.

In 1952, when the State Planning Commission was created, he became its first Secretary General. In that capacity, he had a hand in the drafting of China's 1st Five-Year Plan (1953–1958), together with Xue Muqiao and others. From 1956, he became deeply involved in designing industrial and mining policies, which gave him knowledge and experience he needed later as manager of China's largest petrochemical plant (early 1970s). In 1961, after the Great Leap Forward was discontinued, under the leadership of Zhou Enlai and Chen Yun, he was responsible for policies and regulations aimed at helping China's economy recover from the disastrous effects of the GLF.

In mid-1977, after Mao's death and the arrest of the "Gang of Four" he returned to the State Planning Commission, this time as director. One of his responsibilities there was to plan for and supervise the commercial exploitation of Daqing oil reserves (first discovered in 1959). About a year later, in 1978, when Deng Xiaoping had been rehabilitated and was influencing economic policy making significantly, Ma founded the Institute of Industrial Economics at the newly established CASS. He became the president of CASS in 1982, succeeding Hu Qiaomu. Ma served in that capacity until late 1985, when Hu Sheng was appointed as his successor (and Hu Qiaomu became honorary president).

It was as a senior CASS manager and president that Ma made his most important contributions to China's early market reforms. For example, in the early 1980s Ma led the team that produced the report *China Toward the Year 2000*, a critically important input into the 7th Five-Year Plan (1986–1990).[39] The report explored Deng's objective to give priority to the development of agriculture, light industries and services and the feasibility of quadrupling GDP by the end of the century. (At Deng's request, this ambitious target was also examined by the World Bank, in an economic report that was published in 1985.) In September 1985, as CASS president, Ma was the most senior government official to participate in the Bashan Lun[40] (boat) conference on macro-economic management and reform with top economists from around the world. (Xue Muqiao was the most senior Chinese professional economist to participate.)

During the 1980s and 1990s, Ma wrote many articles on development challenges facing China and several influential books, one of which, *New Strategy of Chinese Economic Development*, was translated into Japanese and published in Japan in 1985. An earlier book by Ma, *Research on Issues to do with China's Economic Structure* had been translated and published in Russian. Two other books by him, *New Strategy for China's Economy* and *Modern China's Economy and Management*, were published in English (by World Press in Beijing, in 1983, and by Foreign Languages Press in Beijing, in 1990, respectively).

Ma was neither an ideologue nor a theoretician; he was, above all, a practical, research-oriented industrial modernizer, deeply concerned about China's technological backwardness in the 1980s. He promoted the idea of upgrading industrial technology and modernizing SOE governance with the help of foreign investment and sought collaboration with external development agencies, such as the World Bank. He enjoyed Deng Xiaoping's full confidence and, as advisor to SCRES, he was frequently consulted by Zhao Ziyang.

In 1993, Ma was designated honorary director of the State Council's Development Research Centre (DRC), in which role he made additional contributions to China's development and reform. Like most other older-generation reformers (except Gu Zhun), Ma remained a Marxist at heart and never gave up on building a "socialist economic system" (which in his view, was a "planned market economy based on public ownership").

In 2005 Ma Hong received the "China Economics Award for Outstanding Contribution", the same year that Xue Muqiao, Liu Guoguang and Wu Jinglian received this distinction.[41] He died in 2007 (of Parkinson's, which had also killed Xue Muqiao).

B. The in-between generation

8. Dong Fureng (1927–2004)[42]

Dong was one of the intellectual giants of early market-oriented reforms under Deng Xiaoping in the late 1970s and early 1980s, when he worked at the Institute of Economics of the CASS. He also served, as deputy to Yu Guangyuan, on the "Theory and Methodology Research Group" that was established in early 1979, shortly after the historic 3rd Plenum of December 1978. In that function, Dong focused on the then still very controversial issues of "ownership" reform and the need to break down the agricultural Communes as quickly as possible. He was a leading participant in the 1979 Wuxi Conference[43] and the first reform economist to stress the need for clarification of the communist concept "ownership-by-the-whole-people". His work on this topic contributed to the design of the Company Law of 1994/5 (which defined various forms of corporate ownership).

With regard to SOEs, Dong suggested, already in 1979, that a distinction be made between SOEs responsible for the supply of "public goods" (such as utilities) and SOEs operating in a commercial/competitive environment (most manufacturing enterprises). The former category should be subject to strict state control and receive subsidies, if necessary, while the latter should be given as much managerial independence (and responsibility for their own bottom line) as possible.

Dong was born in Ningbo and graduated from the Department of Economics of Wuhan University (1950), where he later became a professor and supervised many PhD studies. He also taught economics at Peking University and at Renmin University in Beijing. He published 10 books and hundreds of academic articles on various aspects of China's economy and reform needs. He went to study in Moscow in 1953, where he earned a "deputy doctorate"[44] in 1957. After that he joined the Institute of Economics of the CAS as an assistant to Sun Yefang, his mentor.

Unlike his colleague at the CASS, Zhao Renwei, who was keen to stay away from politics, Dong became a member of the NPC Standing Committee and Vice Director of its Finance and Economics Committee, immersing himself deeply in the legislative process. He was also a member of the CPPCC for many years. Surprisingly, Dong was never awarded the prestigious Sun Yefang economics prize, but was recognized as an "outstanding Chinese scholar" by the French Government in 1987.

9. *Gao Shangquan (b. 1929)*[45]

Gao was only 20 when the PRC was established in 1949 and is not known to have played an important role in economic policy making before the start of market-oriented reforms under Deng Xiaoping in the late 1970s. However, as a staff member of the Ministry of Agriculture (engineering enterprises division), he argued in favor of greater SOE autonomy, already in 1956 (during the "Let a hundred flowers bloom and a hundred schools of thought contend" campaign that followed the 8th Party Congress in September of that year). SOE reform has remained at the center of his professional interests ever since.

Gao was born in Shanghai and studied at the prestigious St. John's University there until his graduation from the Economics Department in 1952 (which was also the year this University was closed by the Government). After working in the Ministry of Agriculture for many years, he became an economic advisor to PM Zhao Ziyang in 1980 and vice minister of SCRES in 1985, a position he held until 1993. In that capacity, he made many big and small contributions to China's economic reforms. In 1992/3, as head of SCRES' "Market Economy Taskforce", he had an important role preparing for the 14th Party Congress of October 1992 and its 3rd Plenum of November 1993 (which gave specific content to the 14th

Party Congress' decision that China would establish a SOCIALIST MARKET ECONOMY, including a "modern enterprise system"). Gao was instrumental in getting the Party to accept the term "labor market" in its reform vocabulary, a small but important victory; use of the term had been resisted by Party ideologues.

His gift for foreign languages, including English, influenced the direction of his professional career. Even before he left SCRES (toward the end of 1993), he became the heart and soul of a professional non-governmental association called "Chinese Society of Economic Restructuring" and organized many national and international conferences explaining China's economic reforms to Chinese colleagues and to the outside world. He was in fact (and in some ways still is) an unofficial economic ambassador at large.

In 1995 Gao was appointed president of the China Institute of Reform and Development (CIRD), a government-supported think-tank cum research and training institute in Haikou, Hainan, with extensive international relations. He held that position for almost 10 years, when he was succeeded by Chi Fulin. Gao and Chi collaborated in the editing and publication by CIRD of hundreds of reports about China's economic development and reform for national and international audiences. He also produced (together with Ye Sen) four very detailed annual reports in English on China's economic reforms (called *China Economic Systems Reform Yearbook, 1990, 1991, 1992 and 1993*), published by China Reform Publishing House, a SCRES organization.

In 1998, he conducted research on economic development at the World Bank in Washington DC as a visiting fellow. Two year later, as a member of the UN Committee on Development Policy, he published an important report on economic globalization in New York.

10. Wu Jinglian (b. 1930)[46]

I agree with Prof. Barry Naughton that "Wu Jinglian is widely acknowledged to be China's most influential and celebrated economist" today.[47] Unlike many of his older and younger Chinese economists-colleagues, Wu never held a powerful executive position. He always remained an independent professional – as academician and policy advisor. His power and influence derive from his recognized professional excellence, personal integrity, courage and independence.[48]

Wu was born in 1930 in Nanjing (then China's capital) in a relatively well-to-do family of entrepreneurs. When Japanese forces attacked Nanjing in 1937, the family fled to Chongqing, which then became the nation's capital. Wu graduated with honors from Fudan University (economics department) in 1954 and joined the Institute of Economics of the CAS in Beijing soon thereafter. There he got to know Sun Yefang, Yu Guangyuan, Xue Muqiao, Du Runsheng, Gu Zhun, Liu Guoguang, Dong Fureng and other Chinese thinkers on economic development and reform. Although Wu had believed, as a teenager, that Mao Zedong was the right kind of leader for China, he admired Sun Yefang and Gu Zhun for their courage to express reservations about Mao's socialist economic policies and agreed with their view that the "law of value" applied as much to capitalist as to socialist economies.

Gu Zhun (who was 15 years Wu's senior) became Wu's mentor at the CAS and a friend. It was on Gu's advice that Wu decided to learn English and study Western economics.

The two periods of Wu's most direct and consequential involvement in economic policy making in China were the mid-1980s (when he was an advisor to PM Zhao Ziyang) and the 1990s/early 2000s (when Zhu Rongji was vice PM (1991–1998) and PM (1998–2003). Wu was the intellectual leader of a group of young Chinese economists, including Zhou Xiaochuan, Guo Shuqing, and Lou Jiwei, who in the early and mid-1980s, as staff members of SCRES, established by Zhao Ziyang in 1982, did much to provide direction to China's early economic reforms. After Wu attended Yale University (1983/4), studying Western economic theories as a guest scholar, he returned to China, joining the State Council's DRC, as a researcher.[49] In that capacity he continued to collaborate closely with the same group of young Chinese economists he had worked with before he went to Yale. Under Wu's leadership, the group produced a very influential report for the State Council *Conceptual Framework for an Overall Restructuring Plan* in 1985. The report, in the preparation of which Ma Hong (then president of the CASS) was also deeply involved, became a key input into China's 7th Five-Year Plan (1986–1990). This is the plan that (for the first time since 1949) aimed at promoting private sector development and at making the economic reform agenda *comprehensive*, in the sense that issues of pricing, fiscal, financial system and trade policy reform, as well as SOE management and SOE ownership reform, would be addressed simultaneously in a consistent, overall framework.

In the 1990s, when Zhu Rongji was Vice PM responsible for the economy ("economic czar"), Wu Jinglian became the unofficial leader of Zhu's unofficial inner circle of Chinese economists who advised him on economic management and reform. Apart from Wu himself, the circle's principle's members were Zhou Xiaochuan, Lou Jiwei, Li Jiange, Guo Shuqing and (initially also) Wang Qishan. Wu took issue with the Party's concept of socialism as a system in which the means of production are publicly owned; in his opinion, the essence of socialism was *the* pursuit of social justice and common prosperity, not ownership of the means of production. In 1993, he and Qiang Yingyi (who became Dean of Tsinghua University's School of Economics and Management in 2006) wrote an article "On Corporatization" arguing that SOE reform should include the legal incorporation of SOEs. The next year (1994), the NPC passed the Company Law (which became effective in 1995), under which SOEs could be "incorporated". The Law defined various forms of corporate ownership and set minimum capital requirements for new companies. (The revised Company Law of 2005 set lower capital requirements to facilitate the entry of private enterprises.)

Also in 1993, Wu co-authored another important article, "A Comprehensive Design for the Near and Medium-Term Reform of the Economic System", with Zhou Xiaochuan. Essentially, that article became the agenda for the 3rd Plenum of the 14th CC of the CPC in November of that year. This 3rd Plenum gave specific content to the decision of the 14th Party Congress of October 1992 to establish a SOCIALIST MARKET ECONOMY, a term that had originally been proposed by Wu Jinglian.

Wu is not only passionate about China's economic development and reform efforts, he is, perhaps above all, a teacher. In China, his nicknames are "Market Wu" and "Teacher Wu". He teaches and guides PhD students at the CASS and at the China Europe International Business School (CEIBS) in Shanghai. He is a much sought-after guest lecturer at Chinese universities and around the world; in the West, he lectured, e.g., at Stanford, MIT, Duke and Oxford. In 2005, he published an English language textbook on China's economic reforms that explains not only what happened, but also why (including the domestic political context in China); it is widely used internationally.[50] In 2011, Wu was named honorary president of the International Economic Association (IEA).

Another factor distinguishing Wu from other important Chinese economist-reformers is the emphasis he places on the need for political reform. This may be the reason he is distrusted by some senior Party members, as became evident in 2008, when it was rumored that Wu was a spy for the US. Those rumors died down relatively quickly, but returned later in circles of contemporary Chinese "Maoists". Wu doesn't explain in his publications exactly what he means by political reform, but it seems that he is echoing Deng Xiaoping's repeated calls for political reform, which then meant (1) the need to strictly separate the Party from Government and (2) the need to strictly separate government administration from SOE management. In his latest book (co-authored with Ma Guochuan, chief commentator of the influential Chinese magazine Caijing, in the form of a dialogue between them),[51] Wu expresses concern that, due to inadequate market reform, China has become a "rent-seeking society" with pervasive corruption and high social inequality. He blames the slowdown in market reforms during the past decade on the growing power of special interest groups in China. He is worried that without deeper economic reforms, there is a serious risk that China's economic system will slide off to some form of "crony capitalism" and that "the dream of generations of Chinese people" to develop China into a prosperous and civilized modern country based on "Constitutionalism, democracy, and rule of law" cannot be realized.

11. Li Yining (b. 1930)[52]

Like Wu Jinglian, Li Yining was born in Nanjing in 1930. There are other similarities between the two as well: when they were young children, their parents fled Japanese occupation forces in eastern China during the Sino-Japan war (1937–1945). Wu's family went to Chongqing (in what was then Sichuan province), whereas Li's family went to Hunan; both Wu and Li became highly respected academic economists committed to market-oriented reforms and are based in Beijing; neither ever held a powerful executive position in government; both have an undergraduate degree in economics (Wu from Fudan; Li from Peking University); and both were attacked by Red Guards during the Cultural Revolution when they suffered humiliations and had to do forced manual labor for "re-education". Both are prolific writers (of books and articles) and served as advisors to the government in the

1980s and 1990s; more of Wu's work was translated and published in English than of Li's work which may have contributed to the fact that Wu is better known in the West than Li. The main professional differences between them appear to be: (1) to improve the efficiency of China's economy, Li assigned priority to SOE ownership reform (through the introduction of shareholding systems) and to strengthening land user-rights for farmers, while Wu focused on price reforms and the need for a *comprehensive* approach to economic reform, (2) Wu traveled widely in the West, became comfortable expressing himself in English, while Li studied Japanese, (3) Li, having worked as a teacher and researcher at Peking University ever since he graduated there in 1955 (except for periods of "re-education" through labor in rural areas during the Great Leap Forward and the Cultural Revolution) is even more a pure academic than Wu, who has worked in a variety of government Commissions and think-tanks and (4) Wu was opposed to continue the "dual-track" pricing system in the late 1980s, insisting that *comprehensive* pricing reforms were needed as soon as possible; Li, on the other hand, found the "dual-track" pricing system perfectly acceptable as an transitional mechanism. In addition, one might say that Li, having written extensively on the role of customs, ethics and morality in China's economy, is more philosophically inclined, while Wu tends to focus more on the role of politics in the economy and the need for political reform.

Li wrote extensively about macro-economic (im)balances and the business cycle and the need for ownership reform but was also strongly interested in firm-level management. He was the driving force behind the establishment of a Business School at Peking University in 1993[53] (named Guanghua School of Management in 1994). Already in the early 1980s, long before the current Shanghai and Shenzhen stock exchanges were officially opened), he tried to convince Party leaders that the best way to improve SOE efficiency was to turn them into independent enterprises responsible for their own bottom line and to subject them to the discipline of a shareholder system. However, Li was keen to preserve the socialist character of China's economy and opposed the full privatization of large SOEs. He recommended that the Chinese state (through the central and local governments, as well as state organizations) retain majority ownership (about 70/30, state/private) of listed SOEs, which is precisely what happened after SOEs began to list on domestic stock exchanges after their official establishment in 1990 and 1991.[54] Li's active promotion of the shareholding system throughout the 1980s earned him the nickname of "Mr. Shareholding". Li regards the market and government as the "dual mechanism" for China's socialist economy; the economy should be "regulated" by the market first and, at a higher level, by the government second.

12. Zhao Renwei (b. 1933)[55]

Zhao is known in China as the economists' economist. He stayed away from politics whenever he could and promoted market reforms from his perch in academia and think-tanks. After his tenure as director of the Institute of Economics of CASS (July 1985–April 1991), he concentrated on issues of income and wealth distribution in China. He graduated from the Economics Department of Peking University in 1957 and joined the Institute of Economics of the CAS (while Sun Yefang was its acting director) that same year, switching to CASS after its establishment in 1977. At CAS he got to know Gu Zhun (who encouraged him to learn English so as to be able to study Western economics), Wu Jinglian, Liu Gouguang, Dong Fureng and, of course, his boss, Sun Yefang. He then became utterly convinced of the need for market-oriented economic reforms in China.

He studied Western economics and perfected his English as a visiting fellow at Oxford's St. Anthony's College, 1982–1984. After that, he returned to China to join the CASS and became a popular interlocutor for visiting foreign economists. As professor of economics at CASS (from 1985 until his retirement in the late 1990s), he taught a generation of younger Chinese economists, many of whom became leading reformers and/or senior government officials. In 1986, together with Wu Jinglian, he published a famous article on China's "dual-track" pricing system for non-agricultural enterprises, arguing that the system was distortive and could at best be accepted as a short-term interim mechanism to facilitate China's transition "from plan to market".[56] His seminal work is a 2001 book *China's Retreat from Equality* (published in the US), which he co-edited and co-authored with Carl Riskin and Li Shi. Zhao's professional work includes many other books and articles, some of which he co-authored with fellow Chinese economists such as Liu Guoguan, Wu Jinglian and Jingji Yanyu.

13. Wang Mengkui (b. 1938)[57]

Compared to most other "in-between" and "older" generation reform economists, Wang stands out as a Party insider, focused on *practical* economic management and institutional reform issues. After graduating from Peking University's School of Economics in 1964, he served in a variety of Party-linked positions, starting as editor of *Red Flag* magazine (1964–1969), a notorious, official organ of the Party. He became director of the DRC (the State Council's in-house think-tank) in 1998 and Chairman of the DRC Foundation[58] in 2007. He participated in the 14th Party Congress (1992–1997) as an alternate member of the Central Committee and in that capacity had an important role in drafting the "Decisions on the Socialist Market-Economy System" of the pivotal 3rd Plenum of November 1993. He was a full member of the Central Committee during the 15th Party Congress (1997–2002) and had an important role in preparing for the 3rd Plenum of the 16th Central Committee of the CPC in November 2003. At that Plenum, the Party decided to reorient its development strategy toward greater regional, social, environmental development and macro-economic balance. It gave a big boost to the ongoing drive for accelerating the development of western provinces.

Wang's articles on China's economy and reform needs are typically non-technical, non-theoretical, and pragmatic. They all focus on clearly defined practical management, policy and institutional issues that arose in China's transition to a market-oriented economic system. In the early 1980s he was especially interested in SOE reform, arguing in favor of what was then called the "one-boss" system. (It meant that top SOE managers had to be professionals with enough power to manage their enterprise top-down, that they should be held accountable for enterprise performance and that "democratic or collective" leadership of SOEs had no place in China's socialist economic system.) Later in the 1980s and beyond, Wang focused on many other practical economic management and institutional development issues such as strengthening the fiscal system, improving income distribution, strengthening land-user rights for farmers, designing a modern social security system (applicable to both state- and non-state parts of the economy), the implications of China's accession to WTO, the need for a clearer definition of property rights and urbanization. Being very persuasive in his articles and his speeches, Wang influenced economic policy making in China in many direct and indirect ways, always in the direction of pragmatic market orientation.

C. *The younger generation*

14. Lu Mai (b. 1947)[59]

In China, Lu Mai is best known for his research on rural development issues and his contributions to rural development policies. For example, Lu is one of the main architects of the abolition of China's millennia-old agricultural tax in the first decade of the 21st century during the government of President Hu Jintao and PM Wen Jiabao. Internationally, Lu Mai is better known for his research on social aspects of globalization, such as, e.g., labor conditions, education, early childhood development, mother and child health care and public welfare institutions in general. On China's behalf, he collaborates frequently with international agencies such as the World Bank, ADB, OECD, ILO and UNDP and is a regular at prominent Western think-tanks such as the Brookings Institution in Washington, D.C.

To illustrate the intellectual distance that members of China's younger generation of reform economists, such as Lu Mai, traveled from the Mao days, when development was equated with industrialization, I quote from a chapter by Lu in a forthcoming book on aspects of globalization.[60]

> Poverty and other deprivations, such as insufficient nurturing and care, or limited social interaction and stimulation, have devastating, life-long effects on young children. Neglect in children's early years is particularly potent and is often manifested as lack of attachment between children and their parents or caregivers. In our ever changing and increasingly mobile world, families are being torn apart by conflict, natural disasters, migration and emigration – all of which take a toll on children's health and development, not only in the short term, but also over a life time. China offers a prime example, for over the past 30 years it has experienced the largest rural-to-urban migration in human history – a migration that has resulted in 61 million children left behind in rural areas under the care of persons other than their parents.

Lu was a baby when the PRC was established in 1949. He did his undergraduate studies in economics in the late 1970s and early 1980s at the Beijing College of Economics and earned an MA in Public Administration at Harvard's Kennedy School of Government in 1991. Before returning to Beijing in 1995, to join the State Council's DRC, he did research for the Harvard Institute of International Development in Cambridge Massachusetts and for the China Business Center of the Hong Kong Polytechnic University. He was appointed Director General of the DRC Foundation – a semi-independent department of the DRC – soon after its establishment in late 1997 and has served in that capacity since, making numerous contributions to China's development and international relations. He is a frequent guest lecturer at Chinese and at foreign universities.

To mark the 30th anniversary of the historic 3rd Plenum of the 11th Central Committee of the CPC of December 1978 – generally considered the start of China's market-oriented reforms under Deng Xiaoping – Lu put together selected writings by Chinese economists on various aspects of the country's economic history since 1949. The writings were published in China (in Chinese) in 15 volumes in 2008. Ten of those volumes were translated into English and published by Routledge in the UK between 2011 and 2017. The availability of this DRC-sponsored series has done much to make the story of China's struggle for economic development (before and after the introduction of market-oriented reforms under Deng Xiaoping in the late 1970s) better known internationally. Lu Mai deserves most of the credit for this.

15. Zhou Xiaochuan (b. 1948)[61]

Apart from Xue Muqiao and Sun Yefang, there are probably no economists covered in this chapter who had greater influence on China's market-oriented economic reforms since the 3rd Plenum of December 1978, than Wu Jinglian and Zhou Xiaochuan, governor of China's central bank since December 2002. He is the longest serving central bank governor of any major country. Although his demeanor is unassuming, as one of the most experienced central bank governors in the world, he has a truly global profile.

Zhou was born in Heilongjiang (about a year before the PRC was established), and raised in Beijing, where his father was a senior government official. Long before Zhou became governor of the PBoC, he was deeply involved in economic policy making in China (as an analyst, advisor and in various senior executive positions). As governor of PBoC, the most important contributions to China's economic reform and development he made (in my opinion) are:

(1) Masterminding the reform, recapitalization and listing of China's state-owned commercial banks;
(2) Gradually liberalizing China's domestic interest rates and the exchange rate;
(3) Setting in motion a process to gradually "internationalize" China's currency;
(4) Conducting monetary policy in such a way that inflation did not become a serious problem, while providing adequate liquidity to support economic growth;
(5) Supervising the emergence and development of domestic capital markets (including a market for corporate bonds).

Zhou started his higher education at the Beijing Institute (now University) of Chemical Technology (from where he graduated in 1975 with an engineering degree). After earning a PhD (in "economic system engineering") at Tsinghua University in 1985, he joined the Ministry of Foreign Trade and Economic Cooperation (MOFTEC, predecessor of MOFCOM), where he served as an assistant minister for 3 years, from December 1986. In 1986, he was also assigned to SCRES (then still under PM Zhao Ziyang), where he worked until 1991 and collaborated closely with a group of fellow reform-minded economists in sister institutions (including, inter alia, Lou Jiwei, Guo Shuqing and Li Jiange) under the intellectual leadership of the more senior Wu Jinglian. This group became the heart of Vice PM Zhu Rongji's inner circle of unofficial advisors in the 1990s. As a student in Beijing, from the late 1970s until joining MOFTEC in 1985, Zhou was already actively involved in thinking and writing about China's structural economic transformation.

In June 1993, when he was a vice president of the Bank of China (BoC), Zhou published an article, co-authored by Wu Jinglian ("A Comprehensive Design for the Near and Medium-Term Reform of the Economic System"), that became one of the most influential papers on economic reform in the 1990s. The "Decision" of the 3rd Plenum of the 14th Central Committee of the CPC of November 1993 and most institutional and reform policy initiatives in 1994 were inspired by that paper. Zhou also authored or co-authored over 100 other academic articles and 14 books. He is a recipient of the Sun Yefang Economics Prize and many other professional awards.

From the time he left SCRES in 1991, until he was appointed governor of PBoC (December 2002), Zhou served in various senior executive positions, including vice president of BoC, deputy governor of PBoC, director of the State Administration of Foreign Exchange (SAFE), president of China Construction Bank and chairman of China Securities Regulatory Commission. During that period, Zhou played an important role in China's joining (as a member) the Bank for International Settlements (BIS), in 1996, and accession to the World Trade Organization in 2001. After China joined BIS, Zhou oversaw the development of domestic financial accounting- and loan risk classification standards consistent with international standards. Earlier, as vice president of BoC (1991–1995), he was deeply involved in the drafting of China's first Central Bank Law and first Commercial Banking Law, both of which became effective in 1995.

Apart from the unification of China's multiple exchange rate system on 1 January 1994, Zhou's biggest contribution to China's development and reform was masterminding the recapitalization and listing of state-owned commercial banks, from the late 1990s through 2010 (when the last of the five Central-Government-owned commercial banks, Agricultural Bank of China, launched its IPO). The Asian financial crisis of 1997/98 significantly increased the perceived urgency of drastic bank reform in China. As vice governor of PBoC (1996–1998) and later governor (from 2002), Zhou played a major role in the design and execution of one of the world's largest and most successful banking reform plans.

A key element of China's strategy for banking reform (Zhou's brainchild) was to seek minority participation by major international banks in state-owned commercial banks prior to their listing.[62] At first, the strategy threatened to become a failure, as the major state-owned commercial banks had a reputation for poor management and were thought to have negative net-worth. But when Bank of Communications (BOCOM) in Shanghai succeeded in selling a minority share to HSBC, many other international banks followed HSBC's example by buying minority shares in other Chinese state banks prior to their listing. Within a few years, after substantial capital injections from the government and with the help of foreign minority shareholders, the largest state-commercial banks were all listed (usually in Hong Kong and Shanghai). Apart from the pre-IPO sale of minority shares to foreign banks and significant internal bank governance changes, China's bank reform process involved, inter alia:

(1) establishing (in 1998) four state-owned asset management companies (AMCs to purchase, hold, auction and/or convert into equity) the state banks' huge portfolio of non-performing loans. Later, one more AMC was added);
(2) auditing of all major state banks to international standards.

Zhou was among the main proponents in China of accelerating domestic financial sector liberalization after the global financial crisis of 2008/9, including a gradual opening of the capital account and removal of interest rate controls. Considerable progress was made, but political considerations and fear of significant capital outflows in recent years seem to have (at least temporarily) interrupted the process. Political opponents of further financial liberalization compared the process to bringing in a "Trojan Horse" that would ultimately undermine Party power.

In March 2009, Zhou proposed reforming the international monetary system such that it would no longer be dependent on the national currency of any particular country (i.e. the US dollar). He referred to the so-called "Triffin Dilemma" as the rationale for his proposal. Partly because Zhou's proposal was effectively ignored by the US, China decided to push the "internationalization" of its own currency a few months later. The IMF's decision to include China's currency, renminbi (RMB), in the valuation base of its Special Drawing Right (SDR) in 2016, enhanced the RMB internationalization process.

Given the importance of China's financial sector and Zhou's contributions to its reform and development, it is not surprising that he was asked to stay on as PBoC governor in 2013, when he reached the mandatory retirement age for senior officials just after a new government had taken over. He is now expected to be replaced as governor in 2018.

16. Li Jiange (b. 1949)[63]

Outside China, Li Jiange is probably the least well-known of the younger generation reform economists included in this chapter. Inside China, however, he is well-known as one of the main architects of the country's economic reform efforts during the 1990s and beyond, especially in the areas of pension system reform, urban housing privatization, mortgage-loan system development and capital market development. Like Wang Mengkui, Li is a Party insider. He was a member of Zhu Rongji's inner circle of informal advisors, together with Zhou Xiaochuan, Lou Jiwei and Guo Shuqing. Internationally, he is best known as chairman and CEO of China International Investment Corporation (CICC), China's first investment bank, during the second term of the Hu Jintao-Wen Jiabao government (2008–2013).

Li was born in Jiangsu, the year of the PRC's establishment. He earned a bachelor's degree in mathematics from Nanjing Normal University in 1981 and a master's degree in economics from the Graduate School of CASS (where he was a classmate of Lou Jiwei) in 1984. He joined the government before the start of Deng Xiaoping's economic reforms and witnessed the dramatic policy changes of the late 1970s as a staff member of the State Planning Commission. During the 1980s, he served in a variety of senior government positions, including the State Council's Secretariat, where he attracted attention as an independent thinker and gifted administrator. His main involvement in economic reform policy making was during the 1990s when he became a member of Zhu Rongji's informal and unofficial inner circle of economic advisors. His expertise in financial and social security issues (including housing finance, pension reform and capital markets) was a major factor in the design and implementation of some of Zhu's most important policies. Li also served in several key executive positions, including director of the China Securities Regulatory Commission (CSRC, China's SEC), 1994–1998, chairman and CEO of China International Capital Corporation (CICC, China's first investment bank), 2008–2013 and deputy chairman of Central Huijing Investment Ltd. (established in 2003 as a financial holding company, owning and managing the state's shares in financial agencies, which in 2007 became a subsidiary of CIC, China's Sovereign Wealth Fund).

Li published many influential academic articles and half a dozen books (all in Chinese) on aspects of China's economic reforms. He teaches at several Chinese universities and is a much sought-after speaker at economic conferences on China's economy around the world. Before he became president of the Sun Yefang Economic Science Foundation in 2009, he was awarded the prestigious Sun Yefang Economics Prize for outstanding economic research three times.

17. Lou Jiwei (b. 1950)[64]

After Zhou Xiaochuan, Lou Jiwei was the highest profile "younger generation" reform economist in China until he stepped down from his post as Finance Minister in November 2016, having reached the mandatory retirement age. He was then appointed president of China's Social Security Fund. Some press reports speculated that he was asked to step down as Finance Minister, allegedly because he pushed too hard for free-market economic reforms.

Although he likes to keep a low profile, Lou tends to be very outspoken (some say "tough-talking", "blunt" or even "pugnacious"). He publicly challenged

Donald Trump's pre-election ideas on trade policy and rejected criticism of China's industrial policies by Jack Lew, his US counterpart until the Trump administration took office.

Internationally, Lou became well-known as chairman and CEO of CIC, China's main Sovereign Wealth Fund (2008–2013). During those years, he was ranked amongst the world's most influential people by *Time* magazine, *Forbes* magazine and *Bloomberg Markets* magazine. Domestically, Lou is best known as a successful Minister of Finance (2013–2016).

Lou was born in Zhejiang (after the PRC had been established) and educated at Tsinghua University (where he earned a bachelor's degree in computer science in 1982) and at the Graduate School of CASS (where he was a classmate of Zhao Renwei and earned a master's degree in econometrics in 1984). Thereafter, he became a key member of an informal group of young economists (including Zhou Xiaochuan and Guo Shuqing) who, in one way or another, worked for PM Zhao Ziyang in the 1980s. As pioneers of market-oriented economic reforms in the early and mid-1980s, under the intellectual leadership of Wu Jinglian, they wrote *Conceptual Framework for an Overall Economic Restructuring Plan*, a very influential report that later underpinned the 7th Five-Year Plan (1986–1990) aimed at promoting *comprehensive* economic reforms, including private sector development. In September 1985, Lou participated in the Bashan Lun (boat) conference on macro-economic management and reform with top international economists. Lou authored or co-authored well over 100 academic articles and several books on China's economy and reform needs. He is a recipient of the Sun Yefang Economics Prize and several other awards.

If China today has a reasonably strong fiscal (and budgetary) system, it is in no small measure due to Lou Jiwei's vision and efforts. As director of the Institute of Finance and Trade of CASS (1984–1988), he became deeply involved in debates on public financial policy issues (taxes, budgetary procedures and central-local fiscal relations). For many years, he fought hard for a complete overhaul of China's fiscal system which finally happened on 1 January 1994 under the leadership of Vice PM Zhu Rongji. He had gotten to know Zhu Rongji when he served as deputy director of the Shanghai office of SCRES (1988–1992), while Zhu was mayor of Shanghai.

After Zhu Rongji moved to Beijing to serve as Vice PM (late 1991) under PM Li Peng and President Jiang Zemin, Lou Jiwei, who became head of SCRES' Macro-Control Department upon his return to Beijing in 1992, became a member of Zhu's informal inner circle of economic advisors. Lou was very much involved in the preparation of a package of macro-economic reforms that was introduced on 1 January 1994, including, inter alia: (1) unification of China's multiple exchange rate system at the then prevailing market rate of 8.7 RMB to the USD, (2) creation of an IRS-type *national* tax agency (for the first time in China's history), (3) replacement of various indirect taxes by a modern, dual-rate, value-added tax (VAT) system, (4) introduction of a national personal income tax system and (5) standard formulas for the sharing of revenues between the central and local governments. After this major accomplishment,[65] Lou was appointed vice governor of Guizhou province (1995) where he served until Guo Shuqing succeeded him in that position in 1998. (When Lou first went to Guizhou as vice governor, Guo succeeded him in Beijing as head of SCRES' Macro-Control Department.) In 1998, when Zhu Rongji had become PM and the Asian financial crisis had spread from Thailand to other countries in the region, Lou and a few other members of Zhu's informal inner circle of economic advisors, persuaded the government to launch a fiscal stimulus program to help protect China's economy against the fall-out from the crisis. China thus became the first Asian country to launch such a program, well before the IMF began to recommend stimulus programs to crisis economies in the region. China's stimulus program of 1998 (which was maintained for several years) was quite effective and allowed the government to gain experience that was very useful when the need for another stimulus program arose during the global financial crisis of 2008/9.

Lou Jiwei also left his mark when he served as chairman and CEO of CIC (China's main Sovereign Wealth Fund) from 2008–2013. In that capacity, he (and his Board) made major investment decisions aimed at improving the rate of return on China's huge foreign exchange reserves. In 2010, he visited President Obama in the White House, offering billions of dollars for the upgrading of America's electricity grid, provided the US created a national Infrastructure Bank to process such investments.[66]

During his time as Finance Minister (2013–2016), Lou Jiwei worked hard to further improve China's fiscal and budgetary systems. An important achievement was the Budget Amendment Act of August 2014. Under that law, provincial governments were permitted, for the first time, to issue their own bonds, the proceeds of which could be used to pay off more expensive, shorter-maturity bank debt. This law was aimed simultaneously at solving a local government over-indebtedness problem and at developing domestic capital markets. Lou was less successful at pursuing other reform objectives, including: (1) introducing a national property tax system, (2) improving China's pension system and (3) reforming the *hukou* system[67] (which has significant fiscal implications).

18. Chen Xiwen (b. 1950)[68]

Chen Xiwen, who was born in Shanghai after the PRC had been established, became an internationally recognized expert in China's rural development. He followed in the footsteps of Du Runsheng. Due to disruptions in higher education during the Cultural Revolution (1966–1976), Chen didn't begin his university education (at Renmin University's Department of Agricultural Economics) until 1978. After he graduated in 1982, he was assigned to the CASS' Institute of Agricultural Economics. From then he has served in increasingly senior research and policy-making positions related to rural development.

As an economic analyst and policy maker, he became influential already in the mid-1980s, when he drew attention to the great (unanticipated) benefits resulting from the spontaneous establishment of millions of (mostly collectively owned) small industrial enterprises at the township and village level. These so-called TVEs provided employment for millions of rural workers made redundant by rapid productivity growth in agriculture, thus avoiding a large flow of rural migrants to the big cities before they could absorb such flows. Chen argued successfully that the government should ensure better access for TVEs to financial resources, but otherwise leave them alone. He was one of the drafters of the "Decisions on the Socialist Market-Economy System" of the 3rd Plenum of the 14th Central Committee of the CPC in November 1993. Chen also had important positions as a deputy to the 16th and 17th National People's Congress (NPC) and as deputy director of the Economic Committee of the Chinese People's Political Consultative Conference (CPPCC). He is a recipient of the Sun Yefang economics prize and several other prestigious awards.

Chen joined the DRC's Rural Economy Research Department in 1990 and became its director a few years later. In 2000, he became a vice president of the DRC. From 2003, Chen was the leader of the Party's Central Rural Work Leading Group, an important (minister-level) policy-making position. In that capacity, he focused on a broad range of rural, agricultural and environmental issues, such as fertilizer and pesticide use, food security, new agricultural technologies and extension services, land and water management and reducing the tax burden on farmers.

The fact that China's agricultural sector has performed so well since the start of market-oriented reforms in the late 1970s/early 1980s, is due, in part, to sensible policies promoted by Chen Xiwen. But it is not only the growth of agricultural output that is important for China's overall economic development; food security and social stability are also very important dimensions of "performance". Throughout his career, Chen focused on reducing rural poverty through various projects and the smooth absorption of millions of rural migrants by rural TVEs and later by industries and construction companies in urban areas. With regard to rural-to-urban migration, Chen fought hard for the reform of China's *hukou* system[69] to improve the access of migrants to urban services. In his writings on this subject he stressed that *hukou* reform is not only a complex cultural issue, but also a major fiscal challenge for municipal governments. As a former deputy director of the Party's Leading Small Group on Finance and Economics, he was in a position to advance suitable fiscal reforms. Another critically important policy area in which Chen became deeply involved is the strengthening of farmer land-user rights and making those rights tradable to promote the development of commercial rural land markets.

Chen's deep involvement in *hukou* reform and related fiscal system and rural land market reforms ensured that he has been at the center of economic policy making in China for many years.

19. Lin Yifu (b. 1952)[70]

Justin Yifu Lin is an outlier among the younger generation reform economists covered in this chapter for several reasons: (1) he came to mainland China from Taiwan in 1979 (less than six months after the 3rd Plenum of December 1978), (2) he earned a PhD (in economics) at the University of Chicago, (3) he had a high-profile international job (as senior VP and Chief Economist of the World Bank in Washington, D.C. (2008–2012) and (4) he chose not to become a member of China's Communist Party. Lin was the World Bank's first Chief Economist from a developing country.[71]

About a year after defecting from the Taiwanese military (by swimming from Quemoy Island, where he was stationed, to the mainland a few miles away), he was admitted to Peking University. There he earned a master's degree in political economy in 1982 (after getting an MBA at National Chengchi University in Taiwan in 1978). With support of Nobel Laureate Theodore Schultz, he was awarded a University of Chicago scholarship for PhD studies, starting in 1982. One of his mentors in Chicago was Gale Johnson, a well-known agricultural economist. After earning his PhD in Chicago (1986), he did research at Yale University for about a year, before returning to China, where he became a protégé of Du Runsheng, the famous agricultural economist (also covered in this chapter).

After his return from studies in the US, Lin joined Peking University as a teacher and became deeply involved in domestic economic policy debates. He was a strong advocate of state-sponsored investment in rural infrastructure (to promote domestic consumption dependent on such infrastructure.) In late 1991, after the collapse of the USSR, he was one of 20 prominent Chinese economists who were consulted by Party General Secretary Jiang Zemin on three major questions during a 3-day private conference: (1) why had the USSR collapsed?, (2) why had capitalism proved so resilient in Western countries? (contrary to what many had expected in light of Marx's theories), and (3) what could China learn from other economic systems? On that occasion, Lin explained the economic success of the four so-called "Asian Tigers" (Singapore, Taiwan, South Korea and Hong Kong) and agreed with Wu Jinglian that China should manage its economy in accordance with modern neo-classical economic theory and call its economic system a "socialist market economy".

As a teacher at Peking University in the late 1980s, Lin earned a reputation as a superb educator. After his World Bank assignment (2008–2012), he returned to Peking University as a local hero. His pronouncement then that China's economy could continue to grow at a very high rate (8% p.a.) for another two decades was met with skepticism, because many of his professional colleagues in China had become convinced that the country's old growth model had run out of steam and that major structural economic reforms were urgently needed to sustain high growth.

Lin's greatest contribution to economics education in China, was his initiative to establish (in 1994) the China Center for Economic Research (CCER) at Peking University.[72] Under his leadership, CCER quickly became China's pre-eminent economic research institution and was later (in 2008) converted into the National School of Development (NDS) at Peking University, which offers, inter alia, a highly rated MBA program called BIMBA (Beijing International MBA).

Lin is one of the most prolific writers among Chinese reform economists covered in this chapter. He published 35 peer-reviewed academic articles in Western professional economic journals, close to 100 articles in Chinese journals and 19 books. He lectured at many foreign universities (in the UK, USA, Australia, Singapore and India) and remains a highly sought-after guest speaker around the world. He was awarded professional honors in several countries, including the Sun Yefang economics prize in China.

In some of his articles and books, Lin explained that Deng Xiaoping's "reform and opening-up" policies had succeeded so well, because those policies permitted the exploitation of China's "comparative economic advantage" in low-cost, labor-intensive manufacturing. By contrast, Mao's industrial policies aimed at promoting heavy industry had failed, because they ran against the country's "comparative economic advantage" at that time. The theme of comparative advantage recurs in Lin's latest book[73] which reflects his World Bank experience and the evolution of his thinking on development and international development aid. The book argues in favor of "South-South Development Cooperation" based on joint learning and concerted efforts aimed at poverty reduction and at "dynamic structural transformation" consistent with the developing country's comparative economic advantages.[74]

20. Guo Shuqing (b. 1956)[75]

Guo, youngest in the group of "younger generation reform economists", is probably also the most highly educated and the one with the broadest career experience. To illustrate this point, I present below a summary of Guo's bio:

- 1956, born in Inner Mongolia
- 1974–1977 (during the Cultural Revolution), laborer at an agricultural Commune in Inner Mongolia
- 1978–1985, student at Nankai University
    - 1982, Bachelor's degree in philosophy
    - 1985, Master's degree in law
- 1984–1986, part-time researcher at SCRES
- 1986–1987, visiting scholar at Oxford University (UK)
- 1988, PhD awarded by CASS (thesis on "Comparative Economic Systems")
- 1988–1993, deputy director Economic Research Bureau of SPC
- 1993–1997, director general of SCRES and member of the Party's Leading Group on Structural Reform
- 1998–2001, vice governor of Guizhou (one of China's poorest provinces)
- 2001–2004, deputy governor of PBoC and president of SAFE, (PBoC's State Administration for Foreign Exchange)
- 2005–2011, chairman and CEO of China Construction Bank (CCB, China's second largest commercial bank)
- 2008, leader of China's delegation to the World Economic Forum in Davos, Switzerland

- 2011–2013, chairman of China Securities Regulatory Commission (CSRC, China's SEC equivalent)
- 2012–2017, member of the CPC's Central Committee
- 2013–early 2017, governor of Shandong (one of China's richest and most populous provinces)
- March 2017–present, chairman of China Banking Regulatory Commission (CBRC).

Guo is the author of over 300 articles and 16 books on various aspects of China's economy and transition to a market-oriented economic system. He is a potential candidate for the presidency of China's central bank. He is a recipient of the Sun Yefang economics prize and several other awards.

Guo has been at the center of China's economic reform efforts since the mid-1980s. He was one of the first Chinese economists to fundamentally reject mandatory or "command" economic planning, while arguing for liberalizing consumer prices and terminating the "dual-track" pricing system (because he considered it distortive and a source of corrupt practices). As a young economist working for SCRES, Guo participated in the Bashan Lun (boat) conference (1985) on economic reform and modern macro-economic management, with top international economists. He was a core member of the team that drafted *Conceptual Framework for an Overall Economic Restructuring Plan* (1985) for PM Zhao Ziyang (under the leadership of Wu Jinglian). That important document underpinned China's 7th Five-Year Plan (1986–1990), which aimed, inter alia, at promoting private enterprise. In the late 1980s, Guo fought for accelerating SOE reforms to improve economic efficiency and stimulate innovation. In the early 1990s, when inflation became a major problem in China, he pushed for financial system reforms and monetary restraints. In the early and mid-1990s, as deputy director of the State Planning Commission and director general of SCRES, he was a member of Zhu Rongji's informal inner circle of economic advisors. During those years, he became deeply involved in studies that led to a comprehensive reform of China's social security system. He participated in many national and international conferences to discuss modern macro-economic management and the need for associated institutional development in China. In the late 1990s, Guo served as vice governor of Guizhou province, succeeding Lou Jiwei in that position. There he learned first-hand about rural poverty and experimented with formulas for simultaneously addressing pension reform and urban housing privatization issues in the capital city, Guiyang.

In the early 2000s, Guo served as deputy governor of China's central bank and president of SAFE, the agency responsible for managing China's foreign exchange reserves, administering capital controls and for balance of payments statistics. Thereafter, he served for almost 6 years as chairman and CEO of China Construction Bank, where he introduced many internal governance reforms, turning CCB into China's second largest commercial bank. He then became China's top securities regulator (chairman of the CSRC. In that capacity, he promoted the development of domestic bond markets, improved access of small and medium-sized private enterprises to equity capital and reformed China's IPO process (by changing the old model that favored SOEs). As governor of Shandong, Guo aimed, inter alia, at improving financial and economic management of Shandong's urban centers by assigning an economic/financial expert as deputy mayor to municipal governments. In early 2017, Guo was transferred back to Beijing as chairman of the CBRC where he is, inter alia, trying to control excessive credit expansion and risky shadow banking.

Notes

1 When Mao was in power, Deng was normally careful not to go beyond Mao's economic policy framework. When he tried in 1975, while Mao was still alive, he was opposed by the "Gang of Four" led by Mao's wife, Jiang Qing.

2 Although Deng was recognized as "paramount" Party leader from 1978, he never was de-jure head of the Party.

3 Information in this brief essay on Xue Muqiao is based on many sources, including, inter alia, Fewsmith (1994); Gittings (2005); Xue Muqiao (2011, in the DRC/Routledge series *Chinese Economists on Economic Reform*); and Wu Jinglian and Ma Guochuan (2016) and personal communications with the Chinese economic historian Fan Shitao.

4 Personal communication.

5 Xue Muqiao (2011, p. 162).

6 The May 4th Movement (of 1919) is seen by many as the prelude to the establishment of China's Communist Party in 1921.

7 He was labeled "the number 1 reactionary academic authority among economists".

8 He may have had a hand in launching the renminbi (RMB) in Shijiazhuan (Hebei) in 1948; the record is unclear on this.

9 The 1st FYP (1953–1957) aimed at rapid industrialization, following the Soviet model. The 2nd FYP (originally meant to cover the period 1958–1962, also prepared with the help of Xue Muqiao) was effectively pushed aside by Mao's Great Leap Forward (started in 1958 and discontinued in the Fall of 1960).

10 The book was published in English by Foreign Languages Press (a state-owned publisher) in 1960.

11 This book was published in English (in 1981) and in several other foreign languages by the state-owned publisher Foreign Languages Press, in Beijing.

12 Some ten million copies of the book are reported to have been printed and distributed.

13 Many of Xue Muqiao's articles on economic reform (written from April 1977–August 1992) were translated and combined in a volume dedicated to him in the series *Chinese Economists on Economic Reform* published by Routledge from 2011–2017. The original series of 15 volumes in Chinese (10 of which were later translated and published in English) was published by the China Development Research Foundation (DRCF) in 2008 on the occasion of the 30th anniversary of the start China's market reforms. The Xue Muqiao volume in English (2011), was edited by his daughter Xiaohe after the author's death. The other nine authors included in the English language series are Du Runsheng, Liu Guoguang, Yu Guangyuan, Ma Hong, Guo Shuqing, Lou Jiwei, Wang Mengkui, Zhou Xiaochuan and Li Jiange.

14 Hu Qiaomu was then President of CASS, which had been created in May 1977 to help guide new thinking on economic and social development. His July 1978 report to the State Council (a year after Deng Xiaoping's political rehabilitation) became one of the pillars of Deng's reform proposals to the 3rd Plenum of the 11th Central Committee of the CPC in December 1978.

15 Perhaps because Xue Muqiao was then head of the Sun Yefang Foundation, which had awarded the prestigious Sun Yefang prize for economics (a kind of local Chinese Nobel

Prize) once every two years since 1985, he did not want to be awarded this prize – see also the section in this chapter on Sun Yefang. (The only other recipients of the Award for Outstanding Contribution (a government administered, but privately funded prize) were Liu Guogang, Ma Hong and Wu Jinglian, all in 2005.)

16 Information in this brief essay on Sun Yefang is based on many sources, including, inter alia, Sun Yefang (1981, 1982, 1983/84); Fung (1982); Fewsmith (1994) and a personal communication from Prof. Wang Yan of Peking University.

17 Personal communication from Prof. Fan Shitao of Beijing Normal University.

18 For a fuller explanation of Sun Yefang's ideas on economic reform, see the introduction by K. K. Fung to his translation of six of Sun Yefang's articles in *Social Needs versus Economic Efficiency. Sun Yefang's Critique of Socialist Economics*. M.E. Sharp, Inc., Armonk, NY, 1982.

19 During the Mao era, Chinese officials and economists were afraid to criticize his policies openly for fear of retribution. If reservations were expressed at all, it was usually done indirectly or obliquely.

20 In a capitalist economic system, "law of value", sometimes referred to as "rule of value", means that the cost of production (including standard rates of profit and capital depreciation) will (in the long-run) be equal to the market price. In a planned socialist economy, it has a normative connotation: goods should be exchanged at prices proportionate to the amount of (standard) labor inputs since "value" was thought to be determined by (standard) labor inputs. Older generation Chinese reform economists, including Sun Yefang, wrote extensively about the "law of value", stressing that the "law" should not be ignored in a planned socialist economy, but used in price setting by the government to achieve plan objectives.

21 Information in this brief essay on Du Runsheng is based on many sources, including, inter alia, Du Runsheng (1989, 2006, 2014, in the DRC/Routledge series *Chinese Economists on Economic Reform*); Fewsmith (1994); and Wu Jinglian and Ma Guochuan (2016) and a personal meeting with Du in Beijing not long before his death.

22 Another Chinese leader who is sometimes given this informal title is Wan Li, Party Secretary of Anhui in the late 1970s. Wan openly sided with local peasants who defied official Party doctrine by breaking up their Communes into individual farms.

23 China's agricultural sector has consistently been one of the best performing in the world since the early 1980s.

24 The system of "dual-track" pricing was extended to industrial SOEs in the mid-1980s and discontinued altogether on 1 January 1994.

25 Du Runsheng favored making land-user rights fully tradable and useable as collateral for bank loans. Since 2008, China's land policies have been moving in that direction, but significant challenges remain.

26 Information in this brief essay on Gu Zhun is based on many sources, including, inter alia, an interview with his daughter Prof. Gu Xiulin, in Beijing in 2015, Wang Hai (2011); Naughton (2013); Zhang Shuguang (2015); and Wu Jinglian and Ma Guochuan (2016).

27 The famous Indian economist/philosopher, who teaches at Harvard.

28 The reason for his dismissal from these key positions is not clear, but may be related to Mao's "Three Antis" and "Five Antis" campaigns of late 1951 and early 1952 (see Annotated chronology)' Evidently, Mao did not trust Gu, who was known to favor greater reliance on private enterprise and markets in economic development.

29 The Institute of Economics of the CAS became part of the CASS when it was established in May 1977, after the Cultural Revolution had ended. CASS's first president was Hu Qiaomu, who became an economic reformer after Mao's death. Hu served as CASS president until 1982, when he was succeeded by Ma Hong, a known reformer. Ma served in that capacity until 1985 when he was succeeded by Hu Sheng (with Hu Qiaomu serving as honorary president).

30 In the late 1950s, Gu was banished by the Party to a rural area where he observed and wrote about (in his diary) deep poverty and famine. When he returned to Beijing, he

re-joined the CAS' Institute of Economics. He was again banished in the early 1960s and was made to suffer terribly during the Cultural Revolution.

31 Gu's essays on economic policy weren't published in mainland China until 1994. In recent years, there has been a revival of interest in China in Gu's work.

32 Information in this brief essay on Yu Guangyuan is based on many sources, including, inter-alia, Fewsmith (1994); Yu Guangyuan (2004, 2014, in the DRC/Routledge series *Chinese Economists on Economic Reform*), and a meeting with his daughter Yu Xiaoqing at the World Bank in Washington, D.C. in 2015,

33 He wrote a book on Deng's contributions to China's early economic reforms: *Deng Xiaoping Shakes the World. An Eyewitness Account of China's Party Work Conference and the Third Plenum (November–December 1978)*. The book was edited by Ezra Vogel and Steven I. Levine, and published (in English) with an Introduction by Ezra Vogel, by Eastbridge, Norwalk in 2004,

34 That's the opinion expressed by Xue Muqiao in his 1979 book, *China's Socialist Economy*, not in earlier publications.

35 Information in this brief essay on Liu Guoguang is based on many sources, including, inter alia, Heng Lin (2006), Liu Guoguang's English language publications included in the bibliography at the end of this book, Fewsmith (1994) and various personal communications with Chinese economists and officials.

36 During the "Japanese War" (1937–1945), three major northeastern universities, Beijing-based Peking and Tsinghua Universities, and Tianjin-based Nankai University, combined to continue teaching jointly in unoccupied southwestern China, first in Changsa, Hunan and then in Kunming, Yunnan, creating "National Southwest Associated University" for that purpose.

37 In May 1977, after the Cultural Revolution had ended, this Institute became part of the newly established CASS.

38 Information in this brief essay on Ma Hong is based on many sources, including, inter alia, Ma Hong (1983, 1990, 2014, in the DRC/Routledge series *Chinese Economists on Economic Reform*) and Fewsmith (1994) and personal communications with the economic historian Fan Shitao of Beijing Normal University.

39 This followed the 6th FYP (1981–1985), which effectively replaced Hua Guofeng's heavy-industry-oriented 10-year development plan (1976–1985), which Deng Xiaoping thought was the wrong way forward.

40 This conference, organized by the World Bank at the request of the Chinese Government, was held on a cruise ship (named Bashan) on the Yangtze River. (Lun is the Chinese word for cruise). The conference is remembered in China as a pivotal event in the evolution of China's market-oriented reforms. The event is described in some detail in Gewirtz. *Unlikely Partners: Chinese Reformers, Western Economists, and the Making of Global China*. Harvard University Press, Cambridge MA, 2017).

41 2005 was the only year that this award was issued, and the 4 reform economists mentioned were the only recipients.

42 Information in this brief essay on Dong Fureng is based on many sources, including, inter alia, Fewsmith (1994); Dong Fureng (1989, 1990, 1992, 1997); Wu Jinglian and Ma Guochuan (2016).

43 See Annotated chronology, April '79.

44 US Master of Arts (MA) equivalent.

45 Information in this brief essay on Gao Shangquan is based on several sources, including, inter alia, Gao Shangquan (1996, 2000), and personal conversations with Gao over many years.

46 Information in this brief essay on Wu Jinglian is based on many sources, including, inter alia, Fewsmith (1994); Wu Jinglian (1991/92, 1993, 2005, 2014); Naughton (2013), and personal conversations with Wu over many years.

47 Naughton (2013). This book contains English language translations of selected articles and speeches by Wu, as well as interviews and comments by Naughton.

48 In 1993, when the World Bank informally approached vice PM Zhu Rongji (then known as China's "economic czar") with a suggestion that China establish a high quality, *independent* economic research institution similar to the Korean Development Institute (KDI), Zhu enthusiastically agreed and proposed that Wu Jinglian should serve as its first head. This proposal never materialized, as it was superseded that same year (1993) by a similar proposal from Lin Yifu, who had already negotiated an affiliation (and office space) for his proposed "China Center for Economic Research" with Peking University. The World Bank then dropped its proposal and, together with the Ford Foundation, provided initial financial support to CCER, enabling Lin Yifu (CCER's first director) to attract highly qualified Chinese economists to the new Center. (CCER was transformed into the "National School of Development" in 2008; NDS offers a BIMBA (Beijing International MBA) program at Peking University and is also a think-tank.)

49 Wu Jinglian was still a "senior researcher" at the DRC at the end of 2016.

50 Wu Jinglian. *Understanding and Interpreting Chinese Economic Reform*. Thomson South Western, Singapore, 2005.

51 Wu Jinglian and Ma Guochuan (2016).

52 Information in this brief essay on Li Yining is based on many sources, including, inter alia, Fewsmith (1994); Li Yining (2010, 2014), and an interview with Li in Beijing, 2012.

53 Li Yining was the dean of Peking University's business school until 2005.

54 Following the start of market reforms in the late 1970s, informal, unregulated and mostly very small, securities exchanges were opened in various Chinese cities, including Shenyang, Wuhan, Shanghai and Shenzhen. The current Shanghai stock exchange was officially opened in December 1990 and the one in Shenzhen in July 1991.

55 Information in this brief essay on Zhao Renwei is based on many sources, including, inter alia, Fewsmith (1994); Liu Guoguang (1985); Riskin (2001), and personal communications with Prof. Zhang Xiaotong of Wuhan University, who is translating a book by Zhao Renwei into English

56 An English language version of that article was published in Reynolds (1988).

57 Information in this brief essay on Wang Mengkui is based on several sources, including, inter alia, Wang Mengkui (2014, in the DRC/Routledge series *Chinese Economists on Economic Reform*), and personal correspondence with Chinese economists in Beijing.

58 The DRC Foundation was established in 1997 as a semi-independent department of the Development Research Centre. DRCF has its own research and conference agenda and earns part of its budget from consultancy work.

59 Information in this brief essay on Lu Mai is based on several sources, including, inter alia, Lu Mai, Jefferson & Zhao 1999; Lu Mai & Wiemer 2005; and Lu Mai & Young 2015; and personal conversations with Lu over many years.

60 Chapter 13 in: "A Bright Star for Every Child: Education in Rural China", in Battro, Sanchez-Soronto and Von Braun (eds), *Children and Sustainable Development, Ecological Education in a Globalized World*. Springer International Publishing AG, (forthcoming).

61 Information in this brief essay on Zhou Xiaochuan is based on many sources, including, inter alia, Zhou Xiaochuan (2017, in the DRC/Routledge series *Chinese Economists on Economic Reform*) and Wu Jinglian and Zhou Xiaochuan (1993), and personal conversations with Zhou over many years.

62 The objective was to gain international respectability for China's state-owned commercial banks and thus to increase their market value in preparation for their IPO.

63 Information in this brief essay on Li Jiange is based on many sources, including, inter alia, Li Jiange (2017, in the DRC/Routledge series *Chinese Economists on Economic Reform*), and personal conversations with Li in the 1990s.

64 Information in this brief essay on Lou Jiwei is based on many sources, including, inter alia, (Lou Jiwei (1993, 2008, 2014, in the DRC/Routledge series *Chinese Economists on Economic Reform*), and personal conversations with Lou over many years.

65 One indicator of the success of China's macro-economic reform package of 1994 is that aggregate tax revenues as a percentage of GDP improved from a nadir of 10.7% in 1993 to over 20% a decade later.

66 This information is based on a conversation between a member of Lou Jiwei's delegation and the author. China's proposal for the establishment of a US Infrastructure Bank was based on their concern that it would be too cumbersome for CIC to deal with dozens of state-level regulatory agencies responsible for electricity grids in the US. A US National Infrastructure Bank was not established and CIC financing for grid upgrading in the US did not materialize.

67 Though a decision to fundamentally reform (and eventually eliminate) the *hukou* system was made at the 3rd Plenum of the 18th CC (Nov. '13), actual progress has been slow.

68 Information in this brief essay on Chen Xiwen is based on several sources, including, inter alia, Chen Xiwen (2014, in the DRC/Routledge series *Chinese Economists on Economic Reform*).

69 China's *hukou* (or family registration) system requires citizens to have a residence permit for a particular city or rural area. The system, introduced by Mao in the 1950s to facilitate agricultural collectivization and prevent unwanted migration, has roots in ancient Chinese history. Under the current system, rural migrants (and their families) working in urban centers without a valid residence permit (*hukou*) for that city generally have no or little access to urban services. Migrant workers in urban China without an urban *hukou* are often the first to be laid off in an economic downturn and the last ones to be hired.

70 Information in this brief essay on Lin Yifu is based on many sources, including, inter alia, Lin Yifu, Cai & Li 2003, Lin Yifu & Wang 2017, Osnos (2010, 2014), and personal conversations with Lin over many years.

71 According to Osnos (2010), Lin changed his original name Lin Zhengyi to Lin Yifu, a Confucian term for a persistent man on a long journey.

72 CCER received financial support from the World Bank and the Ford Foundation during its first few years to enable Lin to attract highly qualified Chinese economists (most of whom were living abroad).

73 The book, *Going beyond Aid: Development Cooperation for Structural Transformation,* Cambridge University Press, Cambridge, 2017, is co-authored by Prof. Wang Yan of Peking University, a former World Bank official, teacher at George Washington University and twice recipient of the prestigious Sun Yefang economics prize.

74 It is evident from this book and many other publications, that Lin is definitely not a "market fundamentalist", notwithstanding his PhD from the University of Chicago.

75 Information in this brief essay on Guo Shuqing is based on many sources, including, inter alia, Guo Shuqing (2012, in the DRC/Routledge series *Chinese Economists on Economic Reform),* and personal conversations with Guo over many years.

4 Chen Yun (1905–1995)[1]

Among China's most important political leaders, after Mao Zedong and Deng Xiaoping, Chen Yun had the greatest influence on economic policy making in China since 1949. Chen was the only senior Party leader *primarily* involved in economic work: a political leader on economic matters. After the PLA and the CPC had gained control over most of northeastern China, well before the PRC was established in 1949, Chen Yun was the Party's chief economic officer for the region, based in Shenyang. After the PRC's establishment, he was head of the Central Economic and Finance Commission, which ran China's economy until the creation of specialized economic agencies (such as the State Planning Commission) in 1952 and a ministerial State Council (Cabinet) in 1953. Together with PM Zhou Enlai, he led economic rehabilitation efforts in the early 1960s, following the disastrous Great Leap Forward. In March 1979, shortly after the historic 3rd Plenum of December 1978, Chen Yun became head of the Finance and Economy Commission to lead economic reforms under Deng Xiaoping.

Chen Yun is less well known internationally than Mao Zedong or Deng Xiaoping, but, as one of the eight "immortals" of China's communist revolution, he is well-known inside the country. I did not include him in Chapter 3 because he was more a politician than a technocrat. His lifelong passion for establishing a *fair and efficient* socialist economic system in China may be related to the fact that he grew up in a family of poor, landless peasants in eastern China. Like Xue Muqiao (who also came from a poor family in Jiangsu and who was born only eight months before him), Chen had to find a job to support himself soon after graduating from primary school. He started as an apprentice for a private printing company in Shanghai, "Commercial Press", at age 13. Through that company, he met many writers who helped him become an *educated* person. He learned much about labor relations, which enabled him to become an effective union leader later.

Later in life, Chen taught himself "political economy" and became familiar with the writings of European socialists of the 19th century, including Marx and Engels, who greatly influenced his worldview. Chen attended the Lenin Academy in Moscow for over a year in the late 1930s and again during the summer of 1952, but did not earn an academic degree.[2]

Chen became a political activist early in life and always remained faithful to his socialist ideals. He joined the (anti-West) May 4th movement in 1919[3] and became a member of the CPC in 1925. He also participated in the anti-foreign May 30th movement that year.[4] Although he later promoted the idea that a state-owned, centrally planned, socialist economic system should be supplemented by (limited) free markets and (limited) private enterprise, Chen retained a strong dislike and suspicion of Western capitalism throughout his political career. He held high positions in the Party and in Government, including inter-alia: member of the Central Committee for 56 years (1931–1987, serving as its vice chairman from 1956–1966), member of the Politburo for over 40 years, First vice PM under PM Zhou Enlai (1954–1965), First Secretary of the Party's Central Commission for Discipline Inspection (1978–1987) and chairman of the CPC Central Advisory Commission (1987–1992), a prestigious position that was apparently created for him after his official retirement from senior Party positions at the 13th Party Congress in October 1987 (following Deng Xiaoping's example).

He participated in (part of) the "Long March" of 1934/5 and developed a strong interest in economic development issues after he joined the CPC Central Committee in Ya'nan (Shaanxi). During most of the time he spent in Ya'nan, he was head of the Party's Operations Department, which gave him significant influence on political decisions and on the careers of fellow Party members. In 1944, the CPC put him in charge of finance in the liberated parts of northwestern China. After the Japanese surrender in 1945, during the latter part of China's civil war, Chen was responsible for finance and economics in the northeastern region, much of which had been liberated by the PLA by then. In his capacity as head of the Party's Northeast Finance and Economics Committee, he arranged for strategic infrastructure investments and other economic improvements in the region while ensuring a balanced budget to reduce inflationary pressures.[5] That experience served him well when he chaired the Central Economic and Finance Commission (CEFC) from the time he returned to Beijing in 1949 until the State Planning Commission (created in late 1952) and a ministerial State Council (Cabinet), created in 1953, became operational. One of the top priorities of the CEFC was to control inflation as quickly as possible. This was done by substituting the newly created RMB for the Nationalist Government's currency and other measures that had been used in the northeast. For inflation control and monetary matters in general, both before and after 1949, Chen relied heavily on the economist Xue Muqiao, who in late 1949 became Secretary General of the CEFC.

Although he was deeply involved in managing the national economy from the time the PRC was established (1 October 1949), Chen kept a low profile. However, in June and July 1956, just before the start of the 8th Party Congress, he made several speeches arguing that a successful socialist economy needed a free-market component for (small) private enterprises to supplement the dominant, centrally planned, state-controlled part of the economy. To ensure healthy debate and quality feedback on what was happening in the economy, Chen even called for "capitalists" to be given leading positions in government and recommended administrative decentralization of the government.[6] If Chen did not (explicitly or implicitly) criticize Mao's policy of accelerating collectivization in agriculture and eliminating all private enterprise, he was at least questioning Mao's methods.

A few months later, at the opening session of the 8th Party Congress (September 20, 1956), Chen delivered another major speech[7] in which he spelled out his concerns about the "scope and speed" with which the non-socialist sector of China's economy ("primarily capitalist industry and commerce") had been force-merged into the socialist sector. He seems to have been comfortable then with the idea that the development of "heavy" industries had to be the core of China's economic modernization efforts and that the core of the economy had to be centrally planned (and controlled) by the state. Chen also felt that the state should be responsible for allocating skilled labor in the economy.[8] Although he supported Deng Xiaoping's "reform and opening-up" strategy of the late 1970s, Chen was certainly not a "free marketeer".

Chen's concerns about Mao's socialist transformation officially focused on its "scope and speed", i.e. methods, not objectives. The main points of his seminal speech for the 8th Party Congress in September 1956 were:

(1) Whilst agreeing that "planned" production and distribution had to be *primary* in China's socialist economy, he found that "the market" (including markets for agricultural "subsidiary" products and a wide range of light industry-based consumer goods) had to play a supplementary role in the economy.
(2) Since he believed in the value of free markets for non-core parts of the economy, he felt that the government should not control prices in those sectors.
(3) The government should not waste time and money collecting unnecessary statistical information on the free market parts of the economy.
(4) Non-state agents should be given a role in deciding what (non-essential) goods to import from abroad.
(5) China's economy could benefit from more decentralized economic decision making.

Although Mao may have been supportive in principle of Chen's idea to leave some room for a free market component in China's socialist, planned economy, in practice, there was no follow-up.[9] In fact, by the end of 1956 there was no private enterprise left in China. Chen's decentralization recommendation, however, was acted upon during the Great Leap Forward[10] (1958–1960), perhaps because Mao had made a similar observation in his famous speech on "Ten Major Relationships" of April 1956. Predictably, the administrative decentralization of 1958 didn't solve SOE efficiency problems. It was reversed in early 1962 by the Central Finance and Economy Small Group (created to guide national economic recovery from the GLF), of which Chen Yun was the most important member.

Chen Yun was not the only senior politician who was critical of Mao's decision to eliminate all private enterprise and introduce a fully state-controlled, socialist, planned economy as quickly as possible.[11] Liu Shaoqi was another. However, Chen was apparently so well liked and trusted by Mao that he was never "punished" for his divergent views. On the contrary, during the first session of the 8th Party Congress in September 1956, Chen Yun and Liu Shaoqi were both promoted to vice chairman of the CPC, a position they both held until 1 August 1966. Apparently, Mao did not see Chen as a competitor, or potential competitor, as he saw Liu Shaoqi and (occasionally) Deng Xiaoping.

Chen began to distance himself from Mao's economic policies in mid-1956. The distance grew in the following years. But Chen stayed away from controversial economic issues in his speeches until after the rehabilitation of Deng Xiaoping in 1977, which he helped engineer. In commenting on the Mao era at the Central Party Work Conference in November–December 1978, just prior to the historic 3rd Plenum of December, Chen Yun is quoted to have said:

> Had Chairman Mao died in 1956, there would have been no doubt that he was a great leader of the Chinese people, a respected, loved and outstanding great man in the proletarian revolutionary movement of the world. Had he died in 1966, his meritorious achievements would have been somewhat tarnished, but still very good. Since he actually died in 1976, there is nothing we can do about it.[12]

After the disastrous Great Leap Forward, the Party looked to Chen to mastermind economic rehabilitation. For health reasons Chen declined to chair the Central Finance and Economy Small Group[13] that was created for that purpose, but he was undoubtedly its most important member. He and fellow senior leaders Deng Xiaoping, Zhou Enlai and Liu Shaoqi agreed to deemphasize "heavy" industrial development and to give priority to agriculture and light industry[14] in a market-oriented setting. The size of agricultural Communes was reduced and in some areas, they were dissolved altogether, giving peasants the opportunity to return to private farming under the HRS.[15] Agricultural output and the broader economy began to recover soon thereafter.

After Mao's death (September 1976) and the arrest of the "Gang of Four" four weeks later, Chen vigorously resumed his public advocacy of a "mixed" economy (including a limited role for free-markets and small private enterprises), but his ideas on this met with resistance from more conservative Party leaders. Chen (together with Marshal Ye Jianying and Li Xiannian, deputy chairman of the CPC and chief economic advisor to Party chairman Hua Guofeng) then urged Hua to rehabilitate Deng Xiaoping and to restore his earlier Party and government positions.[16] Chen knew that Deng was a master-economic strategist and would support his ideas on market-oriented reforms. A year later, Deng was rehabilitated at the 3rd Plenum of the 10th Central Committee of the CPC in July 1977. Soon thereafter, he persuaded fellow Party leaders to go along with Chen's economic reform proposals, which indeed were also his own.

In March 1979, a few months after the historic 3rd Plenum of December 1978, when Deng's de-facto ("paramount") leadership of the Party was firmly established, Chen Yun was asked to chair the newly created Finance and Economy Commission[17] to give specific content to the broad economic reform decisions of the Plenum. This time, he accepted. Three sub-committees were formed:

(1) on Economic Reform, under Xue Muqiao;
(2) on Economic Structure, under Ma Hong;
(3) on Technological Development, under Wang Daohan.

These all reported to Chen Yun and his successor as FEC chairman, Yao Yilin. The Finance and Economy Commission (and its four sub-committees – a fourth one, on Theory and Methodology under Yu Guangyuan, was added later) was critical to kick-starting Deng's market-oriented reforms in the late 1970s and early 1980s.

While Deng and Chen saw eye-to-eye on economic policy in the late 1970s and early 1980s, their views began to diverge not long thereafter. Deng was more determined to push market reforms than Chen, who emphasized that China should remain a socialist, centrally planned economy in which the role of the state was dominant.[18] This led to the ironic situation that ideologically, from then on, Chen Yun was (politically) on Deng's left, whereas he had been on Mao's right (after mid-1956).[19] Chen began to publicly criticize some of Deng's economic policies in 1984. For example, he referred to the Special Economic Zones (SEZs), one of Deng's reform initiatives, as "capitalist beachheads". Many economists and Party leaders then began to see Chen as a brake on China's market-oriented reforms. The same caution that had led him to criticize the "scope and speed" of Mao's socialist transformation in 1956 also led him to criticize the speed of Deng's market reforms from 1984. After the Tiananmen disaster of June 1989, Chen Yun led the Party's conservative opposition to liberal market reforms, which Deng overcame with his Southern Tour of early 1992. Still, despite his conservative leanings, Chen publicly endorsed Deng's views on market-oriented reforms until he withdrew from public life and died a few years later, in 1995.

Notes

1 The most important sources used for this chapter are Chen Yun (1988, 1995); Fewsmith (1994); Wu Jinglian (2005); Bachman (1985); Lardy and Lieberthal (1983); and Hamrin (1990) and personal conversations with Chen Yun's son Chen Yuan, a prominent financial sector leader and reformer in China.

2 Chen did not write books or academic articles. The three-volume *Selected Works of Chen Yun* contains speeches, "talks", newspaper articles and government or Party documents drafted by Chen.

3 This was a nationwide protest movement against the way China had been treated at the Versailles Peace Conference after WWII. The movement, which is well remembered in China today, together with the Bolshevik Revolution in Russia of 1917, contributed to the establishment in 1921 of China's Communist Party.

4 This was a violent popular protest (lasting several weeks, spreading from Shanghai to other cities) against deadly shootings by Shanghai municipal police into a crowd of Chinese protesters in the city's International Settlement zone.

5 There is no evidence that Chen Yun masterminded the creation of PBoC or the launch of the RMB in Shijiazhuang in December 1948, but as head of the regional Finance and Economy Committee, he must have authorized those historic developments.

6 Chen Yun's speech for senior government officials dated 21 July 1956, entitled "Making Use of Capitalists and their Representatives", is included in *Selected Works of Chen Yun, Volume II (1949–1956)*, published by Foreign Languages Press, Beijing, 1997.

7 This seminal speech, entitled "New Problems that Have Arisen Following Basic Completion of Socialist Transformation", is included in volume III (1956–1994) of *Selected Works of Chen Yun,* published by Foreign Languages Press, Beijing, 1999. The fact that it was published in the People's Daily the next day, is a powerful indication that Chen's ideas on the economy, though ignored in practice, enjoyed Mao's support, at

least to some extent. Evidently, from the mid-1950s, Chen's relationship with Mao, which was otherwise very good, became more complicated, because of conflicting opinions on key economic policy issues.

8 This led to the establishment of China's "assignment system" (for the allocation of trained personnel to public sector firms and agencies in accordance with plan priorities), a system that wasn't abolished until the mid-1990s.

9 Mao is reported to have seen and tacitly approved Chen's speech for the 8th Party Congress beforehand. If this is true, it is puzzling why he did not follow up on Chen's advice concerning the role of markets and (small) private enterprises.

10 In launching the Great Leap Forward in 1958, Mao may have intended to move from a socialist to a communist economic system (after the 8th Party Congress in 1956 had concluded that socialism had already been achieved), but the record is not clear on precisely what Mao had in mind.

11 Among economists/technocrats, Sun Yefang and Gu Zhun were the only ones who (obliquely) questioned Mao's socialist policies in their publications at that time. Both were punished by the Party for their divergent views before and during the Cultural Revolution.

12 Reported in *Ming-pao* (Hong Kong) of 15 January 1979, cited in Lardy and Lieberthal (1983).

13 This "Small Group" was modeled after the CEFC that ran China's economy during the first few years of the PRC. In lieu of Chen Yun, Li Fuchun, who had been Chen's deputy in Ya'nan, was appointed chairman.

14 Practically, this shift in priorities was necessitated by the withdrawal of Soviet technical assistance by Khrushchev in 1960 when the Sino-Soviet split broke into the open.

15 Under this system, which was strongly promoted by Du Runsheng (see Chapter 3), individual farmers agreed to sell their "contractual" output to the state at controlled prices, leaving them free to sell any output above that level to private buyers at market prices.

16 The "Gang of Four" had placed Deng under house arrest in April 1976 after accusing him of masterminding anti-government demonstrations in Tiananmen Square earlier that month, in the wake of events that followed the death of Zhou Enlai in January. Hua Guofeng was initially reluctant to rehabilitate Deng, because of his fear that Deng might challenge him.

17 Again, modeled after the earlier CEFC.

18 Chen's idea on how the Chinese economy should be organized is often referred to as his "bird-cage" model; the size of the cage could be varied, giving the economy (the bird) more or less space to move around.

19 The use of the words "left" and "right" in Chinese politics can be confusing. In traditional China, the two words mean the opposite of what they typically mean in the West. Because many scholars are aware of this, "left" and "right" are sometimes reversed in translations of Chinese texts, which adds to the confusion.

5 China's entry into the World Bank

On 15 May 1980, the Executive Directors of the World Bank approved the replacement of the Republic of China (ROC, here referred to as Taiwan) by the People's Republic of China (PRC) as China's representative in the World Bank (WB). A month earlier, the same had happened in the Executive Board of the International Monetary Fund (IMF). The WB became a very important partner of China in the design and implementation of its economic reforms and modernization; probably the number one external partner. This chapter describes the most important developments surrounding the WB's Board's decision of 15 May 1980.[1]

Unlike Mao Zedong, Deng Xiaoping was keenly interested in joining the Bretton Woods institutions (IMF and WB). Soon after the normalization of bilateral US-China relations on 1 January 1979, he formalized ongoing informal efforts to get acquainted with these institutions and to replace the ROC as a member and China's representative on their Executive Boards. When the WB opened for business in 1946, China, represented by the ROC, was a founding member. (The ROC participated in the 1944 Bretton Woods conference that gave birth to the IMF and the WB.) This situation remained essentially unchanged until 1980. Earlier, in October 1971, after the secret visit to China by Henry Kissinger to prepare for president's Nixon's official visit in February 1972, the PRC had replaced the ROC in the United Nations, but the ROC (Taiwan) continued to represent China in the Bretton Woods institutions until April/May 1980. With few exceptions, Western countries did not recognize the PRC when it was established in 1949, but continued to recognize the ROC as "China". During the Mao years, there were several attempts by the PRC (led by PM Zhou Enlai) to replace the ROC in the Bretton Woods institutions, but none of them succeeded, mainly because the US opposed it.

Why Deng was keen to join the Bretton Woods institutions is easy to understand – he saw in these powerful, ostensibly politically neutral, institutions important sources of technical assistance and financial support for the economic reforms on which the country was about to embark under his leadership. (The PRC's earlier ban on borrowing from Western countries and agencies had already been lifted in mid-1978, based on recommendations from a study mission to Western Europe led by Vice PM Gu Mu.)[2] The fact that the PRC replaced the ROC as China's representative in the WB is common knowledge, but how Robert McNamara, then WB president, succeeded in avoiding potentially serious financial problems with the ROC (Taiwan), is not. During my tenure as WB representative in China (1993–97), I got to know part of that story.

McNamara was concerned that Taiwan might default on its financial obligations to the WB, if evicted against its will. The ROC had borrowed substantial amounts of money from the WB for infrastructure and other development projects. A default by Taiwan would have jeopardized the Bank's critically important triple-A bond rating, which kept (and keeps) the cost of WB loans relatively low for developing member countries. Already in the fall of 1971, after Henry Kissinger's secret visit to China and the PRC's replacement of the ROC in the UN, when a change in the relationship between the PRC and the US (and the West in general) was "in the air", McNamara took measures to protect the WB's bond rating.

As WB president at the time, McNamara took great care to ensure that the sensitive membership transition (from ROC to PRC) would proceed smoothly and that the WB would provide not only substantial financial support for China's modernization, but also high-quality technical assistance based on international experience and best practice. Prior to the Board meeting of 15 May 1980, he personally visited China to discuss the transition and possible WB assistance for China's economic development with Deng Xiaoping.

Another key actor responsible for bringing China into the WB was Shahid Husain, a Pakistani national. He was the WB's regional vice president for East Asia and the Pacific at the time and enjoyed McNamara's full confidence.

Shahid Husain's first (private) visit to China (in 1978)

Husain was appointed VP for the WB's East Asia and Pacific region in early 1977, not long after his return from Pakistan, where he had served as economic advisor to PM Bhutto while on leave of absence from the WB. Bhutto was keenly interested in China, which may have inspired Husain. As Pakistan's foreign minister in the 1960s, Bhutto had signed a mutual security and border realignment agreement with China, which cemented the (still existing) "all-weather" friendship between the two countries. After Mao's death in September 1976, the arrest of the "Gang of Four" four weeks later and the return of Deng Xiaoping to central leadership positions in 1977, it became clear to China watchers around the world that China would fundamentally change course in its approach to economic development and international relations. This is precisely what began to happen after the historic 3rd Plenary Session of the 11th Central Committee of the CPC in December 1978.

At that time, China was still isolated and essentially a "black box" for the Western world. The country was very poor and underdeveloped. For much of their knowledge on mainland China, Western observers depended on a handful of journalists in Hong Kong who peered across the border and listened to Chinese radio broadcasts to find out what was happening there. In early 1978, Husain decided that, as WB vice president for East Asia, he had to become better acquainted with what was going on in China, but since there was no official relationship between the PRC and the WB at that time, he could not visit the country in his official capacity. With the knowledge and encouragement of McNamara, he approached Pakistan's deputy foreign minister in Islamabad, a family friend, to discuss the possibility of a private visit to China. The visit was arranged by Pakistan's foreign office and took place in the summer of 1978. Husain and his wife Nigar traveled from Washington to Beijing on Pakistan International Airlines via Islamabad and stayed in China for three weeks as guests of the Chinese Government. They visited Beijing, Shanghai, Nanjing, Urumqi and Kashgar (known in China as Kashi). Husain met with senior Chinese officials, but no written records of those meetings are available (except, perhaps, in China). Undoubtedly, he briefed McNamara and senior WB officials upon his return to Washington.

Shahid Husain's second (private) visit to China (in 1979)

About a year later, Husain visited China again in his private capacity, this time alone. The visit was again arranged by Pakistan's foreign office, but this time it was more official, in the sense that Husain was accompanied to the Pakistan-China border by a unit of the Pakistani army and received on the other side by a unit of the People's Liberation Army (PLA), which accompanied him to Beijing. Again, Husain met with senior Chinese officials, but no written records of those meetings are available (except, perhaps, in China). He probably discussed how the PRC might join the WB, replacing the ROC (Taiwan) as China's representative and thus benefit from development assistance from the WB group.[3]

Breakthrough in establishing official WB-PRC relations

The real breakthrough came only after the normalization of bilateral US-PRC relations on 1 January 1979. It was shortly thereafter that the PRC's first ambassador to the US, Chai Zemin, on behalf of the government in Beijing, approached McNamara to officially express the wish of his authorities to join the WB. Since the Chinese knew that they had to be a member of the IMF before they could join the WB, discussions with the IMF (led by Jacques de Larosière, Managing Director and Tun Thin, director of the Fund's Western Hemisphere department) had already started.

In early March 1980, ambassador Chai invited McNamara to visit China to discuss membership with his Government in Beijing, as soon as possible. McNamara accepted the invitation and visited Beijing from 10 to 15 April. He was accompanied by Shahid Husain, Moeen Qureshi (VP Finance), Heribert Golsong (deputy General Counsel) and Caïo Koch-Weser (personal assistant to McNamara). The timing of McNamara's visit was probably related to a mission to Taipei in late March by Sr VP Operations Burke Knapp and General Counsel Lester Nurick to brief the ROC (Taiwan) on the likelihood that the WB's Executive Board would soon approve the PRC's request to join the institution and to discuss the issue of Taiwan's debt to the WB (about which more later).

One month after McNamara's return to Washington, the WB's Executive Board decided that the PRC would represent China in the institution from then on.

Edwin Lim's early involvement in bringing China into the World Bank

Ed Lim, a Chinese-speaking Philippine economist in the WB, played an important role in this. Sometime after the reunification of North and South Vietnam (1975), he became the WB's lead-economist for Vietnam. (His boss in the WB's East Asia and Pacific region from 1977 was Shahid Husain.) The easiest way to travel to Hanoi from the US at that time was via Beijing. The PRC's liaison office in Washington DC issued special transit visas to WB staff for that purpose. As the outside world knew very little about China's economy then, the opportunity to visit Beijing, even if only in transit, was welcomed by WB staff. During one of those visits (in 1979), Ed visited his ancestral village in Fujian Province and was invited to dinner in Beijing with Lin Jixing, director of research of the Bank of China and leader of an interagency team studying the feasibility of the PRC joining the Bretton Woods institutions. The dinner was also attended by Wang Liangsheng (who later became China's director on the WB's Board), Dai Qianding (who later became China's director on the IMF's Board) and Zhang Xiaokang (who later became China's ambassador to Singapore). As part of their investigations, the Chinese study team had already visited Yugoslavia and Romania to learn about their experience in dealing with the IMF and the WB. Ed Lim's impression from the dinner discussion was that the study team's greatest concern was how to obtain "soft" loans (at that time interest-free, 50-year maturity) from the WB's International Development Association (IDA). Ed pointed out that a member country's eligibility for IDA funds had to be established based on the WB's analysis of the country's economy. Much of the dinner discussion therefore was focused on procedures for preparing a WB study of China's economy.[4]

Ed had also been involved in preparing for China's entry into the WB as leader of a study group formed at the request of McNamara, drafting and commissioning briefing papers on China's economy. The group commissioned papers by economic experts from around the world, who were familiar with China's economy, including Wlodzimierz Brus, P.C. Chen, Mark Elvin, Shigeru Ishakawa, Nicholas Lardy, Dwight Perkins, Thomas Rawski, Ashwani Saith, Peter Schran and Christine Wong.

After the May 1980 WB Board meeting, at which it was decided that the PRC would be recognized as China's representative in the WB from then on, Edwin Lim continued to play an important role in shaping the China-WB relationship under the leadership of Shahid Husain. He was deputy chief of the WB's first economic mission to China in the Fall of 1980 (producing a multi-volume report of China's economy, which was mainly *backward-looking* and served as a guide to formulating the WB's initial assistance program for China.[5] In 1984, he was chief of the WB's second economic mission to China (requested by Deng Xiaoping personally), which produced another influential, this time *forward-looking*, report in 1985. The report examined China's economic development potential and reform priorities. These and subsequent WB economic reports were also used by other international agencies and governments as a basis for formulating their own development assistance programs for China.

The WB's first economic mission to China in the Fall of 1980, included three Chinese professional staff members: Shu-Chin Yang (trade economist), Wen-Poh Ting (agriculturalist) and Kuo Chang Ling (power engineer). The first of these three is known to have played an important role in bringing the PRC into the WB and in providing professional training for Chinese economists and government officials in Western economics and development.[6]

The China-Pakistan connection

Shahid Husain was not the only senior Pakistani national in the WB who played an important role in managing the PRC's entry and in shaping the WB's initial assistance program. By coincidence several key positions in the WB were then occupied by Pakistanis, including Moeen Qureshi (then VP Finance), Parvez Hasan (chief economist for the East Asia and Pacific Region) and Syed Kirmani (project director for the East Asia and Pacific Region). Qureshi accompanied McNamara on his mission to China in April 1980 to discuss China's prospective membership with Deng Xiaoping. Hasan (with Ed Lim as deputy) led the Bank's first economic mission to China in the Fall of 1980 – a mission that comprised 30 WB experts and consultants and an equal number of Chinese counterparts, including Zhu Rongji, who was already then, a leading reformer and later became prime minister. Kirmani, who, prior to joining the WB, had been co-responsible for building the huge, WB-supported Tarbela hydro-electric dam in Pakistan, persuaded the Chinese to accept international technical assistance for the development of engineering standards, international- and local competitive bidding, the appointment of an *independent engineer* for conflict resolution during project implementation, as well as the adoption of standard project accounting and reporting procedures.

Given the friendly relations and trust that existed between Pakistan and the PRC, and McNamara's awareness of it, the Pakistani "mafia" in the WB was very important in establishing productive relations between the WB and China quickly. It is impossible to determine precisely how important those factors were, but it is likely that it would otherwise have taken the WB much longer to become effective in China.

The gold equity and Taiwan debt issues as obstacles to the PRC's WB membership[7]

When the PRC was established by Mao Zedong on 1 October 1949, China's membership in the then existing multilateral institutions (UN, GATT, IMF and WB) stayed with the ROC (Taiwan), because the ROC, governed by the Nationalist Government of Chiang Kaishek was recognized as China's legitimate representative in those institutions, by the US and most other Western countries. In 1950, the ROC was expelled from GATT (on the ground that it had no control over the PRC's customs area). On 25 October 1971, about three months after Henry Kissinger's secret visit to China to prepare for president Nixon's visit in February 1972, the UN General Assembly recognized the PRC Government in Beijing as China's legitimate representative in the UN (thereby expelling the ROC from all UN organizations, including the Security Council.)

Before and after 1971, the government in Beijing made several (unsuccessful) attempts – usually through third parties – to expel Taiwan from the Bretton Woods institutions, claiming that Taiwan was a province of China and that the ROC Government was not legitimate. These complex legal-political battles focused primarily on IMF membership as that was (and is) a prerequisite for WB membership. Membership transition in the IMF and the WB did finally occur in April and May 1980, respectively.

Three critical financial issues had to be resolved in connection with membership transition in the Bretton Woods institutions:

(1) what to do with the gold paid into the IMF and the WB by the ROC;[8]
(2) how to adjust China's quota in the IMF; and
(3) how to ensure that the ROC would continue to pay its debt to the WB after the membership transition.

Proper management of membership transition was also important for ongoing efforts to replenish the WB's "soft" loan window (IDA) for the poorest member countries. The US director on the Executive Board of the IMF feared that adverse reactions in the US Congress to improper handling of the transition, might have "deleterious effects" on the pending US contribution to IDA replenishment. This was an important issue, because many of the WB's poorest members were dependent on IDA credits, and the US was IDA's largest contributor.

Regarding the gold issue, both the ROC and the PRC claimed ownership of the equity that China had paid into the Bretton Woods institutions. The ROC insisted that its contribution should be restored to Taipei before membership transition could be considered. However, the IMF legal department concluded that, if gold restitution took place before formal membership transition, the IMF Board could determine whether the gold belonged to Taipei, to Beijing, or to both. The US representative on the IMF Executive Board lobbied hard for a solution that would allow Taiwan to get most of the gold, which commercially was worth a lot more than it had been when it was originally paid in, because the Nixon Administration had abandoned the Bretton Woods Gold Exchange standard in August 1971 and the market value of gold had risen sharply since. In the end, it was decided that Taiwan would receive 470,708 ounces[9] of China's gold in the IMF and 40% of the "profit" due to gold price appreciation; the remainder of the gold and the "profit" would go to the PRC. At the PRC's request, the IMF did not publicly announce that part of the gold would be restored to Taiwan.

At the IMF Executive Board meeting of 17 April 1980 (on the transition of membership from the ROC to the PRC), it was also decided that China's IMF quota would be SDR550 million. Beijing accepted, but announced that it would soon seek a quota increase. An ad hoc IMF board meeting in August recommended an increase of China's quota to SDR1,200 million, which was approved at the IMF's annual meeting in the Fall. China's quota was further increased first to

SDR1,800 million and later to higher amounts) after that annual meeting. However, given the rapidly growing size and global importance of its economy, China's IMF quota remained grossly inadequate. Under US leadership, at the G-20 meeting in Seoul (2010), it was decided to significantly increase China's IMF quota (and to also increase the voting power of some other emerging economies), but the US Congress delayed its ratification of the Seoul agreement until December 2015. All other IMF member countries ratified the agreement much sooner. Since the US has de-facto veto power over IMF quota decisions,[10] the G20 decision of 2010 could not be implemented until after ratification by the US Congress.

The Taiwan debt issue (in connection with the replacement of the ROC by the PRC as WB member)

This was mainly the concern of the WB, though the IMF, as the Bank's sister Bretton Woods institution, was keen to get the issue resolved satisfactorily. At the time of the 1971 UN decision to recognize the PRC instead of the ROC as China's representative in UN organizations, Taiwan's debt to the WB was about $100mn. By the end of 1979, when the transition of China's membership was "written-on-the-wall", it had grown to about $260mn[11] ($245mn IBRD, $15mn IDA), plus a small amount of loans from the International Finance Corporation. By then all World Bank commitments to Taiwan had been fully disbursed.

In 1971 McNamara was already concerned that a problem over Taiwan's debt to the WB could have adverse consequences for the credit rating of WB bonds and hence for the price that borrowers would have to pay for future WB loans. In the fall of that year, after Henry Kissinger's secret mission to China and around the time that the UN General Assembly decided to admit the PRC and expel Taiwan (ROC), fearing that the Taiwan debt issue might seriously complicate the anticipated membership transition, McNamara instructed the director of the World Bank's East Asia programs department, Ray Goodman, to discuss the issue with China's (i.e. then the ROC's) embassy in Washington, D.C. The embassy's representative, Martin Wong, was understanding of the issue and cooperative in finding practical solutions for the (potential) problem.

In December 1971, Ray Goodman and Martin Wong, special advisor to the Chinese (ROC) ambassador, signed an Aide Memoire that included the following key points:

(1) China (ROC) would not apply for new WB loans or IDA credits;
(2) the WB would continue to disburse on existing loan/credit commitments;
(3) China (ROC) would service its debt to the WB group on time "in all circumstances";
(4) China (ROC) would buy WB bonds in the amount of its debt to the WB anytime the WB would request it to do so.

This remarkable document[12] served as the basis for WB – ROC relations until 15 May 1980 when, following the IMF's decision of 17 April, the WB Executive Board unanimously decided to recognize the PRC as China's legitimate representative in the institution. When the membership transition came close and McNamara had accepted an invitation to visit China personally to discuss the matter with the government in Beijing, he sent his deputy, Burke Knapp, together with the WB's General Counsel, Lester Nurick, to Taipei (27–31 March 1980) to brief the ROC government on the likelihood that the WB's Executive Board would soon approve the PRC's request to join the institution. The Knapp/Nurick mission also discussed the Taiwan debt issue and found to its surprise, that finance minister Philip C.C. Chang was unaware of the 1971 Aide Memoire referred to above and even questioned the authority of Martin Wong to have signed it on behalf of the ROC. He insisted that the IMF gold restitution issue should be resolved to Taiwan's satisfaction first and suggested that the WB refrain from making any statements on the Taiwan debt issue, until the gold issue had been settled. McNamara was horrified to hear this and instructed Burke Knapp to discuss the issue as soon as possible with Martin Wong, then the ROC's most senior representative in Washington, DC.

Knapp reminded Martin Wong (who was again understanding and cooperative) of the Aide Memoire he signed on 7 December 1971 and of the need for Taiwan to strictly observe the terms of that agreement, not only to protect the WB's standing in global capital markets, but also Taiwan's own creditworthiness. He indicated that McNamara would be willing to recommend to the Board that Taiwan remain eligible for procurement under World Bank projects after the membership transition.[13] He is also reported to have pointed out that, should Taiwan renege on its financial obligations to the WB, the PRC, as China's representative in the WB, would then have the legal right to send agents to Taiwan to inspect assets created with the proceeds of WB loans to the ROC. This warning was apparently the "deal clincher".[14] However unhappy ROC officials may have been with the membership transition, Taiwan continued to service its debt to the WB faithfully; the WB never exercised the option of requesting Taiwan to buy WB bonds in the amount of debt outstanding. The IMF gold restitution issue was resolved only after Knapp's mission to Taipei and his follow-up meeting with Martin Wong.

The WB-China partnership after May 1980

After the board meeting of 15 May 1980, Shahid Husain visited China many times in his capacity as regional VP. In June/July 1980, he went to explain the need for a baseline WB study of China's economy and to discuss project priorities and procedures for project appraisal, supervision, procurement and the disbursement of funds. Although the PRC's ban on borrowing abroad had just been lifted, there was no bureaucratic infrastructure in China for the processing of WB loans. It was agreed that – for the first time since 1949 – a "Western" agency – i.e. the WB – would undertake a comprehensive study of China's economy, with the active participation of local Chinese experts.[15] The size and importance of the WB's first economic mission to China have few parallels in the history of the institution. Fortunately, the main conclusions and recommendations of the WB's first economic report on China were consistent with the opinions of leading local Chinese economists at the time such as Xue Muqiao, Yu Guangyuan, Liu Guoguang, Ma Hong and Dong Fureng.[16] A few years later, the WB's second economic report on China was similarly well received by Chinese officials and independent economists alike.

The Chinese had indicated to the McNamara mission of April 1980 that they were seeking financial and technical assistance for projects in agriculture, light industry, heavy industry, energy and transportation, especially ports and railways. A few months later, Shahid Husain agreed with the Chinese that the three top priorities for WB assistance should be higher education, agriculture and ports. The WB was encouraged to find that a 10-year, Soviet-style, heavy-industry-oriented development plan championed by CPC chairman Hua Guofeng had been shelved and that China wished to reduce the national investment rate from the (then) unusually high level of 33% of GDP to around 25%, while domestic consumption, agriculture and light industry would be promoted. A follow-up mission to examine China's capacity for preparing and implementing projects suitable for WB support – led by Syed Kirmani – found that China had achieved a much higher level of technical capacity for planning, designing and implementing, even very large and complex projects, than most WB borrowers. Many of China's leaders at that time had been trained as engineers and were inclined to equate economic development with building infrastructure. They looked to the WB to learn about international best practices and engineering standards.

Following the Kirmani mission, the WB designed its projects to address institutional weaknesses that had been identified. In this way the projects became primary vehicles for a large flow of technical assistance from the WB to many sectors of the economy, including basic infrastructure such as highways, railways, hydro-electric dams and irrigation works, thermal power plants, power distribution, seaports and river ports, water supply and wastewater treatment, oil and gas exploration, as well as agriculture, afforestation, grain storage, education, health care, SOE reform, legal system and financial sector development, pension system reform, labor market development, urbanization etc. The first and second higher education projects provided numerous scholarships for study abroad, modern laboratory equipment for technical universities, as well as domestic training programs for economists and government officials (designed and delivered by the WB's Economic Development Institute (EDI). In the process of developing an initial "pipeline" of projects suitable for WB support, both sides were greatly assisted by training programs for Chinese project staff financed by UNDP. Later, training programs for local staff were included as an integral feature of almost all WB-supported projects in China.

The WB's program[17] for China became quickly very large. In the mid-1990s, some 10,000 Chinese were involved full time in the administration and management of WB-supported projects all over China, except Tibet. Numerous WB-supported projects were being implemented almost everywhere else. With the exception of one quick disbursing "adjustment" loan in the late 1980s, all WB loans and IDA credits for China financed investment- or technical assistance projects.[18] The most important part of the WB group's contribution to China's economic success was not financial – though at about $70bn for almost 800 projects,[19] it was important – but policy advice, technical assistance and training through projects and other vehicles. Indeed, the most important WB contribution to China's economic reform and modernization has probably been institution building, i.e. the development of rules, standards, and organizations for the financing, management and supervision of projects in accordance with sound technical and financial standards (including accounting and auditing). For example, in 1994, the WB provided financial support from a modest grant facility – together with the Ford Foundation – to kick-start the China Center for Economic Research at Peking University; CCER was converted into the National School of Development (at Peking University) in 2010.

Except for a one-time drawing on its General Reserve in 1986 (SDR600 million)[20] to shore up its foreign exchange reserves, China never borrowed from the IMF. China's relationship with that institution was mainly centered on macroeconomic analysis and policy consultations.

China's economic performance since the start of market-oriented reforms in the late 1970s has been outstanding. From 1980 through 2016, China's GDP increased no less than 26-fold! It became an "upper middle-income" country, the world's largest economy (measured by "purchasing-power-parity (PPP) exchange rates, the second largest measured by market exchange rates), largest manufacturer and largest exporter in less than two generations. China's economic miracle is widely regarded as one of the greatest achievements in economic development and a turning point in world history.

Notes

1 Not all of the story in this chapter is part of the public record. Some of the information is based on communications with WB staff who played a role in bringing China into the WB, including Shahid Husain, Edwin Lim and Natalie Lichtenstein and Mrs. Nigar Husain, widow of Shahid Husain (who died in 2015). The story is also based on personal memories, WB archives, IMF archives and archives of the Hoover Institution at Stanford University.

2 See Annotated chronology '77–early '80 (1) and July '78.

3 Including IBRD (International Bank for Reconstruction and Development), or WB proper, IDA, (International Development Agency), the WB's cheap loan window for poor countries, IFC (International Finance Corporation), for participation in private-sector projects, MIGA (Multilateral Investment Guarantee Agency) and ICSID (International Centre for Settlement of Investment Disputes).

4 Most information in this paragraph is based on Edwin Lim's Preface for the book *Fifty Economists Look at Thirty Years of Reform and Opening*, which was published (in Beijing, in Chinese) in 2008. Ed prepared an English language translation of this Preface for his non-Chinese-speaking friends and colleagues; see Lim (2014).

5 After translation of this report by the Chinese government, it also served as teaching material at Chinese universities.

6 Shu-Chin Yang(1916–2001) was one of the first Chinese to be awarded a Fulbright Scholarship for study in the US (1946–49) after WWII. (He had earned an MA in economics from Nankai University in 1943.) With the help of a Rockefeller Fellowship, he continued his studies in the US and earned a PhD in economics from the University of Wisconsin in 1954. He then went to work for the UN in Bangkok (ECAFE) and joined the World Bank in Washington DC in 1963. After his retirement from the WB in 1982, he was hired as a consultant to design and deliver training programs in China of the Economic Development Institute (EDI) under the WB's first higher education

project for China. While working in the WB in late 1970s and early 1980s, the Chinese Embassy in Washington DC and senior officials in China informally consulted Dr. Yang on issues concerning WB membership, which helped to build the understanding and trust necessary for the formal relationship to develop. (My source of information on Dr. Yang's career and role in the WB's relationship with China is his daughter, Ms Catherine Yang of Bethesda MD, USA.)

7 A detailed review of the gold equity and IMF quota issues is provided in Bessma Momani (2013). Another important source of information on the transition of China's membership in the Bretton Woods institutions from ROC to PRC is Jacobson and Oksenberg (1990). The Taiwan debt issue was mostly dealt with discreetly by McNamara himself, Moeen Qureshi (VP Finance), Burke Knapp (SR VP Operations) and the Bank's General Counsel Lester Nurick.

8 This gold restitution issue was highly complex for political, financial and legal reasons; not all files in the WB and IMF archives on this subject have been declassified. The matter was complicated by the fact that in 1980, gold was worth a lot more than it had been when it was paid in originally, due to the Nixon Administration's decision of August 1971 to abandon the Gold Exchange standard. A further complication is that the IMF agreed to honor a PRC request not to make public the information that part of China's gold in the IMF was restored to Taiwan. Consequently, the story on the gold restitution issue in this chapter is incomplete and may not be reliable.

9 Information in this chapter on the gold restitution issue is limited to China's gold in the IMF. It is based on Momani (2013) and on a memorandum from the IMF Secretary to the IMF Executive Board on the gold restitution issue, dated April 16, 1980. Taking into account the gold price appreciation between August 1971 and April 1980, a "back-of-the-envelope" calculation suggests that the PRC received about 62% of China's gold in the IMF at that time and Taiwan about 38%.

10 Most important IMF board decisions require a super-majority of 85% of the vote; the US is the largest single shareholder, with 16.74% of the vote.

11 This increase in Taiwan's debt to the WB was due to disbursements on loans that had already been contacted by 1971; Taiwan did not apply for new loans from the WB after 1971.

12 Document retrieved from the Burke Knapp files in the archives of the Hoover Institution at Stanford. (Burke Knapp, who died in 2009 and was no. 2 in the World Bank under president Robert McNamara, at the time of the PRC-ROC membership transition in 1980, left his personal files to the Hoover Institution).

13 This recommendation was accepted by the WB's Executive Board and the WB's "General Conditions" were amended accordingly.

14 This colorful story was related to the author by Shahid Husain and is not part of the official record.

15 Since the withdrawal of Soviet advisors from China in 1960 until the start of market-oriented reforms under Deng Xiaoping in the late 1970s, there had been almost no involvement of foreign advisors in China's economy. Thanks to Deng's leadership and pragmatic decision-making, China's suspicion of Western economic advisors was then soon overcome. The WB's credibility with Chinese leaders was enhanced by McNamara's evident independence from the US government.

16 A remarkable aspect of China's market reforms after 1978 is that the effort was inspired and supported by Chinese economists who had been trained in Marxist economics.

17 WB program here is understood to include investment and TA projects supported by IBRD loans and/or IDA credits.

18 China is exceptional in this regard. From the early 1980s, quick disbursing "adjustment" loans became common for many other developing member countries. China resisted this trend; it did not need balance-of- payments support and preferred to rely on the technical assistance embodied in WB/IDA projects and joint studies.

19 By the end of June 2016, accumulated WB loans and IDA credits to China stood at almost $60 billion for 399 projects. (China's own financial contribution to these projects

was usually a multiple of the WB's.) By then, the International Finance Corporation (IFC), a WB subsidiary for private-sector development, had invested almost $12bn (in loans, equity and guarantees) in 394 projects in China.

20 This was a so-called "first-tranche" drawing (worth $597.7 million at the SDR/USD conversion rate at the time), which did not require approval of the IMF board.

6 Unfinished reform agenda

This is the hardest chapter to write. Twenty years ago, I thought I knew where China was heading and felt reasonably confident that the country was on the right track to achieve its development objectives. Today, I am confused about where China is heading and concerned that the country may no longer on the right track. I believe that significant further system changes are still needed, but am not sure precisely what, when and how. After explaining the reasons for my concerns, this chapter makes some suggestions for further systemic reform, both economic and political. Although there is no obvious model to follow,[1] China should, in my opinion, continue the "reform and opening-up" process that was started in the late 1970s. Because China's economic development over the past four decades has been so amazingly successful, it is possible that some current leaders think that the country's economic system is about as good as it can get and that all that is needed is some "fine-tuning".

How can anyone know when the transition from one economic system to another is essentially complete? The need for change never stops, not in China, not anywhere. No society has ever reached a system of economic and political organization, that is stable and good for all time. The Decision Memorandum of the 3rd Plenum of the 18th Central Committee of the CPC in November 2013 – about which more below – commented: "there can never be an end to the need for the emancipation of individual thought or for continuing reform and opening-up".[2]

Like most China watchers in the West, I was enormously encouraged by the economic and political changes Deng Xiaoping brought in the late 1970s and beyond. By insisting on pragmatic thinking instead of ideological thinking, he was able to re-direct policy making in fundamental ways. Like many outside observers, I felt that it was indeed time for China to put the "century of humiliation",[3] the political confusion that followed the revolution of 1911 and the ideology-driven economic mismanagement under Mao Zedong[4] behind it. We welcomed the idea that living standards in China would rapidly improve and the Chinese economy would gradually integrate with the global economy.

I was impressed by what I observed in China during the years I headed the World Bank's office in Beijing. It was a refreshing and in many ways surprising experience. Government officials were very good at recognizing China's economic problems and at anticipating new ones. They were focused on the long-term, determined to succeed and usually did the right thing for economic development. When things went wrong, they weren't shy to go back to the drawing board and make policy corrections; they didn't blame foreign advisors, as less confident officials of other developing countries might have done. They were competent, hard-working and had no chip on their shoulders; they were keen to learn from international experience. While many international observers believed that China's economic miracle couldn't last and that the economy would eventually crash for one reason or another, I learned not to bet against China.[5]

Deng's "reform and opening-up" strategy and its initial success, triggered an avalanche of official and unofficial development assistance from many sources. The flow of bilateral financial assistance from Japan was the largest, by far. The World Bank was the most important source of multilateral aid. Then came the Tiananmen disaster of June 1989. This tragic event significantly cooled Western enthusiasm to support China's modernization efforts (although the World Bank found a way to continue its operations in and dialogue with China).[6] For a while, it seemed that economic reforms had come to a halt, as the Party was internally divided. But Deng rescued the situation with his "Southern Tour" in early 1992.[7] Private investment from overseas Chinese (especially in Hong Kong and Taiwan), and from Western companies, took off from the second half of 1992, while WTO-entry negotiations went into high gear. After a few years, official and unofficial development assistance from many sources also resumed and became even larger than before "Tiananmen". Private investment from Japan, Korea, the US and Europe accelerated later in the 1990s.

Like many others in the West, I (perhaps sub-consciously) expected that, as a result of Deng's "reform and opening-up" policies, China's political system would turn democratic sooner or later, and that the country would also in other ways become more "like us". We thought that that would be good for China and for the world. We wanted China to be our friend and, although there was (or is) no unique Western economic or political model, we nonetheless expected that China's society would gradually begin to resemble ours.[8] I now realize that that was an unrealistic, even naïve expectation. China is unlike any other developing country. It wants to have good relations with the West, but does not want to be like the West. Its long history, unique culture, large population and geographic size make China a case "sui generis". (The fact that China tried "communism", essentially a Western ideology,[9] might be seen as a historical anomaly.) Only China can determine its future, but what that will be is less clear today than it seemed 20 years ago.

If we accept that China will not become "like us", is there anything the outside world can do to help China find itself and ensure that its role in the global community will be constructive? I believe there is much the West can do, but first I should reiterate that I am no longer as confident as I used to be that China is on the right track.

To illustrate my concerns, I refer to Government Document No. 9 of early 2013[10] – even though it was apparently not officially released and only circulated in inner Party circles – it seemed to signal a fundamental change in Party priorities, from economic development and reform to the restoration of Party power and national prestige. Such a shift in priorities seemed to be confirmed by subsequent warnings against the use of Western textbooks by Chinese universities, as they might promote "Western values".[11] Similarly, President Xi's relentless efforts to restore Party discipline, combined with the fueling of nationalistic sentiments by state media and delays in the implementation of reforms promised by the 3rd Plenum of November 2013, seem to point to a change in Party priorities.

Nonetheless, China's financial authorities continued to push for further financial sector liberalization, including capital account opening, as previously promised. But, when the Shanghai stock exchange slumped in mid-2015 and large net capital outflows occurred later that year, the Government addressed those problems by relying on old-fashioned, heavy-handed state intervention. In November 2016, Finance Minister Lou Jiwei, an internationally respected and experienced technocrat, devoted to sensible market-oriented economic reforms, though close to retirement, resigned.[12] Many outside China saw this as confirmation of their fear that economic reforms had taken a backseat to the Party's political agenda.

So, what can the West do to help China get back on a more promising reform track? It may be naïve, but I believe that it is very important for China to be recognized internationally as a unique *developing* country, growing and modernizing in its own way, not trying to emulate any existing "model". Government officials are very much aware of the country's size and importance in the world, but always stress its relative poverty and the need to catch up with more advanced economies. Security perspectives of China and the West will probably continue to clash; in China's opinion, the country is not aggressive in international relations (not even in the East and South China Seas), but merely restoring its traditional rights and international influence. Chinese leaders often remind foreign counterparts that their country needs a peaceful international environment to complete its transition to modernity and assume a prominent leadership position in the world.

What can China do to get back on a reform track that is not only good for China, but also conducive to stable and positive relations with the rest of the world? In my view, China should complete the economic *system* reforms that were started in the late 1970s and strengthen its economic institutions. Much remains to be done. There are still significant system inconsistencies, and China's economy is not nearly as open to foreign trade and investment as could reasonably have been expected and would be in China's own interest. Also, there still are far too many underperforming, overleveraged SOEs and outright "zombies", which are a drag on the economy. Many regulatory agencies remain weak. Resuming intensive domestic economic reforms involves both policy- and institutional changes, including political changes. Regarding the economy, the "Decision" of the 3rd Plenum of November 2013 provides an excellent agenda.[13] Regarding policies and institutions, China needs to ensure that its economic and political systems are "in sync", or at least on a path toward convergence, which does not seem to be the case at present. Much can be done in the economic arena before political reform is onto the "critical path."

As mentioned, the "Decision" of the 3rd Plenum of November 2013 provides a useful agenda for further economic reform. Obvious priorities, recognized by the Plenum, are:

(1) strengthening the fiscal position of lower-level governments;
(2) pursuing genuine SOE reform (based on hard budget constraints and genuine competition);
(3) accelerating household registration (*hukou*) reform;
(4) further financial system reform;
(5) creating rural land markets.

Although some progress has been made (e.g., a deposit insurance scheme was already introduced and official interest rate controls were lifted), much of what remains to be done lies beyond simple "fine-tuning". If he had been alive, Deng would probably not consider the present economic model satisfactory.

Regarding the Party's overall objective to create a "socialist market economy",[14] the three most important principles included in the 3rd Plenum's Decision of November 2013 are:

(1) A commitment to *deepen comprehensive reform* based on the earlier "reform and opening-up" process.
(2) That "the market" should play a *decisive* role in the allocation of resources.
(3) That the state should continue to have a *dominant* role in the economy.

Depending on what is meant by *dominant* and *decisive*, there can be serious conflict between the second and third principles. In my opinion, potential conflict has already become a reality, which explains the seemingly *schizophrenic* nature of China's current half-reformed economic system.[15] The state (i.e. the Party) and the market cannot both have a leading role in the economy at the same time. (I realize that this is a typical Western perspective on China's situation, but that doesn't make it invalid.)

The key question in my mind is whether China wants to become a genuine market economy. If the answer to that question is affirmative, China should be willing to accept a less prominent role for the state in the economy. This is, of course, not a "black-and-white" issue; nor is it a new one. Already in the 1980s, when Deng Xiaoping called for "political reform", which he did repeatedly, he was referring to the need to strictly separate (1) Party and Government, and (2) government administration and SOE management.[16] Deng never fully achieved these objectives. Neither did PM Zhao Ziyang, who tried several times in the late 1980s, but gave up when the opposition from Party conservatives became too strong. China's present leadership seems to have given up on pursuing Deng's "political reform" objectives.

When we use the term "political reform" today, almost 40 years after Deng Xiaoping first used it in a major policy speech, we usually have more fundamental reforms in mind. However, the question whether China ultimately wants to become a "liberal democracy" is not on the "critical path" today. A lot can be achieved in the economic arena without fundamental political change.

China's future political model

Although a review of political reform options is not on the agenda for this book, it is obviously important that China's economic and political systems are "in sync", or, at least on a path toward convergence. This does not seem to be the case at present. At the risk of revealing my own political biases and ignorance about China, I'd like to suggest the following system changes – all aimed at improving *accountability, transparency* and *the protection of human rights*:

(1) The government should manage the economy primarily through regulation, macro-environment and environmental policies, not through direct interventions such as "industrial policy" and subsidies for SOEs.
(2) If the Party wishes to retain public ownership of certain commercial enterprises or utilities, it should ensure a competitive environment for those enterprises and full separation of government administration from SOE management.
(3) Promote a genuine rule-of-law system based on the Constitution, as envisaged by Sun Yat Sen early in the 20th century.[17] Ultimately, the Party should subject itself to the rule-of-law and accept the principle of "separation of powers" between Party and judiciary. If China decides against having a multi-party political system, other checks on the power of the ruling CPC are needed.
(4) Improve the protection of human rights, including freedom of expression, as per the Constitution.[18] Freedom of expression would require scaling back (and eventually eliminating), censorship functions of the Party's Propaganda Department.[19] Media restrictions should be lifted retroactively, so that a full accounting of historical events, such as the Tiananmen demonstrations of 1976 and 1989 and other controversial episodes, can yet occur.
(5) Allow for the nomination of more than one candidate for senior Party positions and subject appointments to a transparent electoral process.
(6) Establish a system of "downward" accountability in the incentive framework for Party and Government officials. Senior positions should only be filled by people who are known to care for those "below" them, for the community and for the environment. The present system of "upward" accountability remains, of course, necessary, but it is not sufficient.
(7) Establish a system of mandatory assets declaration or other checks on the moral integrity and fiscal probity, for senior Government and Party officials.
(8) If at some point, China decides to adopt a multi-party political system, opt for a parliamentary system with a proportional representation, rather than a US-style "winner-take-all" system.

In the absence of adequate additional economic and associated political reform, there is a serious risk that domestic conflict between political principles and economic principles will lead to domestic instability and/or international conflict. If China stays on the current track, its semi-reformed economic system may degenerate into some form of "crony capitalism".[20]

China's future economic model

It's been a long journey since Deng Xiaoping changed the direction of economic policy making in China in the late 1970s, but the end of the road is not in sight. Almost certainly, China's future economic model will be unlike a US-style laissez-faire, capitalist system. Although never publicly acknowledged, it seems that the US economy did serve as a kind of model for China until about a decade ago, when the global financial crisis, which started in the US (and other factors), sharply reduced China's appreciation for America's economic system.

Will China nonetheless become a genuine market economy? Under its current political system, probably not; current indications are that it will not be recognized as such by leading Western economies anytime soon. Most probably, China will continue to have a large private sector[21] and encourage private entrepreneurship,[22] but, barring unforeseen political change, the state (i.e. the Party through the government) will probably continue to play a central role in the national economy, including research.

The shape and modalities of China's future economic system will not only depend on Party preferences, but also on how the country's rapidly growing middle class influences domestic developments through changes in public opinion and behavior. In the foreseeable future, the main instruments for the Party to exercise control over the economy are likely to remain:

(1) unique political and regulatory powers over the behavior of private enterprises, both foreign and domestic;
(2) public ownership of key industries;
(3) de-facto control over the allocation of production factors (land, natural resources, capital and key personnel in the public sector).

China's current economic system is sometimes called "state capitalism".[23] Uncertainty about its future economic system concerns mainly the *degree* of state control. Obviously, the state has significant economic functions. The challenge is to find a workable and sustainable balance between the Party's political and economic principles and objectives. There are many different economic systems, including different forms of capitalism; maybe China will be the first country to find a "third way"; a workable and sustainable balance between socialism and capitalism. But, whatever the characteristics of its final "model", China should in my view avoid prolonged dependence on "industrial policy" and similar state-directed economic interventions. To guide reforms and long-term economic development, "industrial policy" may be needed. It can be beneficial, provided such policies do not interfere with basic market and efficiency principles. Any direct interventions by the state in the economy should be consistent with China's comparative economic advantages.[24]

China's Belt and Road Initiative (BRI)[25]

This is a is an important initiative, which may play a role in shaping the country's future economic model. BRI has both economic and political dimensions. It is obviously intended to improve China's development prospects and enhance its influence in the world, but, depending on how it is implemented, BRI can also enhance economic development in many other countries. It is based on the expectation that connective infrastructure will promote trade and development all around. It will not "solve" China's current excess capacity problem in many industries, but it may help to reduce it, while creating new markets for China's large, often underutilized, construction companies.

Through BRI, China can share its enormous experience in infrastructure development (and its large construction capacity) with fellow developing countries. OBOR had a slow start but is beginning to morph from "vision" to a network of concrete projects in many countries. China is expected to finance a significant portion of related investment needs. For that purpose, it has already created the Asian Infrastructure Investment Bank,[26] a $40 BN Silk Road Fund (under PBoC) and contributed to the BRICS bank (called "New Development Bank", NDB) in Shanghai and a related (IMF-style) Contingent Reserve Arrangement, CRA.[27] The Chinese Government has tentatively pledged $1 trillion financing for OBOR projects over 10 years and, because AIIB is too small to handle all OBOR financing, has assigned significant financial co-responsibility to China Development Bank and China Export-Import Bank; state-controlled commercial banks are also expected to participate.

BRI/OBOR represents a vision on international development cooperation and on the relationship between infrastructure and development that is based on China's own experience.[28] It has great potential for promoting long – term economic development in Eurasia (including China itself), Africa and the Middle-East. The main risks I see are:

(1) that Chinese leaders may see BRI/OBOR as an alternative to domestic economic reforms;
(2) that China fails to understand why some countries are suspicious of its political objectives and that, as a result, potentially beneficial economic results cannot be realized.

BRI has the potential to become a major, constructive approach to international development cooperation only if it does not become a substitute for (difficult and sometimes painful) domestic economic reforms in China. Should that happen, China may eventually lose the capacity to finance and otherwise mastermind the network of interrelated projects and experience OBOR as burden.

Notes

1 Mao Zedong initially tried to follow the Soviet economic and political model, but after some years began to diverge from that path, because he saw serious problems with it. Communism, as conceived by Marx and Engels in the 19th century and idealized/romanticized by Mao, was essentially a "Western" ideology; a successful communist, economic and political system had never been realized anywhere. Today, more than 40 years after Mao's death and almost 40 years since the start of "reform and opening-up", there is no obvious model for China to follow either.
2 The Decision Memorandum of this 3rd Plenum, containing 60 decisions on many different subjects, is summarized in English in *China Daily*, a government-owned newspaper, on 16 November 2013. The main economic decisions are summarized in the Annotated chronology, Nov.9–12, '13.
3 The period from the first Opium War (1839–42) until the end of WWII in 1945.
4 This is, of course, not to deny that Mao also made significant positive contributions to China's economic development, for example, by vastly improving basic health and education and by promoting women's rights.
5 The "China collapse" theory, promoted by Gordon G. Chang in *The Coming Collapse of China*. Random House, New York, 2001, has remained popular in certain circles.
6 Against the wishes of the US and other G7 shareholders, WB president Barber Conable authorized a visit to Beijing by the director of the bank's China department Javed Burki within weeks after the disaster.
7 See Annotated chronology Jan.–Feb. '92.
8 My expectations and those of many other China watchers in the West, were well captured in James Mann, *The China Fantasy: How Our Leaders Explain Away Chinese Repression*. Viking Penguin, New York, 2007.
9 As Martin Wolf reminded us in an interview with Wang Yang of the FT's Shanghai office on 8 June 2017.
10 For a summary of the main points of document #9, see Annotated chronology April 13. (A Chinese law professor informed me at a conference in the US in 2015 that document #9 had been withdrawn and that the version that was leaked to a Western magazine was only a draft.)
11 See, for example, Chris Buckley. "China Warns against 'Western Values' in Imported Textbooks." *New York Times*, 30 January 2015.
12 Like several previous retired Finance Ministers, Lou Jiwei was appointed chairman of the National Council for China's Social Security Fund.
13 A relatively "bland" Communiqué of the 3rd Plenum of Nov. 2013, was followed a few days later by a detailed explanation of the Plenum's "Decision", comprising 60 decisions in 16 categories.
14 This the term that was adopted at the 14th Party Congress of October 1992. See Annotated chronology 12–19 Oct. '92.
15 For example, the lack of consistency in the government's development plan for manufacturing is clearly laid out in a report by the European Chamber of Commerce in China dated March 2017: *China Manufacturing 2025. Putting Industrial Policy Ahead of Market Forces*.
16 See Annotated chronology, 18 Aug.'80.
17 For an overview of China's ideas about democracy since the revolution of 1911, see Orville Schell (2017).
18 Many articles in chapter II of China's Constitution provide for specific human rights, including freedom of expression, that do not seem to be observed by the Party.
19 Named "Central Publicity Department" in English. See Shambaugh (2007).
20 For an elaboration of these risks see Wu Jinglian and Ma Guochuan (2016).
21 Since the late 1990s, China's private sector has been dominant in terms of its relative contributions to GDP and total employment.

22 In his work report for the NPC of March 2015, PM Li Keqiang referred to "mass-entrepreneurship" as the best hope for China's economy in the long-run (see chronology, March '15).

23 Another term that is sometimes used to describe China's economic system is "Developmental State". In China, the term "state capitalism" was first used in a 1953 report by Politburo member Li Weihan to describe the economic system he thought would enable China to make the transition to socialism safely and quickly (see chronology, 15 June '53).

24 Many advanced economies, including the US and Japan, benefited greatly from government-led "industrial policies" (and government-sponsored basic research), especially during the second half of the 20th century.

25 The official name for BRI is "Silk Road Economic Belt and 21st-century Maritime Silk Road", also known as "One Belt One Road" (OBOR).

26 AIIB, originally a Chinese proposal (made in 2013), has become a genuinely multilateral development institution, owned by 57 member countries. It is based in Beijing and started operations in 2015. It can finance infrastructure projects anywhere in the world.

27 NDB and CRA, originally Indian proposals, are jointly owned by the 5 BRICS countries: Brazil, Russia, India, China and South Africa. They can only lend to member countries; NDB, which is not limited to infrastructure projects, made its first loan at the end of 2016.

28 China has often built infrastructure "ahead of demand". Although there are obvious limitations to this strategy, China has demonstrated that it can trigger broader development under certain circumstances.

Bibliography

Note: All works listed are available in English.

Apter, David E. and Tony Saich. *Revolutionary Discourse in Mao's Republic*. Harvard University Press, Cambridge, MA, 1994.

Âslund, Anders. *How Russia Became a Market Economy*. The Brookings Institution, Washington, DC, 1995.

Bachman, David M. *Chen Yun and the Chinese Political System*. Institute of East Asian Studies, University of California, Berkeley, Center for Chinese Studies, 1985.

Barnett, A. Doak. *Communist China; the Early Years*. Praeger, Santa Barbara, CA, 1964.

Bell, Daniel A. *The China Model: Political Meritocracy and the Limits of Democracy*. Princeton University Press, Princeton, NJ, 2015.

Bradley, James. *The China Mirage: The Hidden History of American Disaster in Asia*. Little, Brown and Company, New York, 2015.

Brahm, Laurence J. *Zhu Rongji: The Transformation of Modern China*. John Wiley & Sons (Asia) Pte Ltd., Singapore, 2002.

Brandt, Loren and Thomas G. Rawski, eds. *China's Great Economic Transformation*. Cambridge University Press, Cambridge, 2008.

Brus, Wlodzimierz and Kazimierz Laski. *From Marx to Market: Socialism in Search of an Economic System*. Clarendon Press, Oxford, 1989.

Chang, Gordon G. *The Coming Collapse of China*. Random House, New York, 2001.

Chang, John K. *Industrial Development in Pre-Communist China*. Edinburgh University Press, Edinburgh, 1969.

Chen Xiwen. *Collected Works*. (Edited by China Development Research Foundation), (in CDRF Series *Chinese Economists on Economic Reform*). Routledge, Abingdon, UK, 2014.

Chen Yun. *Selected Works* (in III volumes, 1926–1994). Foreign Languages Press, Beijing, 1988.

Chen Yun. *A 320-Page Pictorial with about 45 Pages of Accompanying Text in Chinese and in English*. (Edited by the Department for Research on Party Literature of the Central Committee of the Communist Party of China and Xinhua News Agency). Published by Central Party Literature Publishing House, Beijing, 1995.

China Manufacturing 2025. "Putting Industrial Policy Ahead of Market Forces." European Chamber of Commerce in China, Beijing, March 2017.

"The China Quarterly." *Special Issue: The History of the PRC (1949–1976)*, December, 2006.

Christman, Henry M., ed. *Essential Works of Lenin: "What Is to Be Done?" and Other Writings*. Dover Publications, Inc., New York, 1966.

Coase, Ronald and Ning Wang. *How China Became Capitalist.* Palgrave, New York, 2012.

D'Amato, Paul. *The Meaning of Marxism.* Haymarket Books, Chicago, 2006.

Deng Liqun. "On the Correct Handling of the Relationship between the Planned Economy and Market Regulation." *Chinese Economic Studies*, Spring, 1993.

Deng Xiaoping. *Fundamental Issues in Present-Day China.* Foreign Languages Press, Beijing, 1987.

Deng Xiaoping. *Selected Works* (in III volumes, 1938–1992). Foreign Languages Press, Beijing, 1992.

Department for Research on Party Literature of the CPC CC and Xinhua News Agency, ed. *Chen Yun.* Central Party Literature Publishing House, Beijing, 1995.

Dikötter, Frank. *Mao's Great Famine: The History of China's Most Devastating Catastrophe, 1958–1962.* Bloomsbury, New York, 2010.

Documents of Chinese Communist Party Central Committee, September 1956–April 1969, Volume 1. Union Research Institute, Hong Kong, 1971.

Dong Fureng. *Rural Reform, NonFarm Development, and Rural Modernization in China.* World Bank, Washington, DC, 1989.

Dong Fureng. *Industrialization and China's Rural Modernization.* St. Martin's Press, New York, 1992.

Dong Fureng and Peter Nolan, eds. *The Chinese Economy and Its Future.* Polity Press, Cambridge, UK, 1990.

Dong Fureng and Peter Nolan, eds. *Market Forces in China: Competition and Small Business.* Zed Books, London, 1997.

Donnithorne, Audrey. *China's Economic System.* Praeger Publishers, New York, 1967.

Du Runsheng. *China's Rural Economic Reform: Many People, Little Land.* Foreign Languages Press, Beijing, 1989.

Du Runsheng. *The Course of China's Rural Reform.* International Food Policy Research Institute (IFPRI), Stanford University, Palo Alto, CA, 2006.

Du Runsheng. *Collected Works.* (Edited by China Development Research Foundation), (in CDRF Series *Chinese Economists on Economic Reform*). Routledge, Abingdon, UK, 2014.

Eaton, John. *Political Economy: Marxist Textbook.* International Publishers Co., Inc., New York, 1966.

Engels, Friedrich. *Anti Duhring, Herr Eugen Duhring's Revolution in Science.* Wallachia Publishers, New York City, 2015.

Evans, Richard. *Deng Xiaoping and the Making of Modern China.* Hamish Hamilton, London, 1993.

Fallaci, Oriana. "Deng: Cleaning Up Mao's Mistakes" (Interview). *Washington Post*, 31 August and 2 September, 1980.

Fang Lizhi. "The Chinese Amnesia." *The New York Review of Books*, 27 September, 1990.

Fang Lizhi. *The Most Wanted Man in China: My Journey from Scientist to Enemy of the State.* (Translated by Perry Link, the book was written in 1990 when the author and his wife were refugees in the US Embassy in Beijing, following the Tiananmen "Disturbances" of 1089). Henry Holt and Co., New York, 2016.

Fewsmith, Joseph. *Dilemma's of Reform in China: Political Conflict and Economic Debate.* M.E. Sharpe, Armonk, 1994.

Fewsmith, Joseph. "The Third Plenary Session of the 16th Central Committee." *China Leadership Monitor, No. 9, the Hoover Institution*, Winter, 2004.

Fewsmith, Joseph. *China Since Tiananmen: From Deng Xiaoping to Hu Jintao.* (Second edition). Cambridge University Press, Cambridge, UK, 2008.

Friedman, Milton and D. Rose. *Two Lucky People: Memoirs*. (Chapter 30 and Appendix C). The University of Chicago Press, Chicago, 1998.

Fukuyama, Francis. *Political Order and Political Decay: From the Industrial Revolution to the Globalization of Democracy*. Farrar, Straus and Giroux, New York, 2014.

Fung, K.K., ed. and trans. *Social Needs versus Economic Efficiency in China: Sun Yefang's Critique of Socialist Economics*. M.E. Sharpe, Inc., Armonk, NY, 1982.

Gao Shangquan. *China's Economic Reform*. MacMillan Press Ltd., UK and St. Martin's Press, Inc., USA, 1996.

Gao Shangquan. *Economic Globalization: Trends, Risks and Risk Prevention*. UN, Development Policy Analysis Division, New York, 2000.

Gao Shangquan and Ye Sen. China Economic Systems Reform Yearbook. SCRES, China Reform Publishing House, Beijing, 1990, 1991, 1992, 1993.

Gewirtz, Julian. "Milton Friedman's Misadventures in China." *The American Scholar*, Winter, 2017.

Gewirtz, Julian. *Unlikely Partners: Chinese Reformers, Western Economists, and the Making of Global China*. Harvard University Press, Cambridge, MA, 2017.

Gittings, John. *The Changing Face of China: From Mao to Market*. Oxford University Press, Oxford, 2005.

Gittings, John. "Xue Muqiao (1904–2005), Architect of China's Market Transformation: Obituary." *The Guardian*, 16 August, 2005.

Gregor, James A. *Marxism and the Making of China: A Doctrinal History*. Palgrave, New York, 2014.

Guo Shuqing. *Collected Works*. (Edited by China Development Research Foundation), (in CDRF Series *Chinese Economists on Economic Reform*). Routledge, Abingdon, UK, 2012.

Hamrin, Carol Lee. *China and the Challenge of the Future: Changing Political Patterns*. Westview Press, Boulder, CO, 1990.

Harrold, Peter, E.C. Hwa and Lou Jiwei, eds. "Macroeconomic Management in China." Proceedings of a Conference in Dalian. The World Bank, Washington, DC, June 1993, 1994.

He Weifang. *In the Name of Justice: Striving for the Rule of Law in China*. The Brookings Institution, Washington DC, 2012.

Helleiner, Eric. *Forgotten Foundations of Bretton Woods: International Development and the Making of the Postwar Order*. Cornell University Press, Ithaca, NY, 2014.

Helleiner, Eric and Bessma Momani. "The Hidden History of China and the IMF." Chapter 2 in E. Helleiner and J. Kirshner, eds. *The Great Wall of Money: Power and Politics in China's International Monetary Relations*. Cornell University Press, Ithaca, NY, 2014.

Heng Lin. *Liu Guoguang (Short Bio and Interview)*. (Translated by Xi Xiujun). China Academy of Social Sciences, Beijing, 2006.

Hinton, Harold C., ed. *Government & Politics in Revolutionary China: Selected Documents, 1949–1979*. SR Scholarly Resources, Inc., Wilmington, DE, 1982.

Hu Angang. *Roadmap of China's Rising*. Tsinghua University, Beijing, 2007.

Hu Angang. *China in 2020: A New Type of Superpower*. The Brookings Institution, Washington, DC, 2011.

Hu Jichuang. *A Concise History of Chinese Economic Thought (221 B.C. – 1919)*. Foreign Languages Press, Beijing, 2009.

Hu Shuli, Huo Kan and Yang Zheyi. "Setting Economic Reform in Stone, China's Way: In Four Parts (Paving the Way; Shifting Winds, the Words That Changed History; Shaping Decisions, Taking Action)." *CaixingOnline*, 11, 18 and 25 January, 2013.

Jacobson, Harold K. and Michel Oksenberg. *China's Participation in the IMF, the World Bank, and GATT*. The University of Michigan Press, Ann Arbor, 1990.

Ji Zhaojin. *A History of Modern Shanghai Banking: The Rise and Decline of China's Finance Capitalism*. M.E. Sharpe, Armonk, 2003.

Jiang Zemin. *On the Three Represents*. Foreign Languages Press, Beijing, 2002.

Joiner, Lynne. *Honorable Survivor: Mao's China, McCarthy's America: And the Persecution of John S. Service*. Naval Institute Press, Annapolis, 2009.

Karl, Rebecca. *The Magic of Concepts. History and the Economic in Twentieth Century China*. Duke University Press, Durham, NC, 2017.

Kitano, Naohiro. "Japanese Contribution in Supporting China's Reforms: A Study Based on ODA Loans." China Report, *Centre for the Study of Developing Societies, Delhi, Sage Publications India Pvt. Ltd.*, 2004.

Kocka, Jürgen. *Capitalism: A Short History*. Princeton University Press, Princeton, NJ, 2016.

Kornai, János. *Economics of Shortage*. North Holland Publishing Co., Amsterdam, 1980.

Kornai, János. *The Road to a Free Economy: Shifting from a Socialist System: The Example of Hungary*. W.W. Norton, New York, 1990.

Kornai, János. *The Socialist System: The Political Economy of Communism*. Princeton University Press, Princeton, NJ, 1992.

Kornai, János. "Ten Years after 'the Road to a Free Economy': The Author's Self-Evaluation." Keynote Address, World Bank Conference on Development Economics, 2000, World Bank, Washington, DC, 2001.

Kroeber, Arthur. *China's Economy: What Everyone Needs to Know*. Oxford University Press, Oxford, 2016.

Kuhn, Robert L. *The Man Who Changed China: The Life and Legacy of Jiang Zemin*. Crown Publishers, New York, 2004.

Lampton, David M. *Same Bed Different Dreams: Managing U.S.: China Relations*. University of California Press, Berkeley, 2001.

Lampton, David M. *The Three Faces of Chinese Power: Might, Money, and Minds*. University of California Press, Berkeley, 2008.

Lampton, David M. *Following the Leader: Ruling China from Deng Xiaoping to Xi Jinping*. University of California Press, Berkeley, 2014.

Lardy, Nicholas R., ed. *Chinese Economic Planning: Translations (by K.K. Fung) from Chi-Hua Ching-Chi*. M.E. Sharpe, Armonk, NY, USA and Wm Dawson & Sons Ltd., London, 1978.

Lardy, Nicholas R. *Market Over Mao: The Rise of Private Business in China*. Peterson Institute for International Economics, Washington, DC, 2014.

Lardy, Nicholas R. and Kenneth Lieberthal. *Chen Yun's Strategy for China's Development*. M.E. Sharpe, Armonk, NY, Inc., 1983.

Lenin, Vladimir I. *The State and Revolution*. (Translated and Introduction by Robert Service). Penguin Books, London, 1992.

Li Jiange. Selected Works. (Edited by China Development Research Foundation), (in CDRF series *Chinese Economists on Economic Reform*). Routledge, Abingdon, UK, 2017.

Li Lanqing. *Breaking Through: The Birth of China's Opening-Up Policy*. Oxford University Press, Oxford, 2009.

Li Yining. *Economic Reform and Development the Chinese Way*. Foreign Language Teaching and Research Press, Beijing, 2010.

Li Yining. *Beyond Market and Government: Influence of Ethical Factors on Economy*. Springer Verlag, Germany, 2014.

Lieberthal, Kenneth G. and David M. Lampton, eds. *Bureaucracy, Politics, and Decision Making in Post-Mao China*. University of California Press, Berkeley, 1992.

Lieberthal, Kenneth G. and Michel Oksenberg. *Policy Making in China: Leaders, Structures, and Processes*. Princeton University Press, Princeton, NJ, 1988.

Lim, Edwin. "Learning and Working with the Giants." In Indermit S. Gill and Todd Pugatch, eds. *At the Frontlines in Development*. World Bank, Washington, DC, 2005.

Lim, Edwin. Preface to *Fifty Economists Look at Thirty Years of Reform and Opening: Retrospective and Analysis*. (Edited by Wu Jinglian). China Economic Publishing House, Beijing, 2008. A shorter version of this Preface was published (in English) in *The Oxford Companion to the Economics of China*. (Edited by Fan Shenggen et al.). Oxford University Press, Oxford, 2014.

Lin, Cyril. "The Reinstatement of Economics in China Today." The*China Quarterly*, March 1981.

Lin, Justin Yifu. *Benti & Changwu: Dialogues on Methodology in Economics*. Peking University Press, Beijing, 2005.

Lin, Justin Yifu. "Development and Transition: Idea, Strategy and Viability." *Marshall Lecture at Cambridge University*, 31 October 2007.

Lin, Justin Yifu. *Demystifying the Chinese Economy*. Cambridge University Press, Cambridge, 2012.

Lin, Justin Yifu. *Against the Consensus: Reflections on the Great Recession*. Cambridge University Press, Cambridge, 2013.

Lin, Justin Yifu, Fang Cai and Zhou Li. *The China Miracle: Development Strategy and Economic Reform*. (Revised edition). The Chinese University Press, Hong Kong, 2003 (the original edition was published in 1992).

Lin, Justin Yifu and Yan Wang. *Going Beyond Aid: Development Cooperation for Structural Transformation*. Cambridge University Press, Cambridge, 2017.

Liu Guoguang. "A Brief Discussion on Problems of Planned Adjustment and Market Adjustment." *Jingji Yanjiu*, No. 10, 20 October, 1980, 3–11.

Liu Guoguang. "Adhere to the Basic Direction for Reforming the Economic System." *Renmin Ribao*, 6 September, 1982.

Liu Guoguang. "A Great Historical Turn: Studying Expositions Concerning the Shift of Work Focus in the 'Selected Works of Deng Xiaoping'." *Renmin Ribao*, 12 August, 1983.

Liu Guoguang. "Eradicate the Idea of Natural Economy, Establish the Concept of Commodity Economy." *Renmin Ribao*, 16 November, 1984.

Liu Guoguang. "Remolding the Model of the Economic Structure and Perfecting the Socialist System: An Understanding of the CPC CC Decision on the Reform of the Economic Structure." *Jingji Yanjiu*, No. 12, 20 December, 1984, 16–24.

Liu Guoguang. "Several Difficult Problems Confronting Reform of the Present Economic System." *Jingjixue Zhoubao*, 22 September, 1985.

Liu Guoguang. "A Third Discussion on the Buyers' Market." *Renmin Ribao*, 15 September, 1986.

Liu Guoguang. "Carry Forward the Marxist Economic Theory during the Practice of Reform: Part I." *Renmin Ribao*, 31 July, 1987.

Liu Guoguang. "Carry Forward the Marxist Economic Theory during the Practice of Reform: Part II." *Renmin Ribao*, 3 August, 1987.

Liu Guoguang. "Certain Important Developments in China's Economic Theories since Reforms Were Initiated." *Hongqi*, No. 16, 16 August, 1987, 8–14.

Liu Guoguang. "Several Points of Basic Experience in the Theoretical Study of Economic Reform." *Qiushi*, No. 5, 1 September, 1988, 16–21.

Liu Guoguang. "On the Relationship between Improving the Economic Environment and Straightening Out the Economic Order, on the One Hand, and Deepening the Reform, on the Other." *Chinese Economic Studies*, Winter, 1991–92.

Liu Guoguang. "Several Problems Concerning the Development Strategy of China's Special Economic Zones." *Chinese Economic Studies*, (Spring, 1992).

Liu Guoguang. "Several Theoretical Issues in Respect of the Socialist Market Economy." *Jingji Yanjiu*, No. 10, 20 October, 1992, 8–18.

Liu Guoguang. "Comments at a Symposium to Discuss the Planned Economy as Primary and the Market Economy as Supplementary." *Chinese Economic Studies*, (Spring, 1993).

Liu Guoguang. "Difficulties and Strategies in Economic Reform." *Nanjing Xinhua Ribao*, 19 August, 1994.

Liu Guoguang interview with the Economic Observer on the Meaning of Liu Guoguang's Controversial Speech on "Some Issues in Economics Teaching and Research", Published in the Economic Observer of 10 December, 2005.

Liu Guoguang and Wang Xiangmin. "A Study of the Speed and Balance of China's Economic Development." *Social Sciences in China*, (1980): 15–43.

Liu Guoguang and Zhao Renwei. "Several Questions Concerning the Relationships between Planning and the Market." *Red Flag*, 2 September, 1979.

Liu Guoguang and Zhao Renwei. "On the Relationship between Planning and the Market in the Socialist Economy." *Chinese Economic Studies*, (Summer, 1980).

Liu Guoguang and Zhao Renwei. "The Question of Dual Structure in the Course of Pattern Transformation." *Guangmin Ribao*, 2 November, 1985.

Liu Guoguang and Zhao Renwei. "The Share System, a New Task in Changing the Ownership Relations." *Jingji Ribao*, 2 November, 1985.

Liu Jianhui and Wang Hongsun. "The Origins of the General Line for the Transition Period and the Acceleration of the Chinese Transformation in Summer 1955." *The China Quarterly*, September 2006, 724–731.

Lou Jiwei. *Collected Works*. (Edited by China Development Research Foundation), (in CDRF Series *Chinese Economists on Economic Reform*). Routledge, Abingdon, UK, 2014.

Lou Jiwei, Peter Harrold and E.C. Hwa, eds. "Macroeconomic Management in China. Proceedings of a Conference in Dalian, June 1993." *World Bank Discussion Papers, Washington DC*, 1993.

Lou Jiwei and Wang Shuiling, eds. *Public Finance in China: Reform and Growth for a Harmonious Society*. World Bank, Washington, DC, 2008.

Lu Mai. *FDI in China's Agro-Processing Sector*. OECD, Paris, 2000.

Lu Mai. *China's Social Reform and Rebuilding the Welfare System*. DRC Foundation, Beijing, 2008.

Lu Mai. *Poverty Eradication in China: A New Phase*. DRC Foundation, Beijing, February, 2011.

Lu Mai and Feng Minglian. "Reforming the Welfare System in the PRC." *Asian Development Review*, (2008/Vol. 25, # 1&2): 58–80.

Lu Mai, Gary Jefferson and John Zhao. "Reforming Property Rights in China's Industry." In Gary Jefferson and Inderjit Singh, eds. *Enterprise Reform in China: Ownership, Transition and Performance*. The World Bank, Washington, DC and Oxford University Press, Oxford, 1999.

Lu Mai and Calla Wiemer. "Putting Farmers First: An End to China's Agricultural Tax." *EAI Background Brief No. 231*, March, 2005.

Lu Mai and Mary Young. *Early Child Development for 2030: China's Post-MDG Plan*. The Brookings Institution, Washington, DC, February, 2015.

Ma Hong. *New Strategy for China's Economy*. New World Press, Beijing, 1983.

Ma Hong, ed. *Modern China's Economy and Management*. Foreign Languages Press, Beijing, 1990.

Ma Hong. *Collected Works*. (Edited by China Development Research Foundation), (in CDRF Series *Chinese Economists on Economic Reform*). Routledge, Abingdon, UK, 2014.

Ma Ying and Hans-Michael Trautwein, eds. *Thoughts on Economic Development in China*. Routledge, Abingdon, UK, 2013.

MacFarquhar, Roderick, ed. *The Politics of China, 1949–1989*. Cambridge University Press, Cambridge, 1993.

MacFarquhar, Roderick. *The Origins of the Cultural Revolution. 3: The Coming of the Cataclysm 1961–1966*. Oxford University Press, Oxford and Columbia University Press, New York, 1997.

Mann, James. The China Fantasy: How Our Leaders Explain Away Chinese Repression.Viking Penguin, New York, 2007.

Mao Tsetung. *Quotations from Chairman Mao Tse Tung. (Little Red Book)*. Foreign Languages Press, Beijing, 1966.

Mao Tse-tung. *Selected Works* (in IV volumes). Foreign Languages Press, Beijing, 1975.

Mao Tse-tung. *A Critique of Soviet Economics*. (Translated by Moss Roberts, annotated by Richard Levy, with an Introduction by James Peck). Monthly Review Press, New York and London, 1977.

Mao Tse-tung. *On New Democracy*. University Press of the Pacific, Honolulu. Hawaii, 2003. (Originally published in Chinese in Chinese Culture, Ya'nan, January 1940).

Marx, Karl. *Critique of the Gotha Programme*. Progress Publishers, Moscow, (eighth printing), 1978.

Marx, Karl. *The Civil War in France*. Charles H. Kerr and Co., Chicago, 2014.

Marx, Karl. *Das Kapital*. First Rate Publishers, New York, 2016. (Originally published in German in 3 volumes in 1867, 1885 and 1894, the last two volumes posthumously, by Friedrich Engels).

Marx, Karl and Friedrich Engels. *The Communist Manifesto*. (From the English edition of 1888). Verso, London and Brooklyn, NY, 2012.

Meisner, Maurice. *The Deng Xiaoping Era: An Inquiry into the Fate of Chinese Socialism, 1978–1994*. Hill and Wang, New York, 1996.

Momani, Bessma. "China at the International Monetary Fund: Continued Engagement in Its Drive for Membership and Added Voice at the IMF Executive Board." *Journal of Chinese Economics*, (2013/Vol. 1 #1).

Nathan, Andrew J., and Perry Link, eds. *The Tiananmen Papers*. (Compiled by Zhang Liang). Public Affairs, New York, 2001.

Naughton, Barry. *Growing Out of the Plan: Chinese Economic Reform 1978–1993*. Cambridge University Press, Cambridge, 1995.

Naughton, Barry. *The Chinese Economy: Transitions and Growth*. The MIT Press, Cambridge, MA, 2007.

Naughton, Barry, ed. *Wu Jinglian: Voice of Reform in China*. The MIT Press, Cambridge, MA, 2013.

Naughton, Barry. "SOE reform: Missing in Action." The *China Economic Quarterly*, June 2016.

Nove, Alec. *Was Stalin Really Necessary? Some Problems of Soviet Political Economy*. Routledge, Abingdon, UK, 1964.

Osnos, Evan. "Boom Doctor: Can the Chinese Miracle Continue without Reform?" *The New Yorker*, 11 October 2010.

Osnos, Evan. *Age of Ambition: Chasing Fortune, Truth and Faith in the New China*. Farrar, Straus and Giroux, New York, 2014.

Paulson, Henry M., Jr. *Dealing with China: An Insider Unmasks the New Economic Superpower*. 12 Hachette Book Group, New York, 2015.

Peng Dehuai. *Memories of a Chinese Marshall*. Foreign Languages Press, Beijing, 1984.

Perkins, Dwight H. *The Economic Transformation of China*. World Scientific, 2015.

Raichur, Satish. "Economic 'Laws', the Law of Value and Chinese Socialism." *Australian Economic Papers*, (December, 1981): 205–218.

Reynolds, Bruce L., ed. *Chinese Economic Reform: How Far, How Fast?* Academic Press, Inc., San Diego, 1988.

Riskin, Carl. *China's Political Economy: The Quest for Development since 1949*. Oxford University Press, Oxford, 1987.

Riskin, Carl, Zhao Renwei and Li Shi, eds. *China's Retreat from Equality: Income Distribution and Economic Transition*. M.E. Sharpe, Armonk, NY, 2001.

Roach, Stephen. *Unbalanced: The Codependency of America and China*. Yale University Press, New Haven, CT, 2014.

Rozman, Gilbert. *The Chinese Debate about Soviet Socialism, 1978–1985*. Princeton University Press, Princeton, NJ, 1987.

Russell, Jesse and Ronald Cohn. *Gu Zhun*. Lennex Corp., Edinburgh, 2012.

Saich, Tony, ed. *The Rise to Power of the Chinese Communist Party: Documents and Analysis*. M.E. Sharpe, Armonk, NY, 1996.

Saich, Tony. *Governance and Politics of China (Comparative Government and Politics)*. (Fourth edition). Palgrave, New York, 2015.

Schell, Orville. *Mandate of Heaven*. Simon & Schuster, New York, 1994.

Schell, Orville. "China's Once and Future Democracy." *The Wall Street Journal*, 1 April, 2017.

Schell, Orville and John Delury. *Wealth and Power: China's Long March to the Twenty-First Century*. Random House, New York, 2013.

Schumpeter, Joseph A. *History of Economic Analysis*. Oxford University Press, New York, 1954.

Shambaugh, David. *The Making of a Premier: Zhao Ziyang's Provincial Career*. Westview Press, Boulder, CO, 1984.

Shambaugh, David. "China's Propaganda System, Institutions, Processes and Efficacy." *The China Journal*, No. 57, 2007.

Shambaugh, David. *China's Communist Party: Atrophy and Adaptation*. University of California Press, Berkeley, 2008.

Shambaugh, David. *China Goes Global: The Partial Power*. Oxford University Press, Oxford, 2013.

Shambaugh, David. *China's Future*. Polity Press, Malden, MA, 2016.

Shirk, Susan L. *The Political Logic of Economic Reform in China*. University of California Press, Berkeley, 1993.

The Sixth Five-Year Plan of the People's Republic of China for Economic and Social Development (1981–1985). Foreign Languages Press, Beijing, 1984.

Snow, Edgar. *Red Star Over China*. (Revised and Enlarged edition). Grove Press, New York, 1968.

Sowell, Thomas. *Marxism: Philosophy and Economics*. William Morrow and Co., Inc., 1985.

Stalin, Joseph V. *Problems of Leninism*. International Publishers Co., Inc., New York, 1934.

Stalin, Joseph V. *Economic Problems of Socialism in the U.S.S.R.* International Publishers Co., Inc., New York, 1952.

Stedman Jones, Gareth. *Karl Marx: Greatness and Illusion.* The Belknap Press and Harvard University Press, Cambridge, MA, 2016.

Stent, James. *China's Banking Transformation: The Untold Story.* Oxford University Press, Oxford, 2017.

Sun Yefang. "Admitting Mistakes and Self-Confidence." *Beijing Review*, (27 July, 1981/#32): 18.

Sun Yefang. "A Discussion of Some Prerequisites to the Overall Balance of the National Economy." *Chinese Economic Studies*, (Fall, 1982/Vol. 16, #1): 41–52.

Sun Yefang. *Social Needs versus Economic Efficiency in China.* (Translated and Edited by K.K. Fung). M.E. Sharpe, Inc., 1982.

Sun Yefang. "On Quadrupling Output in 20 Years." *People's Daily*, 19 November, 1983.

Sun Yefang. "To Raise Production Four-Fold in Two Decades Is Not Only Politically Probable, but Technologically Feasible." *Chinese Economic Studies*, (Winter, 1983–84/Vol. 17, #2): 50–67.

Sun Yefang. "Letter to the CCP Central Organization Department, December 27, 1979." *Chinese Law and Government*, (July–August, 1998/Vol. 31, #4): 89–91.

Swinnen, Johan F.M. and Scott Rozelle. *From Marx and Mao to the Market: The Economics and Politics of Agricultural Transition.* Oxford University Press, Oxford, 2006.

Teiwes, Frederick C. and Warren Sun. *China's Road to Disaster: Mao, Central Politicians and Provincial Leaders in the Great Leap Forward, 1955–59.* Routledge, Abingdon, UK, 2015.

Tuchman, Barbara. "If Mao Had Come to Washington: An Essay in Alternatives." *Foreign Affairs*, October 1972.

Vogel, Ezra F. *Deng Xiaoping and the Transformation of China.* The Belknap Press and Harvard University Press, Cambridge, MA, 2011.

Wang Hai. "Gu Zhun: Greek City States and the Origin of Its Democracy." *Perspectives*, (2011/Vol. 1, #3).

Wang Huijong. *China's Development and Reform.* Foreign Languages Press, Beijing, 2003.

Wang Mengkui. *Collected Works.* (Edited by China Development Research Foundation), (in CDRF Series *Chinese Economists on Economic Reform*). Routledge, Abingdon, UK, 2014.

Wei Jingsheng. *The Courage to Stand Alone: Letters from Prison and Other Writings.* Viking, 1997.

White, Tyrene. *China's Longest Campaign: Birth Planning in the People's Republic, 1949–2005.* Cornell University Press, Ithaca, NY, 2006.

World Bank. *China: Socialist Economic Development.* (3 volumes). The World Bank, Washington, DC, 1983.

World Bank. *China: Long Term Development Issues and Options.* The World Bank, Washington, DC, 1985.

World Bank. *China 2020: Development Challenges in the New Century.* (7 volumes). The World Bank, Washington, DC, 1997.

World Bank. *Oral History Program.* (Transcripts of interviews with senior staff conducted from the early 1980s through 2005). Available at http://oralhistory.worldbank.org

World Bank and DRC. *China 2030: Building a Modern, Harmonious, and Creative Society.* The World Bank and the DRC of the State Council, Washington, DC, 2013.

World Bank and DRC. "Urban China: Toward Efficient, Inclusive, and Sustainable Urbanization." The World Bank and the DRC of the State Council, Washington, DC, 2014.

Wu Jinglian. "Economic Development Faces a New Stage in Which Reform Will Promote Readjustment." *Chinese Economic Studies*, Winter, 1991–92.

Wu Jinglian. *Understanding and Interpreting Chinese Economic Reform*. Thomson South-Western, Singapore, 2005.

Wu Jinglian and Fan Shitao. "China's Economic Reform: Processes, Issues and Prospects." In Gregory C. Chow and Dwight H. Perkins, eds. *Handbook of the Chinese Economy*. Routledge, Abington, UK, 2014.

Wu Jinglian and Ma Guochuan. *Wither China? Restarting the Reform Agenda*. (Translated by Nancy Hearst and Hua Xiaofeng). Oxford University Press, Oxford, 2016.

Wu Jinglian and Zhou Xiaochuan. "A Comprehensive Design for the Near- and Medium-Term Reform of the Economic System." Originally published (in Chinese) in *Gaige*, June, 1993; Reproduced (in English) in "Wu Jinglian: Voice of Reform." (Edited by Barry Naughton). The MIT Press, Cambridge, MA, 2013.

Xi Jinping. *The Governance of China*. Foreign Languages Press Co. Ltd., Beijing, 2014.

Xiao Geng and Zhang Yansheng. *The Future of China: The Foshan Model*. Fung Global Institute, Hong Kong, 2016.

Xu Dixin. *China's Search for Economic Growth: The Chinese Economy since 1949*. New World Press, Beijing, 1982.

Xue Muqiao. *The Socialist Transformation of the National Economy in China*. Foreign Languages Press, Beijing, 1960.

Xue Muqiao. *China's Socialist Economy*. Foreign Languages Press, Beijing, 1981.

Xue Muqiao. *Current Economic Problems in China*. (Translated and Edited by K.K. Fung). Westview Press, Boulder, CO, 1982.

Xue Muqiao. "Remember Historical Experience: Resolutely Implement the Policy of Improving the Economic Environment and Straightening Out the Economic Order." *Chinese Economic Studies*, Winter, 1991–92.

Xue Muqiao. *Collected Works*. (Edited by China Development Research Foundation), (in CDRF Series *Chinese Economists on Economic Reform*). Routledge, Abingdon, UK, 2011.

Yang Yao. "The End of the Beijing Consensus: Can China's Model of Authoritarian Growth Survive?" *Foreign Affairs*, 2 February, 2010.

Yu Guangyuan. *Deng Xiaoping Shakes the World*. (Edited by Ezra F. Vogel and Steven I. Levine). East Bridge, Norwalk, CT, 2004.

Yu Guangyuan. *Collected Works*. (Edited by China Development Research Foundation), (in the CDRF Series *Chinese Economists on Economic Reform*). Routledge, Abingdon, UK, 2014.

Zhang Shuguang. "The Explorations and Contributions of Gu Zhun." (Translation of a Chinese paper published on the occasion of the 100th anniversary of the birth of Gu Zhun.). *China Academy of Social Sciences*, Beijing, 2015.

Zhao Renwei, Carl Riskin and Li Shi, eds. *China's Retreat from Equality:*Income Distribution and Economic Transition. M.E. Sharpe, Armonk, NY, 2001.

Zhao Ziyang. *Prisoner of the State: The Secret Journal of PM Zhao Ziyang*. (Translated and Edited by Bao Pu, Renee Chiang, and Adi Ignatius, with a foreword by Roderick MacFarquhar). Simon and Schuster, New York, 2009.

Zheng Xinli, ed. *Economists' Analysis of China's Economic Transformation*. Foreign Languages Press, Beijing, 2012.

Zheng Xinli, ed. *Seeing the Real China in the Economic Perspective*. Foreign Languages Press, Beijing, 2014.

Zhou Xiaochuan *Collected Works*. (Edited by China Development Research Foundation), (in CDRF series *Chinese Economists on Economic Reform*). Routledge, Abingdon, UK, 2017.

Zhou Xiaochuan and Wu Jinglian. "A Comprehensive Design for the Near- and Medium-Term Reform of the Economic System." Originally published (in Chinese) in *Gaige*, June 1993; Reproduced (in English) in "Wu Jinglian: Voice of Reform." (Edited by Barry Naughton). The MIT Press, Cambridge, MA, 2013.

Zhu Rongji. *Zhu Rongji Meets the Press*. Oxford University Press, Oxford, 2011.

Zhu Rongji. *On the Record: The Road to Reform, 1991–1997*. Brookings Institution Press, Washington, DC, 2013.

Zhu Rongji. *On the Record: The Road to Reform, 1998–2003*. Brookings Institution Press, Washington, DC, 2015.

Index

www.ingramcontent.com/pod-product-compliance
Ingram Content Group UK Ltd.
Pitfield, Milton Keynes, MK11 3LW, UK
UKHW011014180926
475701UK00004B/733
9780367438494